Education Development and Leadership in Higher Education

In today's highly competitive, globalized higher education market, higher education leaders and managers have to address such issues as widening participation, the potential of new technologies, quality assurance and quality enhancement to improve standards of teaching, learning and leadership. Education development has a central role to play in each of these areas and should be a core element in the strategic positioning of all higher education institutions.

This book is packed with research and case studies on what education development can offer higher education. It draws from experiences of leading education developers worldwide and illustrates the numerous ways in which education development strategies, structures and processes can make a difference to an institution's effectiveness and reputation.

Education Development and Leadership in Higher Education provides insights to anyone with an interest in and responsibility for determining strategy within their institution – whether education developer, head of department, dean, pro-vice chancellor (teaching) or vice-chancellor.

Dr Kym Fraser is the Director of Education for Warwick Diabetes Care in the Medical School at the University of Warwick, UK.

The Staff and Educational Development Series

Series Editor: James Wisdom

Education Development and Leadership in Higher Education

Developing an effective institutional strategy

Edited by Kym Fraser

RoutledgeFalmer
Taylor & Francis Group

LONDON AND NEW YORK

First published 2005
by RoutledgeFalmer
2 Park Square, Milton Park, Abingdon, Oxon OX14 4RN

Simultaneously published in the USA and Canada
by RoutledgeFalmer
270 Madison Ave, New York, NY 10016

RoutledgeFalmer is an imprint of the Taylor & Francis Group

Typeset in Baskerville by
HWA Text and Data Management, Tunbridge Wells
Printed and bound in Great Britain by
Biddles Ltd, King's Lynn

British Library Cataloguing in Publication Data
A catalogue record for this book is available from the British
Library

Library of Congress Cataloging in Publication Data
Education development and leadership in higher education :
developing an effective institutional strategy / edited by
Kym Fraser.
    p.   cm. – (SEDA series)
  Includes bibliographical references.
  1. College training–teaching Great Britain. 2. College teaching–
Australia. 3. College teachers–In-service training–Great Britain.
4. College teachers–In-service training–Australia. I. Fraser, Kym,
1956– II. Series.
    LB2331.E364 2004
    378.1´2–dc22   2004007070

ISBN 0–415–33524–8 (hbk)
ISBN 0–415–34969–9 (pbk)

Contents

Illustrations

Contributors

Denise Chalmers is the Director of the Teaching and Educational Development Institute (TEDI), University of Queensland, which employs approximately 50 staff. TEDI is responsible for academic and general staff development, multimedia and learning resource development, and evaluation of teaching. She is an experienced university lecturer, teaching students both on- and off-campus. She has researched and published on teaching and learning and professional development at university. She has recently led two national Australian University Teaching Committee (AUTC) projects, *Teaching large classes* and *Training, managing and supporting sessional teachers* and is currently a member for a national project on the teaching of psychology.

John Dearn is the Pro Vice-Chancellor (Academic) at the University of Canberra. He was the immediate past Director of the Centre for the Enhancement of Learning, Teaching and Scholarship (CELTS). In 1994 John was awarded an inaugural National Teaching Fellowship by the Australian Federal Government. In 1997 he was awarded the inaugural Australian Award for University Teaching in the category science teaching and in 1998 was appointed to the national Committee for University Teaching and Staff Development (CUTSD). He is currently an auditor for the Australian Universities Quality Agency (AUQA) and President of the Higher Education Research and Development Society of Australasia.

Kym Fraser is the Director of Education for Warwick Diabetes Care in the Medical School at the University of Warwick. She has worked in the field of education development in the USA, Hong Kong, Australia and the UK. She is a past editor of the Higher Education Research and Development Society of Australasia Green and Gold Guides and is a member of the UK Centres for Excellence in Teaching and Learning assessment panel. Her current research interests include 'rewarding teaching in research intensive universities' and 'investigating the experiences, perceptions and conceptions of teaching professional development of academics in research intensive universities'.

Ray Land is Professor of Higher Education Development and Director of the Centre for Higher Education Development (CHED) at Coventry University. He is a Fellow of the Staff and Educational Development Association (SEDA) and was one of the first national accreditors for the Institute for Learning and Teaching in Higher Education (ILTHE). His current research interests include orientations to educational development, threshold concepts and troublesome knowledge, and theoretical aspects of education in cyberspace.

Robyn Lines is the manager of the Central Curriculum Innovation and Development group at RMIT University, Australia. She has been involved in education development for ten years primarily through faculty-based support roles. She was awarded a National Teaching Fellowship in 1998 to study implementation approaches for teaching innovation and improvement in Australian universities. Understanding successful approaches to effecting teaching change in an increasingly managerialised university sector is a continuing research interest.

Peter Ling is Deputy Director, Learning and Teaching Support at Swinburne University, Melbourne. Peter contributes to policy and planning in learning and teaching. He convenes the Graduate Certificate in Teaching and Learning in Higher Education. Peter holds a PhD relating to public education policy in Australia. Peter has undertaken national research projects on flexible provision of higher education, multiple modes of delivery, resource-based learning and competency-based assessment. He is co-author of *Delivering Digitally: Managing the Transition to the Knowledge Media* (Kogan Page, 2002). Peter is past co-editor of *Higher Education Research and Development* (Australasia) and is on the editorial board of *Innovative Higher Education* (USA).

Bob Matthew is the Director of the Teaching and Learning Service at the University of Glasgow. Originally a civil engineer by discipline, he taught the subject at universities in the UK and Ireland for 17 years before taking up his present position. His current research interests include what is research-led teaching, and developing student autonomy. He is a keen hillwalker and cyclist in his spare time.

Carmel McNaught is Professor of Learning Enhancement at The Chinese University of Hong Kong. She has had three decades of work in eight universities in Australasia, southern Africa and Britain. During the 1990s much of her work was as a designer and evaluator in multimedia and web-based education projects. Such a breadth of experience leaves her well-placed to work across a variety of discipline areas. The changes in her own academic life across discipline boundaries, countries and cultures have led to her current research interests in the evaluation of innovation in higher education and understanding the broader implementation of the use of technology in higher education.

Mia O'Brien is a Lecturer in Higher Education with the Teaching and Educational Development Insititute (TEDI), University of Queensland. Mia is an experienced teacher in both teacher education and more recently in educational development. She has responsibility for the induction programmes for academic staff including teaching and learning and career progression. Mia's teaching and research interests include professional learning for university teachers, design of flexible learning environments, development of academic expertise in curriculum development, pedagogical models for research-led teaching and learning, and the facilitation of communities of practice within university teaching and learning contexts.

Kate Patrick has been working in education development and educational research for nearly 20 years at the University of Melbourne and RMIT University, Melbourne, Australia. As well as running central induction and teaching programmes and a mentoring programme for recently appointed academic staff, she has led a range of development projects, including nationally funded projects on internationalising the curriculum and teaching with electronic simulations. She has an ongoing research interest in the teacher's impact on what their students learn. Kate is currently Manager, Program Quality Assurance, in the Quality Consultancy Unit at RMIT.

Margot Pearson is a Reader in the Centre for Development and Academic Methods, at the Australian National University. Her main research interests and responsibilities currently focus on research education and supervision, however, as the former director of the Centre she was involved for some years in providing leadership programmes for Deans, Directors and Heads of Departments.

Alex Radloff holds an MA in Psychology and a PhD in Education. She is currently Professor and Dean of Academic Development in Science, Engineering and Technology at RMIT University, Australia. Alex has over

25 years' experience in university teaching, has presented training programmes and workshops, and worked as a consultant. Her research interests include self-regulated learning, student academic writing and staff development. She has authored and co-authored papers and book chapters on teaching and learning and has been a recipient of teaching development grants. Alex is an Australian Universities Quality Agency (AUQA) auditor and a past President of HERDSA (Western Australia).

Yoni Ryan is Associate Professor in Higher Education and Deputy Director of the Centre for Learning and Teaching Support at Monash University, Melbourne. She has extensive experience in staff development, and educational design and development with new technologies, at various universities in Australia and the Pacific, and consults for state and federal governments on education policy. She was operational manager and lead author for the major Australian government-commissioned report, *The Business of Borderless Education* in 2001. A recent publication is 'Teaching and learning in the global era', in R. King (ed.) *The University in the Global Era* (Palgrave Macmillan, 2004).

Ellen Sanders has worked in the disability field in Australia and the UK for over twenty years and is currently the Disability Policy Advisor at The University of Nottingham, England. In her position she influences key policy decisions and undertakes strategic developments to promote access and inclusive environments for all students who have a disability. She engages in advisory, developmental, monitoring and evaluation work on a university-wide basis, co-ordinates the Disability Liaison Officers' network in academic departments, oversees a range of projects, assists in devising student surveys and participates in a number of appropriate committees.

Brenda Smith is Head of the LTSN Generic Centre in York and leads a team dedicated to developing enhanced teaching, assessment and learning practice in the UK HE sector. The role of the Generic Centre is to promote and disseminate effective practices in learning and teaching, to co-ordinate national network groups and to promote high-quality learning and teaching across the UK. This role involves working with 24 Subject Centres, working at strategic level with key change agents in universities and other key national network groups such as employers, faculty developers, quality agencies and student groups.

Chris Trevitt is Senior Lecturer at the Centre for Educational Development and Academic Methods at the Australian National University. With a PhD in the physical sciences, and a Graduate Diploma in Higher Education, Chris has 20 years of teaching, research and development experience across the physical and human sciences. Key areas of focus include technology as a trigger for educational and curriculum change, staff development for flexible learning, and embedding an ethos of continuous professional learning and institutional and personal capacity development through action research and action learning.

Acknowledgements

In January 2001 I met with my colleagues Peter Ling and Alex Radloff in a wonderful coffee bar in south-east Melbourne to discuss the idea of developing this book. It's been a long road to its fruition and I wish in particular to thank them both for their enthusiasm and support in nurturing and developing the ideas that underpin this book.

I have been fortunate in my career to have developed excellent 'collegial' relationships with a significant number of individuals from whom and with whom I have learnt a great deal about our profession and our discipline. 'Collegial' is the overwhelming sense that I have of these individuals and I am grateful for their friendship, sense of fun and thoughtfulness.

Thank you to my co-authors for their unfailing support, good humour and willingness to respond to my increasingly long and sometimes frantic email messages. Without you, this book wouldn't exist.

I am grateful for the efforts of Stephen Jones and James Wisdom in bringing this book to publication.

Alec, I have known and loved you for all of my life. You always had faith in me and for that, your friendship and support, I am truly grateful.

My heartfelt thanks and more to Susie for your unfailing moral and intellectual support, your kindness and good humour, the reassuring 4 am conversations, the everyday things that you took on so I could 'work on the book' and the not so everyday things – like your willingness to move country with me.

My mother left school in 1936 at the age of 16. In spite of not having a tertiary education she always maintained that 'an education was no load to carry'. I am indebted to her for always encouraging and supporting me to continue my education. This book is dedicated to my Mum, Hazel Fraser.

Finally, acknowledgements are made to the Higher Education Division of the Commonwealth Department of Education, Science and Training in Australia, to Norris Publishers who publish the *Journal of Computing in Higher Education*, and to Blackwell Publishing who publish the *International Journal of Training and Development* for permissions to use tables and a figure in Chapter 7.

Introduction

The genesis of this book came through my 2001 sabbatical during which I visited a number of education development centres[1] that were initiating exciting and innovative endeavours in the field. My sabbatical took me to a dozen different centres in several different parts of the world. Towards the conclusion of that sabbatical, as I pulled together the key elements from the different centres that I had visited, I could see a framework that, for me, represented different elements of a coherent picture of the field. Pivotal to education development is a recognition of the multi-layered context in which we work, the complex structures that both support and constrain our work, and the variety of processes and strategies that we develop to engage university 'teachers',[2] the university and the higher education sector in education development.

These elements influence our work regardless of where in the world we engage with the discipline of teaching in higher education. Although practice is situated, exploring practices and approaches to education development in different settings is important in extending our understanding of the possible. It is through sharing approaches and practice that education developers are building an international perspective on education development in a world where higher education is becoming a global enterprise.

The book is structured in terms of the elements of context, structures, strategies and processes. Chapters 1, 2 and 3 discuss the higher education contexts in which education development centres operate. Chapters 4 and 5 portray different ways in which education development may be located within the university structure. Chapters 6–11 discuss different strategies and processes that can progress the work of education development.

The higher education context is a highly competitive global one in which university decision-makers need to position their institutions to meet an increasingly complex future. Education development has a role to play in this positioning of universities and this book provides insights into the different ways in which the profession can address many of the issues that higher education institutions face.

In a highly competitive global context the key issues facing the higher education sector include: quality assurance; an increasingly diverse student body; the challenges of teaching on offshore campuses; tight funding; international competition; the changing profile of the academic population; and flexible, student-centred learning. In Chapter 1, Ling reviews the global challenges that face higher education institutions and the changing nature of the institutions themselves. He identifies key changes in the environment in which universities operate and key developments in higher education. Ling concludes with a discussion of the consequences of a dynamic higher education context for education development.

In Chapter 2, Smith discusses the UK higher education sector and the role of the government and national organisations. She revisits the initiatives of the 1980s and 1990s and their impact on learning, teaching and education development. She then looks towards the future of learning and teaching in UK higher education with the creation of the Higher Education Academy.

Patrick and Lines introduce the quality assurance/improvement context of the higher education sector in Chapter 3. They explore the design and implementation issues for the development of quality systems that effectively support education development. They discuss the ways in which they have sought to address the issues raised in their work at the Royal Melbourne Institute of Technology (RMIT) University.

Chalmers and O'Brien in Chapter 4 discuss the structures of education development from the remit of a centrally located unit. They argue that in order for education development units to significantly contribute to the enhancement of university teaching both within the university community, and across the higher education sector, they need to be engaged in four concerns maintaining corporate memory of teaching innovations; systematic implementation of teaching and learning initiatives; facilitating communities of learning; and investigating and disseminating scholarship on teaching, learning and education development.

In Chapter 5, Radloff investigates the position of decentralized approaches to education development. She uses as a case study the approaches taken by an education development group located in the Faculty of Life Sciences at the Royal Melbourne Institute of Technology (RMIT) University. The focus of education development in this approach is programme development and renewal in the context of a quality assurance framework, emphasizing a capability driven, learner-centred curriculum that uses emerging technologies. Radloff explores the issues for decision-makers who have to both prove and improve the quality of teaching and learning in institutions within a context of increasing student–staff ratios, reduced budgets and declining staff morale.

In Chapter 6, Pearson and Trevitt argue that the way leadership is enacted is critical to education development, especially at the academic development unit level. They propose a multifaceted, multi-level approach that allows for, and coordinates, both top-down and bottom-up strategies for education reform. Through the chapter and a case study, they focus on five issues key to achieving such reform through education development: the nature of the work of leadership for education development; the significance of people and process in change management and education development; the potential of a multifaceted approach to education development; the importance of capacity building for adaptive change; and ways to share leadership and work collaboratively to effect change.

In the last decade 'new' technologies have heavily influenced teaching and learning across the sector. Anecdotally it would appear that in many if not most universities, IT infrastructure is developed with little reference to teaching and learning principles. In Chapter 7, McNaught explores the integration of teaching and learning principles with IT infrastructure and policy. She provides case studies from two very different universities, one in Hong Kong and one in Australia, to demonstrate how technology can inhibit or facilitate effective educational practice. She investigates the issues that arise for education development staff who provide advice related to decision making about IT infrastructure and policy in their institutions, outlining broad implications of the two different models for planning IT infrastructure and policy.

Participation and access of students is of increasing concern in many countries and in Chapter 8 Fraser and Sanders look specifically at the disability discrimination legislation in the UK and Australia. The chapter outlines the legislation and the implications of this legislation for universities. A case study describes a particularly effective way that the central education development unit at Monash University used to teach academics about facilitating the learning of students who have a disability. The case outlines the impact the intervention had on the academics, in terms of confidence, knowledge, and changes to practice.

Chapters 9 (Fraser) and 10 (Matthew and Land) focus on two particular strategies/processes that universities and governments use to encourage academics to develop the teaching component of their academic role: graduate university teaching programmes, and funded teaching development projects. In Chapter 9, Fraser argues that award-bearing university teaching programmes need to: model the learning environments in which academics teach; enrol participants who are at a stage in their academic career at which they can cope with the scholarly nature of the discipline of teaching in higher education; be accessible to academics who already have an exceptionally heavy workload; take into account the different disciplinary and local contexts of academics; be articulated with higher degrees; and be linked to institutional structures that promote teaching.

In the last 15 years governments and many universities have provided significant funding for education development projects. Smith in Chapter 2 provides a summary of UK programmes and in Australia examples include the funding from the Committee for Australian University Teaching, the Committee for University Teaching and Staff Development, and the Australian University Teaching Committee. The effectiveness of these projects in terms of their adoption, impact and transferability has been highly variable (Alexander *et al.*, 1998; Murphy, 2003). In Chapter 10 Matthew and Land discuss how education development can be more successfully facilitated through funded projects, highlighting the issue of engaging colleagues. They conclude that education development practice 'needs both to include and to be informed by research, with a clear awareness of the theoretical perspectives and conceptual frameworks on which education developers draw' (Fry *et al.*, 2004: 167).

The book concludes by considering the changing nature of the academic role at the turn of the century. In Chapter 11, Ryan, Fraser and Dearn discuss the implications of many of the contextual changes described by Ling in Chapter 1 for the professionalization of university teaching. They draw upon data collected in a 2002 study of the provision of professional development for university teaching in Australia. From that study they portray the attitudes of Australian academics towards the accreditation of university teaching. They conclude that the attitudes and factors that militate against the professionalization of university teaching are strong and that it is unlikely that professionalization will be achieved in a single country in the current climate. They suggest that the most likely way for the accreditation of university teaching to proceed will be through an international body, such as the International Consortium of Education Developers, which could act to accredit university teaching through agencies such as the UK Higher Education Academy and the National Institute of Learning and Teaching in Australia.

The editing of this book and working with other authors to complete it has taught me a great deal about education development in this ever-changing higher education context. I hope that you both enjoy and find value in reading this book and that it helps you to think about our discipline and improve your practice.

Kym Fraser

NOTES

1   The term 'education development' is a contested term that means different
    things in different contexts. In the context of this book the term is used to
    refer to the developmental activities informed by the discipline of teaching
    and learning in higher education. This discipline is underpinned by research
    into university teaching and learning (Fraser, 2001).
2   A broad range of university staff directly support student learning. Increasingly
    the remit of education developers is widening to include working with each
    of these groups.

1

From a community of scholars to a company

Peter Ling

THE CONCEPT OF EDUCATION DEVELOPMENT WITHIN UNIVERSITIES

This book is concerned with education development. Development within organizations in general may be viewed as contrived change in the behaviour of people, processes and the organizational environment to improve the efficiency and effectiveness of the institution in meeting its purposes. Likewise, within universities development relates to the behaviour of people who constitute the organization, the processes in which they engage, and the conventions and resources that enable and constrain them in carrying out their functions.

This book focuses on one area of development within universities – the development of learning and teaching. This does not mean that education development is confined only to the development of academics as teachers. For one thing, learning is facilitated by an increasingly complex array of personnel and technologies and for another, teaching takes place within organizational systems and structures that have a bearing on the efficacy and efficiency of the university in providing for learning. The book is concerned with development of the environment in which teaching occurs as well as with the development of academics and others who play a role in facilitation of learning. This environment includes organisational missions and goals, plans and strategies, structures and support systems, and quality assurance and improvement measures. Chapters 3, 6 and 7 address quality assurance, leadership and policy issues.

So is there a conventional wisdom about the function of education development and the means of achieving it? There are a number of features of the current era that render a single approach problematic. In this chapter some key changes in the environment in which universities operate and some of the developments in higher education are identified. These can be seen both as responses to change in the environment and as generators of change. A number of forms of education development suited to the dynamic environment and to various forms of provision of higher education have emerged. The chapter concludes with a description of approaches to education development as a preamble to the various contributions to good practice presented in this book.

THE CONTEXT

Education development takes place in the twenty-first century in what Rowley, Lujan and Dolence (Rowley *et al.* 1998: 3) have described as a 'paradigm shift from what we have known as the "industrial age" to a new "information age"'. The information age shifts the very locale of universities from the regional to the global. As Giddens (1999: 19) puts it 'globalization is not incidental to our lives today. It is a shift in our very life circumstances. It is the way we now live.' It has been argued that the effects of globalization on education are overstated; that education systems are still mediated by the structures of nation states (Reid 1999). Globalization, however, impinges on the sovereign law and administration of the states in which we live (Habermas 2001) and the higher education sector at least is acutely aware of the universality of its environment. Globalization is one element of change in the 'Western' world that has altered the way in which work is undertaken. The work of academics is no exception. The work of academics now involves everything from physically teaching on campuses in foreign countries, to collaborative research, and development across national boundaries, to conducting 'virtual' classes with students in a variety of locations.

ACCOUNTABILITY OF UNIVERSITIES

The dynamics of the environment in which universities operate generates tensions. There is a growth in the demand for higher education and a change in the clientele accessing universities (Tierney 1999; Katz 1999; Palmer 2001). At the same time, public financial support has been con-strained as the political pendulum in the context of global competition swung to the right at the close of the twentieth century and moves now only tentatively to the left, and even then with a focus on flexibility and entrepreneurial culture (Giddens 2000). As public funding becomes a smaller proportion of the resources available to universities, the account-ability of academics for their teaching increases through devices that range from performance appraisal systems within universities to quality audits of universities imposed by governments (see, for example, Nelson 2003). This context is further developed in Chapter 2.

That public accountability should increase as public funding decreases could be seen as a paradox. On the other hand it could be seen as the corollary of higher education being recognized as a key component of the economy, both through the production of the intellectual workforce required in the post-industrial era and as a contributor to export earnings through the fees of foreign students (see, for example, Nelson 2003). In addition universities, taking on the corporate characteristics that align with their economic role, assume other marketing trappings such as conspicuous quality assurance systems. The result is a mix of in-house quality systems, accreditation by professional bodies and government-imposed quality assurance mechanisms, some of which specifically target teaching and learning. These various approaches to quality assurance and improvement in relation to university learning and teaching are taken up in Chapters 2 and 3.

THE CHANGING NATURE OF UNIVERSITIES

In this environment it is not only the operation of universities that is undergoing change. The *raison d'être* for universities, always contentious, becomes further confused. Some universities might be represented as seeking to maintain their traditional image. Some appear to operate as multinational, profit-oriented corporations. Some appear set to take on the role of electronic publishing houses.

The technical developments that have propelled universities into a globalized environment, at the same time open the door to new sources of competition both large and small. Commercial publishing concerns not only produce textbooks with self-help quizzes, as they have in the past, but now provide CD-ROM and website support, including links to other resources, discussion forums and online testing. As universities enter global markets adopting the same format for their course delivery as do these publishers, the distinction between universities and publishers focuses on the accrediting role of universities. It is a role that becomes difficult to protect through regulation both because electronically provided education permeates national boundaries and defies national regulation and because, in a world of change, lengthy set-piece programmes, such as bachelor degrees, are less pertinent to meeting ongoing educational needs. Universities must compete with small-scale providers who have an opportunity to enter the market electronically without requiring much in the way of capital or marketing ability. They must compete also with indus-trial organizations that have new techniques for provision of training and education, some of which are recognized by universities for accreditation purposes. The role of the university in the current era is ambiguous.

Technological development has not only influenced the space in which universities operate, it has influenced the pace of change. As Giddens observes, we suffer from a chronic revision of practice (Bryant and Jary 2001). As universities seek to respond to new possibilities for their operations that are opened up by technological developments, react to competition, and adjust to changes in available financial resources, they redefine their mission, revise their strategies and restructure their operations, setting in place revisions and reviews before changes cycle through. It generates a 'manufactured uncertainty' (Bryant and Jary 2001: 22) in the academic work environment.

The traditional university and the present day university are sometimes styled as fitting within differing paradigms (for example, by Kathy Tiano in AVCC 1996).

The concept of a change in paradigm draws attention to some of the features emerging in universities but is problematic in that it suggests a new orthodoxy where there are many possibilities and contesting views of the nature of organizations that provide higher education. Consistent with contemporary views of learning – which recognize that understandings and meanings will vary between individuals – there are many under-standings of what now constitutes a university. One is to envisage the university as an organization, a device which can be seen as a means by which humans attempt to 'write' order into a world that is in a constant state of flux and movement (Hancock and Tyler 2001). In Giddens' terms, the university as an organization is 'constituted' by those who notionally interact with it (Giddens 1984). The people who constitute universities – using the term constitute to mean not only to populate but to frame the phenomenon through their understandings of the institution – are many. They include the leadership of universities, managers and administrative staff, academics, maintenance workers, students, and all sorts of individuals and bodies that have dealings with the university. Each actor will have his or her own perception of the organization. That of the chief executive officer, and those of individual academics, administrative officers, and so on will vary. What the organization is then depends on individual perceptions that may overlap but are bound to vary and may be contra-dictory in some respects (see Figure 1.1).

One consequence of this understanding is that one should expect to find tensions and contradictions in the expectations of education develop-ment in university settings. As Parker puts it, the world in which we operate is 'multiple, contradictory' (Parker 1997: 116). While some academics may still view universities as autonomous – if not anarchic – communities of scholars, their managers may well view the organization as a business

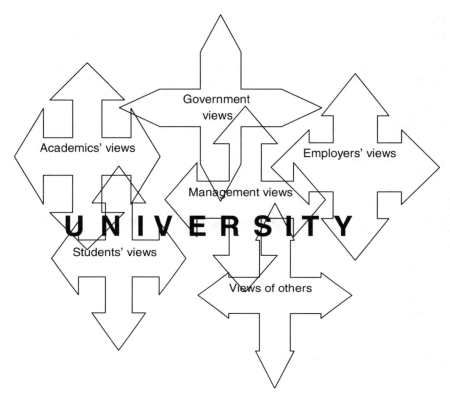

Figure 1.1 *Universities are constituted by numerous interested parties who perceive them in a variety of ways*

enterprise (Margison and Considine 2000) with a defined mission, a strategic plan, and key performance indicators. Views of the nature of academic work may vary from the orthodoxy of Boyer's scholarships of discovery, integration, application and teaching (Boyer 1990). Certainly the balance struck between these activities is likely to be influenced by factors other than purely academic concerns. Academics can also find themselves engaged in management, in public relations and marketing, fund raising, publishing for commercial purposes and a range of political activities.

OUTCOMES OF HIGHER EDUCATION IN THE CURRENT ERA

In this environment what should be the outcome of the learning and teaching aspect of higher education is contested. Is it about being knowledgeable in a select discipline area? Is it about mastering the methods of a discipline? Can it be about becoming competent in some profession? Is it about a learned, rounded individual? Is it about the acquisition of learning and problem solving skills? Is it about acquiring a range of generic skills for economic and social life such as communicating effectively, and working collaboratively?

The outcomes of higher education are influenced in part by perceptions of the nature of a university. John Henry Newman's vision of the university of the 1850s as a centre for teaching rather than research – a community of scholars sharing their understandings with students – still has some currency. In fact the idea of some universities specializing in teaching is raised from time to time. Abraham Flexner's (Flexner 1930) review of American, English and German universities in the 1930s saw the functions of the institutions as including research, the advancement of knowledge – and teaching – the preservation of knowledge. Flexner, however, did not see universities as being concerned with the application of knowledge (except that they may engage in 'training' at the highest level in the learned professions of medicine and law as distinct from 'the make believe professions' such as business) (Kerr 1991: 76). Clark Kerr saw the university as a pluralistic organisation: 'Flexner did not realise how many functions can be combined into a single university – even apparently inconsistent functions', Kerr stated (Kerr 1991: 75). Flexner did not appreciate the populist drive for education nor 'the desire of a technological society for knowledge' (Kerr 1991: 77). Kerr saw the rise in the popularity of university education as being associated with a recognition of the importance of knowledge in economic and social growth. Reflecting on the twentieth century Kerr saw universal access to higher education, a move to a market-driven orientation and the global role of research as outstanding features in the development of American higher education (Kerr 2001; Palmer 2001). As the embrace of universities continues to grow and the definition of higher education becomes ever more challenging, Kerr cautions against a 'free for all' approach where external influences drive internal decisions (Palmer 2001). This may be difficult to eschew. Universities are at least sensitive to the external environment if not driven by it.

The global context of higher education and the competitive environment has some universities attempting to define – and market – their product or outcomes with statements of graduate attributes or capabilities. These include generic capabilities such as being able to work collaboratively as well as individually, being able to communicate effectively, and being able to engage in problem solving (e.g. University of Leicester, University of South Australia). They may include having subject knowledge and understanding, or being informed and skilled in a discipline or professional area (e.g. Swinburne University and the University of Hertfordshire).

The declaration of graduate outcomes, together with demands for attainment of minimum standards, such as the UK Higher Education Quality Council's Graduate Standards Programme, has implications for programme design, learning and teaching activities and the assessment of student attainment. These developments in higher education provide challenges, opportunities, and some would say distractions, for education developers.

LEARNING IN A POST-MODERN WORLD

The majority of students at most universities may remain young people exiting secondary school and undertaking a basic undergraduate programme but, unlike many of their forerunners, this will not be their only contact with university. In a changing environment, curriculum based on knowledge requirements of the world of today is unlikely to suit the world of tomorrow. Changing social and work environments not only generate a need for new knowledge and skills but also a need to access education incrementally, fragmentally and immediately. Lifelong learning brings challenges for universities in programme design and administration, in curriculum approaches, in teaching methods and in assessment (Watson and Taylor 1998).

Changing understandings of the process of learning at this level present a challenge to education developers and require a thoughtful approach to the use of technology in facilitating learning. Current understandings of effective arrangements for learning in higher education focus on the construction of meaning by the individual and emphasize active participation by learners in the learning process. They envisage teaching and learning as interactive/ communicative processes in which it is as important for the teacher to appreciate the learner's understandings, skills and attitudes, as it is for the learner to appreciate the teacher's position. Some current approaches, given the rate of change, emphasize learning processes rather than learning content. The willingness of the Massachusetts Institute of Technology to make the content of its courses openly available online and the willingness of other universities to make courses available on public television indicates that, for these providers, what they market at a fee is more than information; it is accreditation and it is interaction with experts.

Technology (which ironically is reliant on the consistencies of modern science for its operation and advancement) has produced change and instability in the learning environment, the content of learning and approaches to learning (AVCC 1996). Technology, which provides new possibilities for accessing information, opens up potentials for information overload and indeed information bombardment. It has contributed to approaches to learning requiring short concentration spans – the three-minute culture (Lash and Urry 1994) – and to the fragmentation of learning. Do new learning and teaching approaches devised to suit changing times – for example the construction of electronic 'knowledge objects', which are tagged for retrieval against a profile of the immediate learning needs of the individual – meet or defeat the purposes of higher education? There is a risk that technology may be used in teaching simply to expose students to information or that it may generate teaching based on the simplistic behaviourist approaches that computer-based programmed learning undid in the 1960s and 1970s. The capacity of electronic systems to grade student attempts at certain assessment tasks and provide some automated feedback can lead to approaches to assessment suited only to lower order cognitive attainment. Technology, then, provides challenges for learning and teaching in higher education that are developed in Chapter 7.

CHANGING APPROACHES TO LEARNING AND TEACHING

Tensions in the context of university operations are bound to generate contesting approaches to the teaching component of academic work. On the one hand, as Tierney (Tierney 1999) points out, teachers still stand in front of classrooms and lecture to a roomful of students. Classes are still structured to run for a quarter or a semester, and classes meet one, two or three times a week. Students take courses to accumulate credits. Academics assess student work and assign letter grades. On the other hand the virtual classroom and the video-connected remote classroom are with us. The use of online course materials and online communications systems to support or replace classroom teaching is becoming commonplace and the mix of personnel who help to facilitate student learning widens and includes instructional designers, computing and audio-visual technicians and graphic artists and librarians.

In which direction are we heading and how far are we going? There is a push for flexible approaches to provision of higher education that offer choices to learners about the time, place and pace of their learning, about content, and about entry and exit points. We are generating client-oriented systems employing electronic warehouses of metadata-tagged learning objects retrievable on a just-in-time basis to satisfy the ever-changing lifelong learning needs of the individual. Academic input is one component in facilitating learning transactions but it is accompanied by instructional design, multimedia programming, information and content management systems, corporate planning and resource allocation, and client liaison and marketing services. The community that facilitates learning comprises more than scholars.

CONSEQUENCES FOR EDUCATION DEVELOPMENT

There are many approaches to education development and many organizational arrangements for its provision as Chapters 4 and 5 indicate. Organizational arrangements may be more or less centralized. They may be configured with a range of other activities such as educational media production and services, instructional design activities and general human resource development.

Approaches to education development may be seen as falling into various schools. In the past we could distinguish between approaches that focused on teaching and those that focused on learning. The literature of the teaching-oriented approaches includes publications of the UK Staff and Education Development Association (SEDA) and the Higher Education Development Association of Australasia (HERDSA) on lecturing to large groups, teaching small groups and the like. It includes the *53 Interesting Things to Do In Your Lectures* and similar publications of the Bristol Technical and Educational Services, now surpassed by *2000 Tips for Lecturers* (Race 1999). Teaching-oriented approaches include incentive schemes such as institutional and state awards for excellence in teaching (see, for example, Nelson 2003). The literature of learning-oriented approaches includes publications of SEDA such as *Never Mind the Teaching, Feel the Learning*, and the writing of John Biggs (Biggs 1999), which focuses on what the learner does rather than what the teacher does. Learning-oriented approaches to education development are often associated with research into learning in higher education, such as the research based on phenomenography. Incidentally, where education development involves research as well as staff development, it may be styled as a discipline in its own right.

These approaches to education development continue in the current context but they are joined by strategic approaches, adopted by universities with an executive leadership that sidelines old collegial structures (Margison and Considine 2000). Strategic approaches to education development are driven by university mission statements and detailed strategic planning, and evaluated against performance indicators. Strategic approaches may address educational processes, educational outcomes or both. They are likely to involve a wider compass than traditional approaches to education development, which have focused on classroom and laboratory activities. They may address aspects of the learning environment ranging from online and library facilities, to student support, and to the management of learning resources, including the management of staff. They are likely to involve quality assurance and quality improvement measures, a matter taken up in Chapter 3. Teaching input-oriented measures may include a requirement that teaching staff hold formal qualifications in teaching in higher education as discussed in Chapter 9. Strategies may include quality improvement

Table 1.1 *Approaches to educational development*

Approach	Focus of educational development activities
Teaching orientation	Teaching strategies / teaching tips
Learning orientation	How students learn and what students learn
Strategic orientation	Strategies to assure institutional objectives are met

incentives such as awards for good teaching. In this universities have been urged on by governments.

The strategic approach is driven in part by increased public accountability for the quality of university provision. Professionalism in university teaching has been demanded by the Dearing Report in the UK, and the Institute for Learning and Teaching in Higher Education was established to ensure that it occurs. The creation of the Higher Education Academy – merging the Institute for Learning and Teaching in Higher Education, the Learning and Teaching Support Network and the TQEF National Co-ordination Team – continues the government commitment to support quality enhancement and the student experience in higher education. Likewise, in Australia the government established the National Institute for Learning and Teaching in Higher Education to enhance learning and teaching in universities by, amongst other measures, promoting and supporting strategic change in higher education institutions.

Each of the approaches to education development operates in a dynamic environment. Strategic approaches, though often framed in three- and five-year plans, are not necessarily associated with stability, for they present in a context of organizational change. Schools, departments, and 'super-faculties rise and fall, informal assemblies appear and disappear, DVC [Deputy Vice Chancellor] and PVC [Pro Vice Chancellor] offices seem to be equipped with a revolving door' (Margison and Considine 2000). Traditional approaches to education development, focusing on the ongoing functions of learning and teaching, may be more stable, but in their case theories and understandings change over time, along with teaching approaches and technical possibilities.

This environment suggests that a review of contemporary practices may be valuable. The chapters that follow reflect on the dynamics of the current environment of education development and present a range of responses to it.

2

The role of national UK organisations in enhancing the quality of teaching and learning

Brenda Smith

Over the last two decades there have been many changes in educational policy worldwide, with an increasing emphasis on public accountability. Alongside this, student numbers have increased globally, as well as the student body becoming more diversified in terms of age, background, qualifications and culture. Consequently this has led the higher education sector in the UK needing to rethink and adapt many of its practices, thus helping to ensure that all students receive a positive learning experience. Support for these changes has come from a number of directions including funding by the UK government and other national organisations.

The aim of this chapter is threefold. The first aim is to take a backward glance and discuss some of the funded initiatives that took place in the 1980s and early 1990s. Lessons learned will be highlighted. The second aim is to explore the current landscape and in particular takes a look at the Teaching Quality Enhancement Fund and its impact on learning and teaching. The third aim is to take a forward look and a 'peep' into the future as the higher education climate moves from one of quality management to quality enhancement and the formation of the new Higher Education Academy.

A BACKWARD GLANCE

Twenty years ago funding to support teaching initiatives was rare. Individuals or small teams of staff usually carried out innovations on learning and teaching in their own time. Central education development units were unusual and few opportunities existed for disseminating learning and teaching initiatives beyond the individual university perimeter walls.

In 1987 the Enterprise in Higher Education initiative (EHE) was launched and funded by the Department for Education and Skills (DfES). The initiative supported 56 institutional projects for five years, with a total funding of £58,000,000. It was designed to encourage the development of qualities of enterprise amongst those seeking higher education qualifications. The DfES did not seek to define these qualities of enterprise, but left the definitions to the individual institutions. This turned out to be a real advantage, as it encouraged discussion within the different universities. These discussions actually helped to frame many of the bids, as each institution had to define what was meant by 'qualities of enterprise'. In reality this brief was interpreted very broadly and the development and embedding of enhanced pedagogical approaches was evident in many project outcomes. So for many staff this was the first time that opportunities existed to share effective learning and teaching practices.

The EHE funding enabled activities to take place that previously had not been possible due to lack of funding opportunities. In many of the EHE projects staff from different departments and subject areas met for the first time in cross-institutional groups. In addition funding was available to run both in-house and off campus events. Some of the events involved being away from the university for a couple of days to devote time to new innovations and to engage in professional development. A number of these events took place in hotels, where, for the first time, staff started to feel valued for the contribution they made. Practices were shared and the interpretation of what was meant by the qualities of enterprise was explored. It created new opportunities for inter-disciplinary, inter-faculty, and inter-site collaboration. The EHE was really the forerunner of the current debate and emphasis on preparing students for employability and developing the skills of lifelong learning.

For some institutions a key feature of the EHE was the involvement of students. Some of the later projects appointed student enterprise co-ordinators. In other universities students were integrated into some of the staff development activities. Students can be highly influential in helping to change practice; having experienced active learning they started to ask other staff why they did not use some of these methods. Indeed some students became active change agents.

As a requirement of the funding, institutions had to state how they intended to continue and sustain the outcomes of the EHE. As a consequence a number of institutions formed new central education development units or extended existing ones. It would be interesting to trace the career progression of staff involved in these projects. Anecdotally, many now hold senior positions within their own or other institutions. The experience of enterprise had given these staff a broader perspective on higher education and many had developed additional professional skills that led to future promotions.

The context of higher education started to change and modularisation and semesterisation began to become accepted by staff in institutions. One of the consequences of this was that programmes and courses were split into smaller units called modules that were generally delivered over a semester. Many staff felt that what they had previously delivered over a whole academic year now had to be compressed into a semester. One of the consequences was that staff felt 'pressurised' to focus on subject content at the expense of previous innovations. Skills development became less of a focus and a number of the innovations lay dormant. EHE initiatives soon became forgotten as staff moved on or back to their previous jobs. The emphasis now was on rewriting courses and programmes to comply with modularisation and semesterisation.

In summary, evaluation of the EHE suggests that the initiative was intentionally instrumental in raising the profile of pedagogy (National Foundation for Education Research, 1991). It opened up a discussion around learning and teaching issues, and stimulated continual financial backing for educational and staff development. There is substantial evidence that the initiative built capacity for staff and education development.

Following on the heels of the EHE programme was the Computers in Teaching Initative (CTI) that was established in 1989. It was initially funded by the Universities Funding Council, and then jointly funded by all UK funding councils. Its aim was to encourage the use of computing and information technology (C&IT), which was to be delivered through 24 subject-based centres. The centres were to provide academic departments with advice and information about the suitability and availability of C&IT for use in the relevant subject areas, and to enable changes in learning and teaching. Later a small central support service was added to the programme.

Support included resource guides, websites, newsletters, workshops, seminars and departmental visits. There is no doubt that the centres increased the pool of experience and skill in C&IT. Although the original emphasis was on the encouragement of computer-aided learning, this gradually changed towards the use of generic C&IT tools. The evaluation found that of those that used the centres 88 per cent described the service as good or excellent (HEFCE 1998). However for some staff the centres were perceived as confined to the 'techies', while few felt that middle and senior managers had been influenced.

> The initiative appears to have made no explicit or systematic relationship to existing networks or associations of education development. Its links with staff or education development units in higher education institutions do not appear to have been very effective (Jackson and Phillips 2002: 11).

Another key initiative was the Teaching and Learning Technology Programme (TLTP), launched in 1992 and funded by the Universities Funding Council (UFC). The aim of the programme was to make teaching and learning more productive and efficient by harnessing modern technology.

The programme was based on competitive bidding from higher education institutions (HEIs). In the first two years of the programme 76 projects were funded for three years. This early phase concentrated on the development of materials. Unfortunately few of these materials failed to migrate beyond the department or consortia that developed them. Later phases were aimed more at the implementation and embedding of TLTP products, rather than the development of new materials.

In the early phases of the programme, dissemination strategies had not been incorporated in the design of the projects, which could be said to be a very expensive form of staff development for the few. However TLTP did contribute to the growth of new networks and increased collaboration as the programme developed, although significant barriers to the uptake of C&IT still existed. By phase three a National Coordination Team had been appointed to offer a much-needed support role for these projects.

There were other funded initiatives such as the Effective Teaching and Learning Assessment Programme (ETAP), which was a joint funding council project launched in 1993 to promote the development of training and consultancy in support of teaching, learning and assessment. Five consortium projects were funded in the areas of resource-based learning, student support or subject-specific learning and teaching. Again it was found that disseminating outcomes did not necessarily change practice.

The initiatives summarised above were funded to meet the perceived needs of the funding councils, or in the case of the EHE initiative, the then Training Agency. Substantial amounts of money were given to these initiatives in order to bring about change in learning and teaching. The long-term effectiveness of these initiatives is difficult to judge as so many factors influence learning and teaching practice. However looking back at these initiatives each seems to have been set up with little reference to previous ones. Learning from one initiative to the next seems to have been lost; many bids were written with seemingly little reference to previous work. Also it is now difficult to obtain copies of all the evaluation reports, for as new staff came in post in the respective agencies, the 'shelves were swept clean'. There is an urgent need to ensure some form of archive in order to learn from all these initiatives. This would enable effective practices to be drawn upon and any lessons learned carried forward.

THE CURRENT LANDSCAPE

Following the UK Dearing Report (NCIHE 1997) the Higher Education Funding Council for England (HEFCE) undertook an extensive high level consultation with the higher education sector on proposals for 'Learning and Teaching: strategy and funding proposals' (HEFCE 1998c). The outcome of the consultation was a high level strategy that focused on five key themes to enhance learning and teaching in England.

The five themes are:

- encouragement and reward;
- coordination and collaboration;
- disseminating and embedding good practice;
- research and innovation;
- building capacity for change.

To deliver this strategy the HEFCE established a Teaching Quality Enhancement Fund (TQEF). One of the strengths of the TQEF is that it is a multi-functional fund that takes a three-pronged approach to enhancement focused on institutions, subjects and individuals, which is clearly its strength. The fund aims to effect change at the three levels of the institution, the subject and the individual.

At the institutional level, all English higher education institutions now produce 'Learning and Teaching Strategies'. The aim is to ensure all institutions have a strategic vision of how they will identify and address learning and teaching issues. They are required to produce annual learning and teaching strategies, along with operational plans. Resources that are based on student numbers are currently provided to support institutions to address the issues they identify. A review of these learning and teaching strategies by HEFCE (Gibbs 2001) indicates that enormous developments have taken place since the instigation of such strategies.

Key findings included the fact that documentation had considerably improved, especially for the implementation components: for example change mechanisms were present in 76 per cent of learning and teaching strategies submitted in 2000, but were only present in 10 per cent in 1998. Change mechanisms most commonly cited were: staff development, Institute for Learning and Teaching membership, exploitation of C&IT, and rewards for excellent teaching. In addition two-thirds of learning and teaching strategies were predominantly or partly strategic with new management and implementation structures and procedures. In 1998 half the strategies relied solely on policies and committees, and did not identify clear implementation procedures or task groups to translate policies into actions. Coupled with this was a lack of devolution to faculties or departments – only 6 per cent adopted this approach – whereas 35 per cent had devolved models by 2000. By 2000 the strategies submitted were more comprehensive and sophisticated (Gibbs 2001: 4).

The second level focused on the subject element that is key to the success of the teaching quality enhancement fund, as it is on a subject basis that most individual academics operate, network and think. The subject based element has two components: the first is a development fund (the Fund for the Development of Teaching and Learning – FDTL) that aims to encourage and fund innovation based on excellence as defined by the subject review process of the Quality Assurance Agency (QAA). The second component is the Learning and Teaching Support Network (LTSN), which aims to provide a comprehensive framework for the promotion, transfer and embedding of good learning and teaching practices.

Invitations to bid for FDTL funding follow on from a subject review of specific discipline areas. FDTL was launched by the HEFCE and the Department for Education in Northern Ireland (DENI) in December 1995 (HEFCE 1995). To date, four phases of funding have been allocated and the fifth phase details were published in October 2003. The aims of the FDTL, in phase one were:

> ... to stimulate developments in teaching and learning: and to secure the widest possible involvement of institutions in the take up and implementation of good teaching and learning practice (HEFCE 1995: 2).

Key to the programme is that funding support is given to those subject providers who performed well in subject review, with the aim of disseminating good practice more widely in the system. Thus FDTL was the first form of funding to be seen to explicitly reward excellence. A National Coordination Team (NCT) supported the FDTL programme providing essential education development expertise and gave support in the planning, dissemination and sharing of effective practices. Indeed the Council and NCT appear to have learned a number of lessons from previous initiatives which helped to ensure a higher level of central guidance and co-ordination of projects (HEFCE 1998a). The evaluation report of 1998 states:

> ... the real impact of FDTL can only be judged in the future on the basis of the effectiveness of the dissemination and implementation of the funded projects, and, as is clear from other initiatives both in the UK and overseas, such dissemination is fraught with difficulty (HEFCE 1998a: 4).

In phases four and five, the LTSN became involved both in supporting the projects in the planning phase and especially in publishing and disseminating the outcomes for the different discipline/subject areas that were represented under these phases. This LTSN support offered better coherence at the subject level and a more coherent dissemination platform. For example in the earlier phases, most projects had listed a number of national conferences to disseminate their outcomes. Many had to be cancelled because of lack of numbers and a plethora of such events across the UK. In phase four, the relevant LTSN Subject Centres had jointly planned seminars and conferences with the current projects to offer a smaller number of events but with parallel streams to accommodate the various themes. These proved to be well attended.

In 1998 the UK funding councils committed £7,000,000 per annum over five years to establish a UK-wide Learning and Teaching Support Network. The idea of the LTSN was to provide a discipline-based model for delivering change and developing collaboration. It also formed a dissemination platform for initiatives and enhancements in learning and teaching. The LTSN is a unique national framework for managing changing times within universities via a network of 24 subject centres hosted by UK higher education institutions and a UK-wide Generic Centre. The LTSN may be one way to transform the university of the twenty-first century from being highly competitive to one that actively encourages partnerships and collaboration to enhance student learning.

The 24 subject centres were a mix of single-site and consortium-based centres all located within relevant subject departments and hosted by higher education institutions. The subject focus recognises that for many staff in higher education it is at this level where most networking and exchange of learning, teaching and assessment practice takes place. The centres were client-centred with high visibility within their subjects and provided both a pro-active and a responsive service to the needs of their communities.

The core activities of each subject centre included:

- collation of information on all aspects of teaching, learning and assessment within the discipline area;

- provision of training opportunities;

- advisory service to practitioners, such as academics, learning technologists and staff that support the student experience within the discipline area;

- support through maintenance of networks and effective contacts;

- liaison with relevant professional bodies and subject associations;

- advice on the implementation of technology in learning and teaching;
- ensuring that all practitioners are aware of current and future developments in learning and teaching;
- collaboration with cognate subject centres to support interdisciplinary and multidisciplinary activity;
- collaboration with the Generic Centre to ensure that subject centre staff are aware of broader issues.

However, there are also many learning and teaching issues common to all subjects that benefit from being disseminated and promoted. As a result the LTSN Generic Centre was established. The Generic Centre built links between the subject centres and was a major national source of information and expertise on learning and teaching practice. Its mission was:

> In partnership with others, the LTSN Generic Centre will broker information and knowledge to facilitate a more coordinated approach to enhancing learning and teaching (LTSN: www.ltsn.ac.uk/genericcentre/index.asp?id=16866).

The Generic Centre focused on two main levels of activity; at the discipline level with subject centres, and at an institutional level with key change agents. Within higher education institutions the Generic Centre worked with senior managers with responsibility for learning and teaching, staff and educational developers, learning technologists and other key staff groups where relevant. For example, the Generic Centre has worked with disability officers in relation to curriculum accessibility and the implications of the new disability legislation. The Generic Centre also worked in partnership with sector agencies to achieve its strategic aims and objectives, and avoid duplication. For example these agencies include the Quality Assurance Agency (QAA) and the QAA for Scotland, the Institute for Learning and Teaching in Higher Education (ILTHE), Joint Information Systems Committee (JISC), Universities UK, the Standing Conference of Principals (SCOP), employers and student groups.

To concentrate its activity the Generic Centre selected four key themes high on the learning, teaching, assessment and curriculum agenda as vehicles to motivate subject centres, higher education institutions and its partner organisations to engage with the Generic Centre. These four themes were: assessment; e-learning; employability and widening participation.

The LTSN network was initially well resourced, but came under increasing pressure to do more, as it demonstrated that collaborative networks do support the academic community and more use is made of its services. The latest evaluation report of the LTSN (LTSN 2002), including the Generic Centre contained some of the following points:

- The constituent parts of the LTSN, namely the Subject Centres, the Generic Centre and the Executive have made progress in cohering and developing their respective roles and have brought alive the concept of a network with a degree of central management and co-ordination. The differences in emphasis between these actors, in terms of their core business, are now emerging with more clarity. The 'branding' of the LTSN is positive, hard won and distinctive. There is a strong argument for sustaining and developing its distinctive approach (LTSN Executive 2002: 6).

- The range and quantity of the activities undertaken by the three parts of the LTSN are impressive. The array of informative, brokering and collaborative activities is creative and wrings more than could be expected from the available resources (LTSN Executive 2002: 6).

- The LTSN punches above its weight in terms of the resources available for direction, management and activities. In this sense it can be seen as excellent value for money; but there is a real danger that the short term and small scale funding of its work will actually destabilise the network in the medium term (LTSN Executive 2002: 7).

It is interesting to note this last statement, as the LTSN is now an integral part of the Higher Education Academy.

The third and final level of support is at the individual level via the National Teaching Fellowship Scheme (NTFS). The aim of the scheme is to provide reward and recognition to individual staff to begin to generate the kudos that is already associated with academic staff undertaking nationally and internationally excellent research activity. Since the year 2000, 20 National Teaching Fellowships have been awarded each year on the basis of outstanding work in the development of learning and teaching. In 2004, 50 NTFS awards were celebrated with two additional categories of rising stars and learning support staff (www.ntfs.ac.uk). Each of the winners receives £50,000 towards a specific teaching development project. The scheme celebrates the excellence in teaching of individuals regarded by their own institutions, in England and Northern Ireland, as being outstanding as teachers and promoters of learning. The fellows are awarded certificates at a high profile and prestigious ceremony each year.

Initially the sector was hesitant about the scheme. Indeed some institutions did not even submit a candidate in the first round. However the scheme has now increased in popularity and held in high regard and, as one winner said, it had changed his life. For once he felt recognised for the contribution he had made to learning and teaching. Hopefully over the coming years the fellowship holders will disseminate the outcomes of their projects to the benefit of higher education.

There is no doubt that the TQEF funding across the three levels of the institution, subject and individual has made a significant impact in terms of teaching and learning. This section highlights the fact that when money is specifically ring-fenced for learning and teaching that innovations and sharing of practice can occur. Not only have more innovations been set up and disseminated, but new and additional posts have been created via the learning and teaching strategy funding. The interesting challenge for the sector, however, will be to sustain these developments if the TQEF funding ceases at the institutional level.

The final 'organisation' in this section is the Institute for Learning and Teaching (ILTHE), which was launched in 1999. The ILTHE came about as a result of recommendations in the Dearing Report (the National Committee of Inquiry into Higher Education). It was a membership body for all who teach and support learning in higher education in the UK. The ILTHE aimed to enhance the status of teaching, improve the experience of learning and support innovation in higher education. Membership was available to individuals either by the initial entry route for experienced staff or by the successful completion of an ILTHE-accredited programme of learning and teaching in higher education. By June 2003 15,000 staff had become members. Benefits of membership included a password-protected web area of resources, the journal *Active Learning*, conference cost reductions, opportunities to bid for project funding and regional network groups. For the first time the higher education sector had a membership-funded body to support its professional needs.

Most of this chapter has focused on developments in England. However developments in Scotland are leading the way in terms of a quality enhancement agenda. The quality enhancement agenda in Scotland has been developed as a partnership between QAA, Scotland, Universities Scotland, student representation, the Scottish Higher Education Funding Council (SHEFC), and many academic partners. Scotland took the opportunity to re-evaluate the whole quality process over two years. It was felt that the present QAA system was time consuming, intensive and would not necessarily lead to enhancements. The previous funding had identified few problems so a decision was made to invest funding in a proactive methodology rather than a reactive one.

A key feature of the new method is to develop two enhancement themes over each academic year. Following consultation with the sector the first two themes selected were assessment and responding to student needs. Two steering committees were set up to decide on the detail. Although it is too early to know the effectiveness of this methodology, it does appear eminently sensible to focus the attention of the higher education sector in Scotland on only two major themes. It is more likely that colleagues will involve themselves in focused activity and that this will lead to enhancement in student learning and sustained change in practice.

All of the above initiatives have been funded via government. However other organisations have played a key role. These include the Staff and Education Development Association (SEDA), Society for Research in Higher Education (SHRE) and the Association of Learning Technologists (ALT). All offer conferences, workshops and other networking opportunities. Their role and influence should not be underestimated as for many years they have offered valuable opportunities for staff to meet and share practices. In fact SEDA was the forerunner in offering accreditation to institutions offering learning and teaching programmes or named awards for new academic staff.

However, with all these initiatives it is very difficult to evaluate the long-term impact in terms of effectiveness and sustainability. Influences on practice come from many different directions and isolating one factor against others is virtually impossible. What can be said however is that these initiatives have contributed to a climate of support for learning and teaching.

Dissemination of outcomes appears to be a key feature of all this activity and yet the impact of this is little understood and under-researched. Dissemination occurs at different levels with different degrees of impact. A dissemination strategy for good learning and teaching initiatives usually includes workshops, conferences and publications. Dissemination of resources for teaching and learning often amounts to little more than a distribution exercise. The materials get shipped but like so many Christmas presents, there is no guarantee that they will be used once they have been unwrapped. Successful adoption requires the acceptance, understanding, valuing, and use of what is being disseminated by those at the other end of the distribution channel. Dissemination is the easy part; ensuring adoption is altogether more challenging.

A FORWARD LOOK

A forward look highlights the fact that higher education is in a state of constant change. Just as the sector gets used to one initiative or policy directive, another one comes along. The third and final section of this chapter focuses on the development of the 'Higher Education Academy'. The formation of the academy arose from an evaluation of the Teaching Quality Enhancement Fund that was conducted in 2002. A committee was established (TQEC) to review the arrangements for support of quality enhancement in teaching and learning in UK higher education. It was also asked to identify any gaps or overlaps in the work of the four main agencies in this field (QAA, ILTHE, LTSN, and the Higher Education Staff Development Agency – HESDA), and to seek ways of improving effectiveness and value for money. The committee commissioned an extensive programme of research with staff, students and other bodies with an interest in quality enhancement.

The outcome of the committee's work was the widespread perception that the arrangements for quality enhancement are complex and fragmented, and insufficiently 'user-focused'. Many observers considered that the sector needed to give a higher profile to the process of continuous quality improvement and professional development for all those who support student learning. As a consequence the committee recommended a new organisation to help to deliver this vision. This new academy would encompass the work of the three existing agencies most directly involved in quality enhancement (ILTHE, LTSN and HESDA), which would permit a more integrated and strategic approach. The academy would work with the whole range of individuals, groups and institutions concerned with the student experience in higher education. However, only the ILTHE and the LTSN formed the Academy; the HESDA Board agreed that HESDA would become part of the Leadership Foundation that was formed in January 2004.

The new Higher Education Academy, formed in May 2004, was officially launched across the UK in October 2004 with the key aim of promoting higher education by:

- providing strategic advice to the higher education sector, government, funding bodies and others on policies designed to enhance the student experience;

- supporting curriculum and pedagogic development across the whole spectrum of higher education activity;

- facilitating the professional development of all staff in higher education.

The focus of the academy is, therefore, on all policies and activities relating to enhancing the student experience. Moreover, the academy is concerned with all staff supporting the student experience and ensuring their professional development. At the time of going to press it is difficult to comment on the academy, as it is still very much in its infancy. However, it aims to promote excellence in supporting the student experience in higher education. It will support, develop and represent those working in higher education, gather and develop information and practice, and offer advice and guidance in an accessible and user-friendly way to the UK higher education community. Although the academy built on the strengths of the work done by the ILTHE, LTSN and NCT, it is a higher profile body with a more strategic role and not just an amalgam of existing activities.

Currently the reader would be forgiven for thinking that government and UK organisations are the only factors impinging on assuring and improving teaching quality. Of course these agencies have an impact and give direction through both policy and funding streams. However, it should not be forgotten that for years, individuals and groups of academics have been dedicated to enhancing and supporting their students' learning. In many cases this has been achieved at great personal cost to themselves. Many have devised curriculum materials of both a paper and electronic nature, engaged in debates, produced new and innovative courses and attended learning and teaching conferences all in their own time. There has been an enormous amount of goodwill in the sector that has never been documented. However, some colleagues would argue that we need not only to assure ourselves that the quality of teaching is appropriate, but that it is improving. Others would contest this statement, and indeed the evidence from the Quality Assurance Agency (QAA) External Subject Reviews clearly indicates that provision across UK institutions of higher education is robust and of high quality. The title also implies that some intervention is needed via UK organisations if this goal of assuring and improving teaching quality is to be achieved. In the UK there are no national standards for teaching in higher education, although there is currently a consultation on professional standards. However the Government's White Paper on 'The future of higher education' (DfES 2003) indicates support for learning and teaching:

> Teaching and learning are central to the purpose of higher education. We are committed to understanding better where and how good teaching and learning take place and to take steps to ensure standards are high and continually improved, and that best practice is effectively shared. All students are entitled to high quality teaching, and to the best possible information to help them make the right choices about what to study and where. And those who teach well are entitled to have their success rewarded (p. 46).

In conclusion it can be seen that educational development has played a key role in enhancing the quality of learning and teaching. Over the last two decades large sums of money have been spent on learning and teaching initiatives, resulting in major developments in this area. However there are three key issues that need continual attention. The first issue is the question of archiving these materials and evaluations produced. Much of this valuable information is lost as organisations change buildings, change their name and new staff become appointed. A national archive of this material would be a great asset to international higher education. The second issue is to really focus on dissemination for embedding and sustainability. More research is needed in this area if we are to truly understand how learning and outcomes from one project or institution can be transferred elsewhere. It is only when we understand this that we can truly say that funded initiatives give value for money. The third issue is have we really evaluated and learnt lessons from all these initiatives and then used this learning to inform the next one? What some of these initiatives have succeeded in doing is not only to develop deliverables for wider dissemination, but also and very importantly they have led to the development of networks, partnerships and special interest groups. Some initiatives such as the LTSN have also used the role of brokerage to bring previously unconnected groups, institutions, partner organisations and individuals together and helped to develop UK-wide discussion on many different issues relating to learning and teaching. The impact of all these initiatives at both an individual and strategic level is difficult to measure when so many factors interact to change practice. Evaluation really needs to focus on what models and strategies are particularly effective and then to apply this understanding to future funding initiatives. What we can say however is that the profile and practices of learning and teaching in UK education has been raised due to the enthusiasm and hard work of many organisations, groups and individuals.

3

Assuring and improving teaching quality

Kate Patrick and Robyn Lines

> *It is the potential of quality management to break th(e) happy anarchy of university life that makes it so significant to the development of universities (Brennan and Shah, 2000: 116).*

In the minds of many academic staff, quality systems have come to be associated with central control, relentless measurement and ever-increasing demands for more accountability to the system. Is it possible to construct a quality system that genuinely supports education development and change? How could a quality system be constructed to do this effectively? What design and implementation issues need to be addressed? This chapter explores these issues, drawing on our experience of trying to negotiate them in a particular university setting.

Our discussion moves from the general to the particular, beginning with a description of the broader context. We go on to identify from our reading and our experience some of the critical issues involved in constructing an effective university quality system. Next we present a case study, discussing how we have tried to address these issues at RMIT. We conclude with some observations about what we have learnt in the process.

CONTEXT

In Chapter 1, Ling has mentioned the regulatory and quality assurance regimes which are increasingly impinging on the work of universities, and an associated shift to managerialism and academic accountability within universities. It has become routine for national quality agencies to monitor the quality of teaching and learning within the 'self-accrediting' university (Dunkerley and Wong, 2001; Brennan and Shah, 2000).

These quality regimes vary in the extent to which they have developed explicit standards which universities are expected to meet. Unlike the UK Quality Assurance Agency, for instance, the Australian University Quality Agency, AUQA, has adopted a distributed approach: their audits focus on the quality system which the university has in place to support the mission and goals it has set. Even this approach, however, is underpinned by an implicit expectation that academic activity within the university should support the university's mission, and that university processes and performance indicators should promote and monitor its realisation.

University leaders (in Australia, the Australian Vice-Chancellors' Committee) have acquiesced in the development of these regimes. Indeed, as Brennan and Shah (2000) point out, it is common for university leaders to use quality assessment and quality systems to serve university goals. The process of external quality assessment has frequently been assimilated as a support for an increasingly centralised approach to university governance (cf. also Marginson and Considine, 2000).

As Ling has pointed out (Chapter 1, this volume), this managerial transformation of universities with its increased emphasis on quality and accountability is a response to significant changes in the material conditions of universities. Individual university responses to these changed circumstances are influenced by a range of factors (the history of the institution, relative wealth, reputation) but have generally been characterised by a shift to centrally determined strategic directions, including the internationalisation of curriculum, increased flexibility in the time and place of learning, and the reconceptualisation of teaching in terms of student outcomes and capabilities. In this context, the challenge for education development is to help academics think about their teaching differently. This may well mean seeking to transform the culture of teaching and learning which prevails within a particular department.

At the same time, we know that academics identify first with their discipline, and then with their department (cf. Hannan and Silver, 2000; Clark, 1996b). Despite the aspirations of university leaders, the university's goals may well be seen as remote, irrelevant, or rhetorical, to be addressed in the formulation of documents for approval or promotion but not directly useful in the lived work of teaching and learning.

Within this context, we argue that the university's quality system can significantly influence the achievement of university strategic goals, and can contribute to the further development of the strategy itself. The extent of this influence depends on the focus of the quality system and the extent to which it is accepted and integrated into the fabric of life in the institution.

This is not to assume that quality processes are necessarily transformative. Even at programme level, connecting quality processes and education development work is a problematic task. Changes in teaching and learning are more often described than achieved – rather like 'progressive' teaching in the 1970s, which penetrated only a few classrooms (cf. Cuban, 1984; Bennett, 1984). In Australia, ten years of ratings on the nationally administered Course Experience Questionnaire (CEQ) by Australian graduates have shown little change in students' experiences of learning in their discipline (see Graduate Careers Council of Australia, 1994; Badhni and Aungles, 2002; Patrick, 2003). Similarly, Brennan and Shah (2000), drawing on their international array of case studies, found little evidence that external quality assessment had directly influenced teaching practice or curriculum.

The particular challenge explored by this chapter is the design and implementation of a university quality assurance system which can both assure and improve teaching quality – that is, which actively supports transformative education development and educational change. We argue that for the quality system to be effective, it must be accepted by the diversity of constituencies within the institution while at the same time framing the strategic direction and nature of change for the whole university.

ISSUES

Defining quality

> With Quality as a central undefined term, reality is, in its essential nature, not static but dynamic. And when you really understand dynamic reality you never get stuck. It has forms but the forms are capable of change ... If you want to build a factory, or fix a motorcycle, or set a nation right without getting stuck, then classical, structured, dualistic subject-object knowledge, although necessary, isn't enough. You have to have some feeling for the quality of the work. You have to have a sense of what's good. That is what carries you forward (Pirsig, 1974: 255).

Quality regimes do not necessarily support transformative change. How quality is defined makes a difference to the capacity of the quality regime to support educational change and development.

Quality is variously interpreted as an outcome, as a property or characteristic, and as a process. Sallis (2002: 13–14) distinguishes between quality as fitness for purpose, which is associated with consistent and effectively documented processes, subject to accountability and audit; and what he calls 'transformational quality' which is 'about improving ... doing things right, not just doing the right things'. Brennan and Shah (2000) use a set of definitions by Daniels (1998), distinguishing between quality assessment, which measures performance and/or outcomes; quality control, which denotes arrangements to verify that teaching and assessment are satisfactory; and quality assurance, which encompasses a system of policies, systems and processes which maintain and enhance quality.

The variety of approaches to quality, and the different senses in which quality is understood, are problematic. Conversation focused on quality can be conducted at cross-purposes or become sterile through an obsessive focus on process, rather than substantive issues of teaching and learning. We have encountered many academics who share Bill Readings' scepticism about 'quality' regimes and the emptiness of excellence as an objective (Readings, 1996; cf. Watts, 2002; Patrick *et al.*, 2002).

There is particular discomfort with the language of quality assurance – hardly surprising, if we consider the diverse discourses which are simultaneously present in a university (cf. Bergquist, 1992; Trowler, 1998). Different ways of framing work within the academy sit alongside the already mentioned managerial approach and the increasingly prevalent market discourse. In designing a quality system it is necessary to recognise the multiple cultures within the university and to develop a system that is balanced between the provision of visible and systematised quality assurance necessary to meet external and internal requirements, and systems that provide significant space for local adaptation such that they are accepted by academics and usefully deployed within different academic cultures.

This implies a distributed approach whereby the diverse communities within the university engage with quality issues in a way which makes sense to them. Seeing quality assurance and improvement as a form of action research may resonate with academics in some disciplines; alternate forms of the language of scholarship may be more effective with others. Different assurance and improvement languages will be required if we are to communicate within the system, and up and down the various levels of the organization. The quality system needs to provide methods of translation that enable university policies to be assimilated into the disciplinary, professional or departmental languages in use.

Building commitment: the need for ownership and trust

As Bowden and Marton (1998) point out, universities cannot be assumed to be learning organisations committed to change processes. Commitment at all levels is critical to the sustainability of an ongoing change process: both unambiguous support from management, and a connection with things that matter to academic staff.

If such commitment is to be fostered seriously, the organisation must be coherent in its support of these ideas. Each arm of management within the organisation needs to be clearly pulling in the same direction, policies and practices should be aligned and resources should be distributed in ways that clearly show support for the direction of change (Mintzberg, 1994; cf. Biggs, 1999).

Commitment is about caring; people cannot be expected to commit to a system. As Senge says:

> ... caring is personal. It is rooted in an individual's own set of values, concerns, and aspirations. That is why genuine caring about a shared vision is rooted in personal visions ... If people don't have their own vision, all they can do is 'sign up' for someone else's. The result is compliance, never commitment (Senge, 1990: 20).

People will, however, commit to ideas that respond to issues of significance for them. The system can then support them through implementation and documentation. An effective system will maximise the amount of responsible autonomy at the programme and subject level while providing support for implementation.

This approach recognises the diversity of cultures within the university and the significance of locally developed practices and indicators. It implies that the overarching policy is seen as providing an interpretive framework for quality improvement/assurance which can be achieved by transformations which are owned and directed by staff at the local level (cf. McNaught, this volume).

Collective commitment to change implies a climate of trust. A punitive or blaming environment will result in defensiveness or token compliance rather than active participation. This is particularly an issue in relation to the design and deployment of feedback and performance monitoring. As a participant in one of our curriculum workshops remarked, there is a tendency within a rapidly changing and somewhat chaotic environment to 'go mad on processes as a substitute for trust'. When does a focus on process become an indefensible organisational defence aimed, in her words, at 'controlling the uncontrollable'?

We need to find a balance between systems focused on data collection, interpretation and use for improvement and the use of data for the measurement of quality and appraisal of staff (both internally and externally driven). While judgements need to be made within an organisation on some basis, using the same data for improvement and measurement runs the risk of one policy or process undermining another.

At the local level, improvement also requires a culture of trust. No-one will reasonably share failures – and achieve Argyris and Schön's 'double-loop learning' (1978) – in a punitive environment. Improvement and innovation require risk taking but this is unlikely in a culture of blame. Support needs to be distinguished from surveillance.

Building change into university practices

> It's a very odd thing –
> As odd as can be –
> That whatever Miss T. eats
> Turns into Miss T.
> (de la Mare, 1913)

For the quality system to be effective in supporting transformative change, the task of 'doing quality' needs to be built into the life of the university and incorporated in taken for granted university practices. This implies that resources are directed to supporting change processes: specifically, data, dialogical support, and time.

Universities typically codify their directions in strategies or plans, but these are nothing more than sloganeering if they are not fully supported by the organisation's systems and resources. To promote continuing commitment, resources need to be allocated not only to the collection of programme performance data and the filing of reports but also to data flow and the activities of improvement and innovation – the means to find meaning in and to act on the data.[1]

Dialogical support is critical to education development. We see it as particularly important that the university allocate resources to collaborative support for groups of staff working on educational change projects.[2] In many disciplines, significant educational change may well mean adopting new ways of representing knowledge and conceiving of the relation between teachers and students. The change process will challenge the epistemology, professional identity and established practices of many academic teaching staff – in effect, it involves cultural change within academic departments (cf. Prosser and Trigwell, 1999; Martin, 1999; Ramsden, 1998b; Trowler, 1998).

We argued above that a distributed approach to educational change makes sense in the light of the diversity of academic discourse. Our experience is that appropriate and effective support can be provided via centrally promoted initiatives, as long as they are themselves predicated on working with and within diverse cultures and on a dialogical model of development. The sustaining of a rich and productive conversation about quality and its assurance can also be fostered by university education development units, which can create a place for reflection and provide opportunities for sharing the variation of experience across cultures and teaching environments.

Even in the medium term, however, support from central units will not be enough. Given current pressures on funding, no central unit is likely to be large enough to provide ongoing dialogical support across the university. Education development units have traditionally dispensed their resources by providing short-term teaching development projects and central activities in which individuals participate; neither of these strategies appears to be particularly apt for supporting transformative change at discipline level in either teaching or curriculum. A successful quality system needs to 'snowball' learning and incorporate models of group development, coaching and mentoring (see, for instance, McNaught, this volume).

We see this as effectively the development of a learning organisation: creating a coherent, supportive environment that is dialogical and open to experiment and development (cf. Senge, 1990; Martin, 1999). A key aspect of this, consistent with the pedagogy being fostered through the system, is that learning is collaborative – it runs both ways. The university should be open to and able to learn from the practices within the faculties to develop its understanding of its objectives in a rich and fluid way. It must be a reciprocal system. This is exceedingly difficult to achieve in practice but is nonetheless a necessary aim.

The other major resource issue for education development is the resource of time. This is the one in shortest supply. It means the organisation needs to have a commitment to the kind of change it desires; it must not lose its nerve and demand that these changes happen too quickly or without the requisite investment of time for change to be initiated and take root and for its impact to be revealed. Pressure for fast results undermines the change process.

Addressing these issues

Before describing how we've approached these issues at RMIT, some background is in order.[3] RMIT is a large technological university, formerly an institute of technology, which incorporates both technical education (TAFE – equivalent to further education in the UK) and higher education. Historically, RMIT has been committed to applied education and work-integrated learning. Nearly half our course-work students in every category are studying part-time, as are most of our research students. This emphasis affects research as well as teaching. While staff involvement in pure research has increased since our designation as a university in 1992, applied consultancy and practice-based research still dominate our research profile. At the same time, the workload of teaching staff has increased significantly over the past twenty years, with a considerable worsening of student–staff ratios. From a management perspective, competing demands on academic staff time are contained by a system of individual staff workplans which are agreed at the beginning of the academic year, following discussions within the department and negotiation between each academic and the head of department.

RMIT offers diplomas and degrees across a wide range of fields: engineering and applied sciences, business, health and para-medical disciplines, design and the fine arts, social science, social work and education. About 40 per cent of our 57,000 onshore students are undertaking technical programmes; about 45 per cent are undergraduates; and the rest are undertaking post-graduate coursework or research degrees (13 per cent and 3 per cent respectively).

In recent years RMIT has been building an international presence. A substantial number of international students come to RMIT in Melbourne to study, mainly in business and engineering programmes (currently a quarter of all enrolled students; a majority of students in some programmes). RMIT also maintains partnerships with a number of institutions in the Asia/Pacific region, involving over 6,000 offshore students studying for RMIT awards.

The key objectives of current education development at RMIT emerge from this history and context. Our most recent strategic plan envisions transformative changes in teaching and learning: in particular, the development of online learning resources, a shift to a student-centred approach to teaching and learning, and the development of capability-based curricula.

In the 1990s, quality initiatives at RMIT focused primarily on quality as fitness for purpose: description, measurement, audit, and incremental change.[4] In the changing environment for universities described above, however, repeated measurement and adjustment or incremental improvement are not enough to achieve the university's objectives.

A new programme quality assurance system has been developed at RMIT to support these changes and to provide a framework for appropriate education development work. Support for the system is provided by university-level units and faculty staff. The quality consultancy unit leads the development of the system, including consultation with staff, and has a continuing role in resourcing, monitoring and improving it. The university programme renewal team offers leadership and support to staff undertaking periodic curriculum review and renewal. In each faculty, associate deans of teaching and learning coordinate and support local implementation of the system, and connect staff in schools and departments with the university's central support services.

Designing an appropriate quality framework

The university's new programme quality assurance (PQA) system is designed to incorporate education development, and supports a shift to student-centred teaching and capability-based curriculum, in line with RMIT policy. Critical elements of our approach are:

- a quality management system focused on educational improvement;
- a quality assurance cycle which incorporates periodic programme renewal;
- stimulus and support for curriculum review and transformative change at programme and subject level.

Both authors are engaged in working to support this system: one as manager of the system overall, the other as the leader of the university programme renewal team.

We see the PQA system as offering a framework which supports the university's development as a learning organisation. It has been designed to work with RMIT's system of devolved responsibilities, to respect cultural differences within the university, and to prompt, support and incorporate education development at programme and subject level. It is intended to be permeable and adaptable, capable of promoting locally owned, sustainable change.

The system is based on a set of seven criteria. These were developed by the associate deans who support programme teams in the Faculties, and endorsed as university policy. The criteria specify that programmes are expected to be useful, effective, well-designed, well managed, and appropriately resourced; meet equity targets; and satisfy relevant professional accreditation requirements (the RMIT website, www.rmit.edu.au/teaching andlearning/pqacriteria, provides more detail). In order to ensure that these criteria are addressed in programme design and implementation, they have been built into the requirements for programme approval, programme management, curriculum review and renewal, and external audit. These have been introduced in stages: in 2001 a single faculty undertook a pilot implementation of quality management (reported by Radloff, in this volume), in late 2001 the criteria were embedded in revised programme approval and renewal processes, and in 2002 they were introduced across the university as a framework for programme management and annual reports.

Figure 3.1 depicts the five-year cycle which is built into the system.

How is this system designed to respond to the issues we have identified as critical?

Below the line in Figure 3.1 are the ongoing and annual improvement and reporting activities of the programme team. At programme level, the system

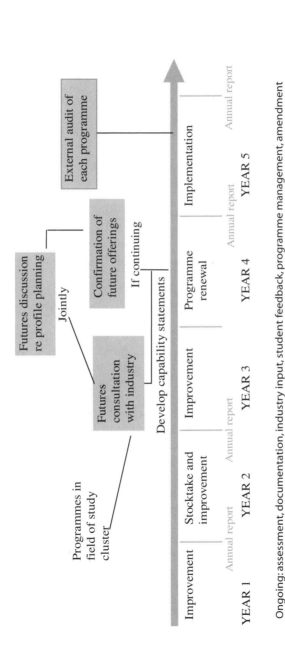

Improvement | Stocktake and improvement | Improvement | Programme renewal | Implementation

Annual report

YEAR 1 | YEAR 2 | YEAR 3 | YEAR 4 | YEAR 5

Develop capability statements

If continuing

Programmes in field of study cluster

Futures consultation with industry

Jointly

Futures discussion re profile planning

Confirmation of future offerings

External audit of each programme

Ongoing: assessment, documentation, industry input, student feedback, programme management, amendment

Figure 3.1 *A five-year cycle for programme quality assurance and renewal*

provides for local development of goals and performance measures. The aim is to support local ownership by staff teaching into the programme (the programme team). While the PQA criteria provide a common framework, programme teams are expected to define quality and undertake continuous improvement in a way which is meaningful for their field of study. To do this, they need to make their own sense of the criteria, to identify and collate relevant measures for tracking performance, and to use data from these measures as input for local improvement planning: [5] for example, staff in one of our undergraduate business degrees are now monitoring the availability of work placements for their third-year students, which gives them early warning of changes in the employment market. The associate dean (teaching and learning) in each faculty supports programme teams in this process of interpretation.

The programme reports are also designed to maintain the confidence of the university leadership. The reports go to deans, who in turn report on the action which faculties are taking and the support they require from the university. They are built into management accountability, and make visible the efforts and achievements of staff and the responses of senior managers. They provide data on the quality, currency and viability of each programme. They identify issues to be addressed and the resources and support which are required. Used constructively, this reporting system should improve communication and increase trust and confidence between staff at different levels.

The processes depicted above the line in Figure 3.1 are the renewal and audit processes which provide external input and inform the university's decisions concerning the profile of programmes it offers. The periodic programme renewal cycle is designed to engage staff in identifying, or re-evaluating, the outcome capabilities which graduates need to develop. This enacts the commitment to capability-based curriculum which is incorporated in the PQA criterion for programme design. Programme renewal provides an opportunity for staff to re-invigorate their approaches and rethink their curriculum. The programme team undertakes futures consultations with community and industry stakeholders, identifying trends and possible developments in the field (Emery and Purser 1996), and revises the curriculum to ensure that future graduates have the capabilities which are likely to be needed. It is also a significant opportunity for education developers to support the change process. They facilitate programme-level reflection and planning, which we see as critical if staff are to engage effectively with the cultural shifts which are implicit in university policy.

The renewal process also provides input for university planning. Staff engaged in the consultation phase of programme renewal collect insights which can significantly contribute to medium-term planning of the university profile. Programmes in the same field of study are scheduled for renewal concurrently, to maximise the reach and effectiveness of the consultation process and its power to provide useful data for planning purposes.

These elements of the system provide an integrated framework which supports sustainable strategic change, as well as the self-monitoring and incremental improvement associated with the 'business excellence framework'. In terms of education development, programme teams are expected to reflect on curriculum and pedagogy as part of their annual action planning processes, and to undertake extensive consultation and curriculum renewal every five years. Faculty staff provide ongoing feedback and support for the improvement planning, and a university-level programme renewal team is available to support the curriculum renewal. In line with McNaught's characterisation of RMIT (this volume), this can be seen as a corporate system, with tightly specified policies to be implemented in a controlled manner (McNay, 1995). RMIT is not tidily corporate, however. As can be seen from the description above, our quality assurance system has been deliberately designed to accommodate local diversity and assertiveness, and the multiple perspectives of policy-makers and academics (cf. Ling, this volume).

So much for the interpretation of quality that is designed into the system. How has it worked in practice?

Fostering trust and commitment

Balancing the requirements of different stakeholders has not been easy. The system makes complex demands. These can be seen as cumbersome by programme teams and as insufficiently focused by university strategic planners. Our challenge now is to streamline the system while preserving and developing commitment to the underpinning criteria and the cyclical approach to reporting and renewal.

The programme annual report, which is meant to facilitate local ownership of the criteria, was initially seen as over-complex. Academics were frequently suspicious of the reporting task: the criteria and the report were seen to be imposed by management, and several people expressed concern at the possible outcome of open discussion of problems or under-performance.[6] To address this concern, faculties were invited to launch the reporting process via discussions with programme leaders about how the report could be useful to them. Staff in some faculties critiqued the report protocol and participated in developing an alternative. The process was broadly successful, in that nearly all programmes provided reports which incorporated achievements, issues and action plans. The deans' reports summarising programme level achievements, issues and action plans are being carefully read, and should contribute to strategic and operational planning for education improvement.

In some areas, staff have been actively using the reporting process to evaluate the performance of their programme against the PQA criteria. Where this has happened, there has been a shift towards reading university performance indicators as potentially helpful data, and seeing the reporting system as part of a meaningful improvement and development cycle. Used in this way, annual reports should help a programme team track the performance of their programme over time, assess where improvements are needed, and evaluate the effectiveness of the changes they make. They will also accumulate a rich, multi-dimensional array of evidence which will make it easy for auditors to attest the quality of their programme.

Staff involved in the pilot implementation of the process, however, continued to express their concern at the workload involved (see Scott 2002), which has tended to impair the confidence of senior management in the process as a whole. An additional complication has been the reorganisation of the university to bring faculties together into portfolios, which involves a redefinition of the role of heads of schools and departments. The role of heads in relation to programmes is changing: they are now becoming key players and their support will be critical in the future (cf. Pearson and Trevitt, this volume).

Next steps involve further simplifying the reporting process and integrating it more effectively into profile planning at university level. This responds both to concern at the detail and workload involved in the first stage of annual reporting, and also a push to connect programme quality management more closely with profile planning.

While it should be useful to programme teams to have a simpler reporting format and locally delivered data, closer engagement with profile planning may well be a two-edged sword, in which accountability will cut across educational objectives. Indicators which are used by the university leadership to determine programme discontinuance may become highly salient to programme teams, but they may also lose their point: they become dis-embodied, emptied of meaning, subject to challenge. Connecting annual report content to profile planning may also encourage window-dressing and undermine the usefulness of the report as a tool for local programme planning.

We will need more discussion about the purposes and uses of the reports, and how they can contribute to improvement at local, school and university level.

Resourcing transformative development

Annual reports support, record and possibly occasion continuous improvement activities, but they are unlikely to provide the challenge which is needed for transformative education development (cf. Bereiter and

Scardamalia, 1993; Marton and Booth, 1997). Within the system, a current opportunity for qualitative change in teaching and learning practices is the renewal of programmes, which is scheduled to take place on a five-yearly cycle. The initial round of programme renewals require the transformation of the curriculum from a traditional discipline format to a capability base, and the consequent redevelopment of all of the subjects within a programme, in accordance with the university's strategic commitment to this form of curriculum.

Our aim here is significant transformation of curricula, teaching and learning. This represents a considerable mindshift for staff who view curriculum in terms of content rather than capabilities. It challenges many of the taken for granted curriculum practices within the university which have been characterised by individual academic 'ownership' of discrete subjects, whose content and underpinning assumptions remain largely private. Programme renewal reverses the traditional approach to creating a programme through the aggregation of individual subjects to one where the role of individual subjects is determined by the team. Developing a team approach to the curriculum requires that the staff interrogate the diversity of views about the nature of the profession and appropriate education for it, and come to some form of consensus.[7] Finally, a capability approach necessarily implies a constructivist approach to course design and teaching as students need to be active in constructing meaning, critically evaluating and developing their capability and shaping their learning experiences. This challenges many current practices that have been more strongly didactic and oriented to the transmission of information.

In line with our system objectives of recognising cultural diversity and fostering local engagement, programme renewal operates within an action-learning framework. A capability-based curriculum is necessarily a holistic and integrated one and the active commitment of all staff who teach in the programme is necessary to develop a deep and collective understanding of the implications of the change and to reinforce, or build, the community of continuous enquiry that will be needed to realise the curriculum design. Members of the collaborative team for each renewal include all staff who teach within the programme, a support person from the university programme renewal group, and consultants from the library and Learning Skills Unit.

Building this collection of people into a team committed to educational transformation has proven to be a challenge. In practice, one complicating factor has been the university's decision to prioritise the first programmes to be renewed according to feedback from graduates on their learning experiences (via the Course Experience Questionnaire, collected nationally). Many staff begin by challenging the reliability of the nationally collected CEQ data which have initially been used by RMIT to prioritise programmes to be renewed.[8] These data appear to contradict their own locally collected student feedback at individual subject level.

To connect the system data to the local context, early work in a renewal project generally involves extensive consultation with students through focus groups. Students are invited to contribute their perceptions of the programme as a whole, their assessments of their most and least effective learning experiences, and the capabilities they see as desirable outcomes from their study. Staff have generally chosen not to participate in these interviews, to enable students to speak more freely. The data from the interviews are, however, discussed by programme teams, with the aim of generating fresh insights into the holistic student experience and identifying the specific local concerns that need to be addressed and that make a renewal a worthwhile initiative. These discussions often surface anxiety – not only the anxiety which staff expect students will experience, but also their own concern about public discussion of criticisms raised by students. We have found that it has been useful to have a detached facilitator to work with the staff group. The facilitator helps to keep the discussion focused on the issues, so that the students' feedback is not treated as evidence of personal failure, but rather as providing clues to a complex situation which is worth addressing collectively. We also get the group to locate readings which describe other staff struggling with similar issues in trying to transform their teaching. This work will continue to be useful where renewal is routinely scheduled as part of the PQA cycle.

Once there is agreement that there is a need and opportunity for change, the nature and direction of that change often becomes the focus for continuing scepticism. At this point there is a tussle between central direction and local ability to take control. From the university perspective, the shift to a capability-based curriculum incorporates local ownership – the university has explicitly decided not to provide a university-wide definition of desirable capabilities. From the staff perspective, however, capability-based curriculum is a prescriptive top-down initiative, and they are unlikely to be confident that students will gain from the significant changes in teaching and learning practice that this will require. They often think that the university has already determined a constraining and limiting approach which they will be required to adopt, and need a lot of encouragement to see that there is a space in which they can construct and develop a curriculum which makes sense to them. In this context, how have we gone about ensuring that staff take ownership?

A key to success in achieving support for centrally devised strategies is the ability to translate these into the language of the group who are to undertake the development. Attention to the metaphors through which participants express their thinking is a useful point of connection between local practice and central goals. This involves the central education development staff member in listening very carefully to the ways in which the group conceptualise and articulate their understandings of what is central to teaching and learning in the specific professional domain. We have found, for example, that some groups with whom we have worked conceptualise curriculum as a linear accumulation of knowledge from foundational concepts to their application in practice-like situations. Developing a capability-based curriculum with such groups requires a focus on the ways foundational concepts might be learned through active strategies in practice-like situations. Other teams have articulated an approach that suggests that learning should develop from a broad and general conceptual base to the progressive achievement of specialised professional skills. The language of capability development in this context will be different from the first case and perhaps focus on the potential to link early learning to conceptions of what being a professional might mean. The point is, that whatever the discipline- and profession-shaped ways of conceptualising and speaking about teaching and learning are, they need to be noticed, respected and made visible in the practice of curriculum change.

Another critical step in building ownership has been to involve staff in talking with outsiders in industry and the community whose enthusiasm for a capability-based curriculum approach has proven contagious. Together, we have run focus groups with external stakeholders which concurrently contribute to the quality system's broader planning objectives. At the programme level, this not only serves to rethink the outcomes for the programme in terms of capability, but also builds or revitalises relationships and opens up new possibilities for external partnerships in teaching, learning and assessment. Often, exciting new ideas are generated.

The processes for developing the curriculum and specification for individual subjects that follow the development of the capability profile are consistently team based and dialogical, and are supported by the participation of an education developer from the university programme renewal team. For transformation of teaching and learning to occur, the aspirations of the curriculum need to translate into significant changes in the design and teaching of individual subjects. Our experience suggests that this is most likely to happen if collaborative practices are extended to this level.

The ability to provide central support for all such developments is unrealistic. We are currently exploring peer-pairing practices, group development through workshops and peer review of course guides following the protocols of academic journal reviewing. These should allow us to draw upon the expertise of our most able teachers in the building of staff capability and programme quality. These strategies require the staff involved to have time and a commitment to learning the specific languages of diverse programme teams with which they work, and to engage with them in their everyday practices so that diversity is recognised and valorised. In effect, a kind of ethnographic engagement is necessary for successful educational support.

At a practical level, effective participation in programme renewal also requires committed local leadership within departments, schools, and faculties. Provision of resources to support renewal, particularly staff time, has proved challenging. We are working towards a better alignment of the scheduling of education development initiatives and staff work-planning within departments so that the necessary time to fully participate in a renewal is allocated. Current policy for programme quality assurance includes a five-year cycle of programme renewal, which should facilitate forward planning for work-plans.

It is too early to fully evaluate the impact of programme renewal on the quality of student learning and outcomes. Evaluations of the processes of programme renewal with participating teams suggest that our approach to the provision of central education development support has, in fact, contributed to some significant rethinking of curriculum, teaching and assessment strategies. Staff team members have said that the participation of an external education developer from the university programme renewal team validated their own significant effort in undertaking the renewal, and that knowing that an outsider was participating helped them to prioritise the necessary time commitment. In addition, including the external member in team discussions and workshops meant more than the injection of a different repertoire of teaching and learning ideas; it was significant in constructing a forum where previously unexamined differences and approaches could be made visible and become a part of team dialogue. Finally, this experience of renewal built confidence in the team about its ability to effect significant change.

REFLECTIONS AND OUTSTANDING ISSUES

Our experience illustrates that, in practice, the key issues we have identified are intimately inter-related. We are still in the process of trying to address them.

First, there are unresolved tensions around the definition of quality itself, and its relation to educational change and development. These are critically related to the issue of acceptance and ownership.

We have posited a view of quality which recognises that conceptions of quality and educational systems are both dynamic. The quality of programmes is constantly being re-evaluated, and the criteria by which quality is judged are always already contestable (Connolly, 1974; Hacking,

1999). From this perspective, active debate about what constitutes educational effectiveness should actually contribute to the development of more effective practices by opening up possibilities for doing things differently (compare Marton and Booth, 1997; Bereiter and Scardamalia, 1993).

If quality is interpreted primarily in terms of the alignment of policy and practice, however, audits become a tool for evaluating compliance. University policies are deployed as criteria against which teaching practices and curriculum can appropriately be audited; there is no space for debating what the policies mean and how they might effectively be taken forward. This fails to acknowledge the contestability of policy, and elides the gap between aspiration and performance, which depends on achieving a degree of agreement about policy objectives. In the imagination, this gap may easily be jumped. For academic staff, however, shifting to a different pedagogy and approach to curriculum is not easy and may not be seen as desirable. In this situation, an approach using the audit as a weapon to impose compliance may well encourage resistance and/or tokenistic window-dressing, rather than conviction and substantive change (cf. Power, 1997). Effective implementation of RMIT's quality system, as we see it, requires that audits are used as a tool to support and attest careful and collaborative work on the implementation of policy issues.

Second, there is a tension between a policy commitment to scheduling the renewal of curriculum in each programme on a five-year cycle, and university planning decisions which give priority to the out-of-cycle renewal of particular programmes. At this stage, when relatively few academic staff have engaged in renewal, expertise in curriculum renewal is scarce and tends to be concentrated in the central academic development unit. Hence programmes being pushed forward for early attention are competing for support with programmes which are scheduled for renewal, jeopardising the concept of cyclical renewal. As we have indicated, the resource aspect of this can be tackled via snowballing staff expertise in curriculum renewal, and recruiting academics as peer mentors in renewal projects. More importantly, however, we see that the quality system needs to demonstrate that university futures planning can gain from programme-level input based on renewal consultations. For this purpose, we are bringing together university planners and staff who have been involved in industry and community consultations, to discuss possible futures and the implications for the programmes RMIT might offer. This is an aspect of the process which is still being developed.

Finally, there is the challenge of converting transformed written curriculum into transformed teaching practice. The programme renewal project operates at the interface between curriculum and teaching; we recognise that programme renewal is only the first step. To make it effective, staff teaching in the programme need to come together to talk over the new directions in curriculum and explore areas of difference. Detailed subject preparation has to be worked through, and staff who were not involved in the renewal process may well be called on to rethink the relation between teaching and learning. Follow-through is needed to ensure that all staff involved in teaching new curriculum have an opportunity to work through its rationale. This means developing tools to help align capabilities and learning outcomes at the subject level. Ideally we would like to link this with sustained support for teaching staff as a collective, at department or discipline level (cf. the *intrepid* project reported by our colleagues Nicolettou and Wright, 2002).

Implicit in all of this is the vital importance of staff commitment and involvement at different levels of management (cf. McNaught, this volume, on vertical integration). In the next stage of implementation, we are aiming to provide opportunities for managers to participate in renewal and curriculum rethinking, so that they appreciate the effort involved and the dangers of being impatient for results (cf. Pearson and Trevitt, McNaught, this volume). In short, we see quality as a collaborative and ongoing enterprise with enormous potential for inspiring education development.

NOTES

1   In passing, we note that it is critical that documentation is seen as useful. This means balancing the time and effort involved in instituting and maintaining a QA system (especially the requirements for documentation that make it visible and auditable) with recognised benefits in terms of improved outcomes and experiences for staff and students.

2   See Bereiter and Scardamalia (1993) and Marton and Booth (1997) for discussion of the importance of noticing variation; Martin (1999) and McNaught (this volume) for case studies of collaboration.

3   Most of the information provided below is available from the RMIT website, www.rmit.edu.au; data on RMIT postgraduate research students is drawn from Barnacle (2002).

4   Over the past ten years, quality at RMIT has involved activities under each of Daniels' headings. Our first educational quality assurance scheme, established in 1994, was a peer-review system based on a commitment to continuous educational improvement. Subsequently, the university achieved certification of teaching and learning under ISO-9001. This meant demonstrating that we had an effective quality management system; the Quality Unit used a modified form of the Australian Business Excellence Framework categories to describe our approach to planning, implementation, evaluation and improvement, and organises internal and external audits of practice against policy and procedure. In line with this, the university leadership

has emphasised the importance of stakeholder input and feedback, sponsors a process for establishing and addressing the Top Ten student concerns every year, and uses data on teaching quality to inform profile planning. These data are obtained from the Course Experience Questionnaire, which is administered to all Australian university graduates the year after they complete their programme.

In the early 1990s, there was also some interest in total quality management, and subsequently groups within the university established improvement projects under this banner; it was not, however, adopted as a university project.

5   In this process, university-generated performance measures can be interpreted as potentially useful sources of evidence. This is an improvement on the common situation where university data are seen as threatening and/or irrelevant, rather than as useful prompts to change.

6   This concern was understandable. In 2002 and 2003, the university's profile planning process was mandated to identify 10 per cent of programmes for 'resting' and renewal or discontinuance, using teaching quality as the primary indicator.

7   For a discussion of the nature of this consensus and its relationship to notions of capability, see Lines (2002).

8   This prioritisation was initiated as part of the profile planning process. It has identified programmes for renewal independently from the programme quality assurance cycle – alignment between the two systems is still being worked through.

4

Education development units and the enhancement of university teaching

Denise Chalmers and Mia O'Brien

THE CORE BUSINESS OF EDUCATION DEVELOPMENT

The increasingly complex and often discontinuous demands on university teaching place education development units in an interesting position. As Ling points out (Chapter 1, this volume), education development is concerned with both the development of teaching and the development of the environment in which teaching occurs. This dual focus on teaching development and the teaching environment takes place in an organisation, which is itself situated in a complex global environment of higher education. This has led us to engage in a critical re-examination of the place of an education development unit within the university, and the central concerns of education development.

Our colleagues in this book have outlined how facilitating the development of teaching engages us in a range of everyday puzzles and problems many of which have been outlined by Ling, and in other chapters in this volume. While these are complex issues in themselves, they are the pragmatic outcomes of a more global and constantly shifting higher education context. It is therefore imperative for education development practitioners to maintain a working knowledge of the socio-economic, cultural, political and philosophical terrain as points of reference for their professional practice.

The role of those engaged in education development is not limited to these familiar issues identified above. Education development endeavours to make a significant contribution to the enhancement of university teaching both within the university community, and across the higher education sector. In order to achieve this, we argue that education development units are primarily engaged in four overarching concerns:

1   maintaining a corporate memory of, and sustained engagement in, the issues and innovations in teaching in higher education;

2   engaging in comprehensive and systematic implementation of teaching and learning initiatives;

3   creating and facilitating communities of learning involved in the iterative and dynamic top-down/bottom-up engagement and management of educational initiatives;

4   investigating, articulating and disseminating scholarship in (and on) teaching, learning and education development.

In this chapter we briefly review each of these four concerns as they have been historically and pragmatically played out within the Australian higher education context. At the same time, we outline our understanding of the key role a central education development unit (EDU) may play within the university context. We argue that if EDUs are to be truly effective within the teaching and learning community, then they need to be positioned across the multiple layers of interactions within their own universities, between collaborative universities, and across the higher education sector itself. To exemplify our discussion, we illustrate the education development approach and practices of the Teaching and Education Development Institute (TEDI), a large, centralised EDU within the University of Queensland. Our approach is holistic in outlook, multi-functional in nature, and interleaved within the many levels of policy, institutional initiatives and educational practices that exist concurrently in today's complex universities. Our conception of education development has emerged as a reflexive response to the four overarching concerns (described above), and a conviction that to do otherwise risks a fragmentation of education development that has often been limited by *ad hoc*, localised and short-lived changes in teaching quality and practices.

There has been an ongoing debate about whether the professional development of university teachers best takes place through central or departmental units (Brew, 1995; Johnston, 1997; Murphy, 1994; Nightingale, 1987; Warren-Piper, 1994; Webb, 1996; Zuber-Skerritt; 1994; Blackmore *et al.*, 1999). Indeed, in this book a number of departmental or decentralised approaches to professional development are described, e.g. Radloff; McNaught; Patrick and Lines. In this chapter we argue that a central university unit is the most effective structure to achieve enhancement of teaching and learning and the agendas of governments, universities, departments and individuals throughout the university.

A FRAMEWORK FOR EDUCATION DEVELOPMENT

Education development is about improving and enhancing student learning and the student experience of learning. Given this assertion, it may seem very strange that students tend to be mentioned only in passing in these pages. This is because education development is primarily concerned with working with university teachers and those who contribute to the students' learning experiences. The ultimate goal is that, as a result of engaging university staff and teachers in education development activities, students will benefit. Therefore, it needs to be stated from the outset that we contend that EDUs should not represent themselves as responsible for the quality of teaching and learning across a university. The ultimate responsibility for this lies with the staff who teach the students, the faculties which offer the programmes of study, and the staff who support the teaching. However, we assert the role of an EDU as central to the effective and sustainable support of excellence in university teaching and learning and, in particular, the attainment of the four fundamental concerns identified above. Through the EDU we aim to provide leadership, advice, scholarship, research, guidance, support and services within a range of key functions. These activities are not simply carried out in a functional or technical way but are framed within an overarching philosophy of education development and teaching enhancement.

Our central assumption is that sustainable transformational change in the quality of university teaching and learning will be more effectively achieved through a holistic and integrated perspective of education development. This perspective holds three interrelated tenets. The first is a commitment to ground all education development activities (including the professional development of teachers, the design of curricula and production of learning resources, and the active contribution to university policy and practices) in a deep understanding of the nature of scholarly teaching and academic learning, and that this is an ongoing and interactive process.

The second recognises that university teachers, learners, and education developers are partners in the task of identifying, articulating, investigating and demonstrating scholarship of practice within the university community. This includes recognising and affirming the integrity and authenticity of the various disciplinary fields. Much of our work is therefore directed at facilitating partnerships throughout the many sites and layers of interaction within the university.

The third is a conceptualisation of the education development unit (EDU) as a dynamic conduit both within the university community, and across the wider higher education sector. Central to this conception is the explicit negotiation of what counts as valued teaching and learning within our university, and the facilitation of both top-down and bottom-up initiatives towards the enhancement of policy and practice related to teaching and learning.

We view this approach as one that positions the EDU in close partnership with the university community and one that can sustain and provide leadership to the ongoing task of developing and enhancing the quality of teaching and learning in universities. Such an approach also permits a reflexive relationship with the broader contexts and culture of higher education and, as such, provides a viable alternative to more traditional, prescriptive paradigms of education development. We agree with Webb's cautionary stance on prescriptive 'models' for education development (1996; Macdonald, 2003), and are conscious that philosophical positioning is inherent within any act of teaching (Barnett, 1997; Delanty, 2001; Gosling, 2003;). However our point is that this positioning is often overlooked or unexamined. Indeed, it is this very positioning that distinguishes the education development endeavour from any other within the university, for, as Rowland (2003) points out, EDUs are engaged primarily in the task of providing a service to an institution. For that service to be truly educational rather than technical, our role must include finding ways to articulate the practice of teaching within an understanding of the philosophy and values inherent within them, and to use this understanding as a basis for active participation in the critical discourses of higher education and the pragmatic decision-making of the university community.

The implications for EDUs is the need to articulate a process of development that facilitates engagement in teaching and learning communities as a central component of our everyday practice, and embedding them within the wider social, moral and political imperatives for teaching and learning. In this way, responding to issues such as flexible learning, student diversity and international education become educative experiences that are philosophically informed within the community of learning, not simply technical outcomes of a teaching initiative.

In this regard, we present a conceptual model of education development (Figure 4.1) as an interactive partnership based on the processes of communication and collaboration, whilst precluding any prescriptive purpose for education development. As Schön (1987) points out, such an endeavour is epistemologically oriented when it elicits questions about the nature of knowledge and our role in the construction of disciplinary domains for study. The components of the model are based upon our perceived need to position the EDU as the conduit for 'communicative action' and negotiation of teaching practices within the often implicit assumptions and values of university education. From this position, the values, theories, methods and structures of knowledge within each discipline are as integral to the process of development and articulation of learning as the philosophies, pedagogical imperatives and educational objectives of

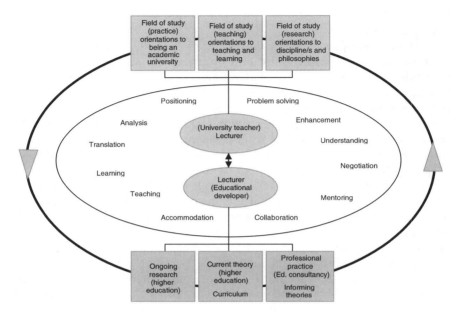

Figure 4.1 *Model of collaborative engagement for teaching and learning*

Source: Figure taken from author's unpublished PhD (O'Brien, 2004).

the university community. Education development is therefore conceived of as a process of negotiating these positions within the task of articulating effective innovations for specific teaching and learning needs.

This model represents the collaborative engagement between a single university teacher and an education developer. However, by substituting the words in the central two ovals to curriculum development team and education development team, or teaching and learning committee and EDU staff, the model can be continually scaled to describe the process of engagement with multiple layers and communities of practice within a university.

Our assertion is that EDUs need to be engaged in a multilayered, multifunctional and interleaved way within the university. We explore this further in the following section, by reviewing each of the four overarching concerns for education development outlined in our introduction. In doing so, we draw out implications for EDUs, and describe how this model facilitates our attempts to respond effectively to these issues.

Maintaining a corporate memory of, and sustained engagement in, the issues and innovations in teaching in higher education

Education development has been characterised by the ebb and flow of the changes within higher education (Brew, 1995; Macdonald, 2003; Walker, 2001). Now firmly taking its place amongst the legitimate fields of study within higher education (Macdonald, 2003), education development brings a suite of traditions of research, scholarship and practices that are the result of decades of engagement in the service of innovation and initiative within university teaching. But while the education development field remains highly diverse in scope, it has been largely homogenic in intention. As a result, central EDUs have become the site of 'corporate' memory of previous research, innovations, practice and policy directions in teaching and learning in many universities. Much of this corporate memory is constituted from the principles of quality teaching and learning derived from educational research, applied to many scholarly endeavours and grounded in the collective wisdom of practitioners whose primary endeavour has been concerned with 'sustaining and enhancing the quality of learning and teaching within the institution' (Hounsell, 1994). As well as the wider scholarly and research-based corporate memory, it also encompasses the ongoing and localised policy developments and teaching and learning initiatives that have taken place within the university and region. This intellectual capital is a valuable part of any university, and of the sector itself (Gosling, 2003).

The importance of the management and development of intellectual capital for teaching and learning has been recently acknowledged by the Australian government, which, in keeping with a similar initiative in the UK, has recently recommended the establishment of a National Institute for Learning and Teaching. This initiative has grown out of the experience of several preceding national government initiatives. The most recent was the formation of the Australian University Teaching Committee (AUTC) established in 2000 to promote quality and excellence in university teaching and learning. The AUTC was preceded by the Commonwealth Staff Development Fund (CSDF), 1990; the Committee of Australian University Teaching (CAUT), 1992; and the Committee of University Teaching and Staff Development (CUTSD), 1997. These organisations provided funding for innovation and change in teaching and learning but utilised different strategies for identifying innovations and allocating their funds. The majority of these committees had a three-year remit, after which they were disbanded and replaced by another. The administration of these committees was provided by the government agency responsible for higher education at the time and, as is typical of governments, was frequently restructured with different portfolios. As a consequence, it has been difficult to maintain a corporate memory of the various higher education initiatives, or to capitalise on (or even archive) their outcomes. With the establishment of a National Institute for Learning and Teaching, it is hoped that the corporate memory of these teaching and learning initiatives can be established, outcomes of initiatives can be disseminated and new initiatives can be identified and implemented.

At the local university level the 'corporate memory' role has not always been well understood. In a number of Australian universities, EDUs have been established centrally, devolved to faculties, moved to different reporting structures with different roles, and disbanded only to be re-established some time later. Other universities have valued their role and these EDUs have experienced greater stability. Interestingly, the recently introduced Australian University Quality Audits have helped raise the profile of EDUs in their own institutions for their ability to provide evidence of policy implementation and sustained engagement in initiatives and innovation in teaching and learning (Nicholls, 2001; Macdonald and Wisdom, 2002).

Understandings about quality teaching and learning, research initiatives and policy developments are not the sole domain of EDUs. These understandings may be distributed amongst many individuals and teams throughout a university. However, we believe that a central EDU such as TEDI can claim an ongoing role in facilitating the careful management, sustainability and dissemination of these understandings in a strategic and mindful manner across a university over an extended period of time. This is a role that brings much responsibility, particularly as such understandings are by nature discontinuitous, dynamic, and highly intersubjective over time and place, and are embedded within political, economic and disciplinary constraints. The enaction of this role is unlikely to be provided by decentralised EDUs or individuals or teams based in faculties, particularly if it is to be sustained over an extended period of time. Our conceptual model aims to reduce the opportunity for fragmentation of teaching innovation, particularly as it makes the values, theories and understandings within teaching practice an explicit part of any education development interaction.

The Teaching and Education Development Institute (TEDI) is a large centralised unit with a mandate to support and enhance excellence in teaching and learning at the University of Queensland. It was first established in 1973 and while it has grown and increased its functions, it has enjoyed the sustained support of the university throughout this time. This has enabled the university to assign roles and delegate responsibility to the unit over these 30 years. In return, TEDI has been able to contribute to, implement and support the university's policies as well as identify, implement and support local and individual initiatives and carry out evaluations related to teaching and learning. The value of this was evidenced in the recent university quality audit where the work of TEDI was featured in all sections of the university's quality portfolio, including its role in policy development and processes and subsequent implementation in teaching and learning, international education, research training and human resources management. The university was able to draw on the intellectual and corporate memory and document its sustained engagement in initiatives and innovations in teaching and learning through TEDI. Gathering this sort of evidence would have been highly problematic (and certainly more difficult) without the existence of an enduring, centralised EDU.

Comprehensive and systematic implementation of teaching and learning initiatives

A centralised education development unit
An ongoing discussion on education development has centred on where the EDU activity is located within the university (centralised or devolved), the relationships that are formed between the departments and the EDU, and the ways in which policies and initiatives can be comprehensively implemented in a meaningful way (McNaught; Pearson and Trevitt; Patrick and Lines; Radloff, this volume). We argue that a centralised EDU with effective and direct links with departments can support both top-down and bottom-up initiatives and achieve effective and comprehensive implementation of teaching and learning initiatives.

A recent trend in education development in the United Kingdom (and to a lesser extent in Australia) has been for departments to take a greater role in providing professional development for their academic staff as the impact of the quality reviews take effect and resource allocation becomes more devolved (Blackmore *et al.*, 1999). This trend is in response to the view that central EDUs provide programmes that are generic and poorly articulated with departmental needs, particularly in the area of teaching. Conversely, departments are viewed as not seriously addressing education development. For example, the traditional role taken by heads of departments in relation to professional development is of individual academic staff identifying their own professional development needs and seeking to address these through attending conferences and undertaking study leave (Blackmore *et al.*, 1999). However, the conference and study activities invariably focus on research and very rarely include teaching development. Indeed, there are instances where heads of schools have not approved requests for teaching development, stating that only research activities will be considered. Education development activities, if undertaken at all, are more likely to occur at their own institution through self-identification of need and participation in a relevant workshop. The focus of departments therefore tends to be on the development of individual staff, albeit in the context of the department's strategic aims and objectives, and can be considered to be a bottom-up strategy where staff needs are identified and provided for through a range of departmental sponsored activities. More often than not, the departmental programmes that are developed do so with little reference to, or collaboration with, the EDU (Blackmore *et al.*, 1999).

Regardless of the perceived adequacy of a centralised or departmental approach to education development, it is generally agreed that linkages between central EDUs and departments have not been as effective as they might in achieving comprehensive and systematic implementation of teaching and learning initiatives. However it should be acknowledged that as our colleagues in this book have indicated (Radloff; McNaught, this volume) faculty-situated education development groups and centralised units have the potential to achieve different and complementary outcomes, particularly where there is collaboration and sharing of resources, expertise and experience.

Balancing individual needs and institutional imperatives
A related issue to departmental and centrally based education development is the extent to which development engages with the agendas of individual academic staff and the institutional imperatives. In the previous example, development was seen as the responsibility of the individual to identify and address. This is more likely to occur in a departmental context but it has also been the traditional model for development activities provided by central EDUs. Johnston (1997) was concerned about this issue, not questioning the value of a central EDU for this was taken as a given, but whether the focus of its activities should be directed at the development of the individual teacher or the development of the organisation. She argued that there should be a balanced approach that recognises that both the individual and the institution should be the legitimate targets for professional development activity by the central EDU. The enhancement of educational practice for both individuals and institutions are now recognised as central to the core business of EDUs (Gosling, 2003; Rowland, 2003), and includes the reconciliation of individual practices with institutional philosophies (Barnett, 1997; Gosling, 2003; Pearson and Trevitt, this volume) and the theoretical development of the fields that inform them (Light and Cox, 2001; Rowland, 2003). Boud captures this succinctly stating, 'any unit established for staff development has a responsibility for responding to diversity but also needs to act strategically when central initiative is required for maximum effectiveness' (Boud, 1995: 213).

Our model aims to embody the principles and practices of scholarly education development whilst preserving the legitimacy of expertise and experience of those with whom we work. This concern is reflected by the inclusion of the disciplinary values, understandings and objectives of our colleagues as a fundamental aspect of education development interaction. This is the case for the development of teaching with individual academics, collaborative teams, as well as the development of institutional policies and initiatives in order to engage in the comprehensive and systematic implementation of teaching and learning issues.

At TEDI, we address this fundamental issue in our operational plans, our range of functions, and in our organisational structure. TEDI currently employs 45 staff, 8 with academic positions. The stated mission of TEDI is to 'support the University of Queensland and its staff in their efforts to pursue excellence in all aspects of teaching and learning'. Functions undertaken to achieve this mission include: teaching development, evaluation of teaching and student experiences, educational resource development and coordination of a whole of university staff development programme (both academic and general staff) and includes teaching, learning and research development and management, human resources and skills development. These are general terms for functions that are complex and multi-layered but can all be considered to fit under the broader umbrella of education development.

It would be misleading to represent the work of TEDI within the UQ context as a neatly ordered, linear and straightforward process, where in fact it is a quite messy and complex affair. In common with all EDUs, the issue is the management of initiatives for teaching and learning for the many varied contexts of a university, and to bring a sense of logic and principled coherence within the complexity. An invaluable role of our model has been the explicit articulation of how that logic and coherence may be achieved within the complexity that is the 'university' itself, and how our development activities are rooted within principles of effective teaching practice. Describing complexity and messiness is very difficult and rarely helpful, so in the next section we provide an overview of our approach to the implementation of teaching and learning initiatives. It is only partially adequate in reflecting the depth and complexity such activities require for effective and sustained implementation within a large university.

As in most universities, the guidelines or policies for teaching and learning are the foundations in which EDUs ground their practices. At the University of Queensland, TEDI has sustained an ongoing role in the development and implementation of the Teaching and Learning Enhancement Plan (TLEP) – a five-year rolling plan – and in the various initiatives of the University Teaching and Learning Committee and the office of the Deputy Vice Chancellor (Academic). The staff from TEDI are actively involved in all levels of initiation, development, implementation and evaluation of these activities and contribute depth of expertise, knowledge and experience in education in a range of tasks for education development. In this regard, TEDI acts as a conduit, bringing the concerns of the TLEP and other initiatives to each of the everyday functions it is engaged with, as well as the experiences and ideals of the teaching community to the many tasks involving the development of university policy and initiatives. These concerns currently include:

- development of high-quality teaching and curriculum development for a research-intensive environment;

- systematic and evidence-based review of curriculum, teaching and learning;

- provision of flexible learning opportunities and environments including the use of educational technologies;

- the internationalisation of curriculum;

- inclusive education and the recognition of diversity within our student population;

- emerging fields of practice for which interdisciplinarity, industry-relatedness and/or external accreditation are a concern;

- rapidly increasing postgraduate coursework programmes designed for professional development within a field.

TEDI plays a central role in identifying and responding to these initiatives in a comprehensive and coherent manner. It does this through working with individuals, programme teams, communities of practice and organisational units, either at their or our instigation.

Education development – formal programmes for teaching, learning and leadership
Most formal courses in teaching and learning are offered as part of the University Staff Development Committee (USDC) programme. This committee's work is guided by the Staff Development Policy, The Teaching and Learning Enhancement Plan and the University's Strategic Plan.[1] The primary method of engagement in this programme is through workshops and seminars, which are offered to both academic and general staff involved in teaching. These are coordinated and delivered throughout the university and across a number of campuses. The programmes provide the university with an opportunity to engage staff with the educational and administrative values it seeks to imbue, and to inform staff how they may develop their roles within the university in congruence with these values and university policies. For example, all academic staff new to university teaching attend a four-day 'Introduction to teaching' programme. Developed and

implemented by TEDI, this programme introduces academics to a range of models of teaching and learning and engages them in reflective discussion of their philosophical underpinnings and practical outcomes for students. The programme provides assistance and direction in curriculum development, educational design, assessment, flexible learning, educational leadership, evaluation, and promotes reflective practice as an orientation for professional development.

Additional workshops are offered to all teaching staff, building on each of these aspects of teaching. All programmes are reviewed and evaluated on a cyclic basis. Finally, a number of scholarships are provided each year for staff across the university who wish to undertake a more extensive formal study within the Graduate Certificate in Education. TEDI academics are regularly invited to teach within this programme, and participants of the certificate programme are often encouraged to continue to enhance their formal learning through the workshop programme (see Fraser, this volume on accredited teaching programmes).

However, it would be naïve of us to think that teaching staff will enthusiastically participate in teaching development programmes for their own value. Academic staff are under great time pressures to research, teach and carry out administrative duties and so while participating in development activities might be 'good to do', when time is scarce these activities tend to be the first to be sacrificed. In recognition of this we have framed our teaching development programme as 'Becoming a UQ Academic' where many of the workshops are contexualised in understanding and evidencing teaching in ways that support the development of their academic portfolio. At UQ, an academic portfolio is used as the base document for annual performance review, mid-term and final review for confirmation of continuing appointment, and applications for promotion, study leave, and teaching awards. Academic portfolios are made up of evidence and reflection on teaching, research and service. In this way the formal workshop programme is directly linked to supporting the university's policies and values while at the same time supporting the individual academic staff in demonstrating and evidencing their teaching development or educational leadership in ways that they can use for career progression.

The formal teaching development programme is further supported by less formal, but nevertheless strategic, institutional and departmental initiatives through education development.

Faculty-oriented education development
TEDI provides support and educational expertise for faculty staff engaged in curriculum development, advising postgraduate students and all aspects related to the enhancement of the quality of teaching at a less formal and

situated level. This type of education development encompasses the design, development and presentation of curriculum at the course and programme level, the design and implementation of innovative assessment approaches, the use and development of teaching and learning technologies and resources, and the evaluation of effective curriculum and teaching. These can be initiated at the university level, and an example is a recent policy to undertake systematic curriculum review on an annual, triennial and septennial basis as identified by the Teaching and Learning Enhancement Plan. TEDI staff were members of the working group that generated this policy and subsequently worked with schools and their teaching and learning committees and teaching programme teams on ways in which they can effectively implement the policy to inform their decisions on curriculum review.

This work is carried out at several levels. On the one hand, TEDI staff work with individual teachers, groups, programme teams or committees on a particular aspect of teaching to provide expert advice, and to support the development of expertise. On the other hand, we work actively across the university as members of committees or programme of study teams on particular initiatives such as curriculum development, renewal and evaluation. In this type of work, the TEDI staff member is a co-developer or member of the team working towards an agreed outcome that has been identified by the group. In other situations TEDI staff are members of university level committees or project groups contributing to policy development and subsequent policy implementation through various faculty- and school-based committees.

A particular variation of education development is education resource development. It is important to note that while we consider this to be an aspect of education development, it is sufficiently distinct and important to warrant its own functional description.

Development of educational resources (and those that use them)
In this function, TEDI particularly focuses on the development of resources for programmes and courses. Our purpose here is to continue to devise resources that provide support for teachers, and to enhance the learning experiences of students. A well-designed resource may guide and facilitate the student learning experience in that course, or be part of a complementary suite of media, self-directed and face-to-face interactions within a course. These resources might be learning guides, websites and resources, CD-ROMs, videos etc. It is recognised that resource development is most effective when it is accompanied by adequate support for the professional learning of the academics who will use them. Once again, we refer to our conceptual model (Figure 4.1) as an effective representation of this task, where the focus of interaction is the concurrent conceptualisation

and development of a resource (or interrelated suite of resources) with the academic's understanding of how they will be most effectively used.

TEDI staff work in teams with university teachers throughout the curriculum planning process, identifying where the best educational outcomes could be achieved, utilising the most appropriate media, and designing a range of interactions for students, both personal and mediated. The resources are then developed by specialised TEDI staff with expertise in instructional and graphic design, computer programming, desktop publishing and media production. This is an iterative process involving ongoing interactions with the teacher and the development team through to completion and the evaluation of the resources. Ultimately, our aim is to support the simultaneous development of both teacher and resource, so that the teachers themselves can undertake ownership and ongoing development of the original and new resources. TEDI provides ongoing support for upgrading or enhancements of the resources, with additional training provided to assist teachers to develop more sophisticated use of the technologies.

Evaluation of teaching and student experiences
An informed understanding of the quality of teaching, learning experiences and curriculum provided by our university is fundamental to ongoing enhancement of teaching and learning. In addition to providing evidence of our strengths and needs, universities build their initiatives around additional information about graduate destinations, employer and community perceptions, and the quality of students' experiences.

For TEDI, this function includes administration and operation of the surveys completed by students on the quality of the teaching and the nature of courses. First and foremost, this function provides an essential service to teaching staff, by engaging them in reflective cycles of gathering data, considering their teaching and courses in light of student feedback, and the ongoing task of enhancement. Initiated by teaching staff themselves, this data also provides first order evidence of their teaching achievements and developing expertise, and is formally acknowledged within the academic portfolio as a component of evidence on the quality of their teaching. To encourage the use of many other forms of data on student learning and teaching quality, TEDI academics integrate evaluation data with other professional development activities, and provide guidance tailored to the individual academic's needs.

The data gathered from these teaching and course surveys are analysed and provided to teachers in several ways to facilitate their interpretation and lead to improvements in teaching. The data set can then be made available in aggregated form to provide programmes of study and schools with information on student perceptions on the quality of teaching, and so provide meaningful information on their programmes of study and school performance.

Other student surveys are administered primarily for the organisational unit and institutional purposes. For example, a whole-of-university survey is administered every two years on students' experiences of their programme of study at different points in their study, e.g. first year, final undergraduate year, and honours and postgraduate study. The data from these institutional-level student surveys can be considered at programme, school, faculty and institutional level as well as allowing for comparisons to be made within the university and with other universities. Another institutional level student survey is administered for all courses on a cyclic basis so that courses contributing to a programme of study are surveyed over a three-year period. Various reports on these different data sets are prepared by TEDI and provided to the university, faculty, school and programme of study for programme, school, quality audit and benchmarking reviews.

Student surveys encompass only one part of the evaluation function of TEDI. It also includes evaluation of curriculum, teaching and assessment practice, and educational resources. These are carried out through gathering and interpreting data from various sources including survey instruments, interview and focus groups, artefacts and interrogating university and national data sources. This type of evaluation work may be carried out by TEDI in a variety of ways, including: as a project with all aspects carried out by TEDI staff; as a member of a team advising and contributing to the evaluation task; and as a consultant providing advice on appropriate methodologies and phases of evaluation.

University-wide development programme
The University of Queensland has an encompassing approach to staff development evidenced by a university policy which recognises the needs of the institution to develop staff skills in order to achieve its mission and the individual's need to develop work-related skills for career advancement and personal growth. To support both the university and individuals' needs, the university provides an extensive programme of professional development available to all staff on general and academic contracts. Over 180 different courses provide a total offering of 400 courses each year. These are grouped under the categories of induction, career advancement, performance enhancement and self-development. A range of programmes are offered under each category, some directed at general staff and others at academic staff while others, such as leadership and management programmes, are equally appropriate for both. The University of Queensland TEDI website shows the full range of programmes offered.[2]

Through these various functions, TEDI is able to engage in the comprehensive and systematic implementation of teaching and learning activities for extended periods of time. This is carried out through an integrated approach to achieving initiatives that are institutionally and departmentally initiated but which are designed to engage individuals in ways that make it a meaningful and developmental experience for them.

Creating and facilitating communities of learning involved in the iterative and dynamic top-down/bottom-up engagement of educational initiatives

Perhaps the most overlooked role is the positioning of EDU staff across various levels of the university in which we engage in the enhancement of teaching and learning. The emerging accountability for university teaching has particular implications for the work of education development. Many EDUs are now experienced in participating in institutional decision-making and management providing advice for both the 'requirements for development, and appropriate institutional structures and strategies for the most effective ways to carry it out' (Brew, 2003b: 174). This is not unproblematic, as these activities can be seen as top-down and disconnected from or imposing on the work of departments and individuals. Within the UQ context, TEDI has been quite purposeful in establishing both a bottom-up as well as top-down endeavour. This has been achieved by facilitating discussion within the university community about what works, what is valued and what is preferred for teaching and learning at UQ. For example, we have been actively working to engage with faculties, schools and programmes of studies through establishing the role of TEDI affiliates and membership on faculty and school Teaching and Learning Committees and flexible learning and curriculum development initiatives.

TEDI affiliates, and Teaching and Learning Committees
In order to be responsive to discipline and department needs, TEDI has actively sought to engage in situated projects and activities. The school, faculty or team of staff involved in teaching a programme of study identifies these projects. Our aim is to engage with staff in team- or project-based activities that have an educational outcome – staff development or student learning – as a member of the team and active contributor to the task. To enact this, each school is invited to nominate a person as their TEDI affiliate. An affiliate's role is to act as a liaison and communication link between TEDI and the head of school, the School Teaching and Learning Committee and school staff. The intention of the affiliate initiative is to provide representation of school needs directly to TEDI and to enable 'point of need' negotiations of professional development agendas and approaches tailored specifically for school-identified programmes and projects. At the time of writing, this initiative was in its formative phase,

and appears reliant upon goodwill and purposeful collaboration between school-based affiliates and TEDI consultants. To date, requests via the affiliates programme have included tailored professional learning workshops in specific topics (such as large-class teaching), centralised professional development workshops in academic service (such as chairing Teaching and Learning Committees), and support from TEDI consultants for school-based curriculum review.

The University Staff Development Committee supports these situated programmes with funding for catering and material costs. TEDI has membership on the USDC and proposes the annual staff development programme and budget. Once the overall programme is approved, TEDI then has responsibility for developing, delivering, evaluating and reporting the teaching development programme.

Another major committee that impacts on teaching development and the work of TEDI is the university Teaching and Learning Committee (TLC). This committee has a reflexive relationship to the faculty Teaching and Learning Committees and to the school Teaching and Learning Committees. The purpose for the TLC is to guide the University in the development and implementation of strategies for pursuit of excellence in all aspects of teaching and learning. The TLC develops the Teaching and Learning Enhancement Plan and TEDI enacts and supports much of this plan through encouraging and facilitating activities within faculties and schools consistent with enhancing and improving teaching and learning.

TEDI staff are represented on the university TLC, the faculty TLCs and a number of school TLCs. In these roles TEDI has opportunities to contribute to policy development and to plan subsequent support for the faculties and schools in enacting these policies. Active membership on university committees is also an opportunity for us to identify issues and trends, and to undertake initiatives, as they may be relevant to perceived future directions. In this regard, it has been these opportunities that have underpinned and informed TEDI's approach to supporting initiatives such as the university-wide articulation of graduate attributes. The development of graduate attributes will be a familiar task to many universities, and at UQ this involved TEDI in the provision of support for the process of articulating discipline-specific graduate attributes at the programme and course level.

It would be misleading to imply that TEDI worked with all schools and programmes of study teams across the university on the implementation of the graduate attributes policy. We did not. While many programme teams mapped their programme graduate attributes with little or no input from us, in this work we: (1) worked across the seven faculties in the university and engaged with teaching staff at many levels, (2) developed tools and processes to help them frame and understand the task, (3) provided a consistent message and level of support of what was involved in the task, (4) collected and shared cases and examples of implementation across the university, (5) were actively involved in the process for many of the large enrolment programmes, (6) worked with staff who would almost never attend a TEDI workshop, (7) were involved in several significant curriculum development initiatives that grew out of the task of articulating graduate attributes as a result of the teaching staff actively thinking about the learning of their students, and (8) documented and evaluated our work in supporting and implementing the policy and identified ways in which we could work more effectively. This work is by no means completed as teaching teams grapple with issues related to embedding the graduate attributes into their courses and assessment, but in many instances there is a member of TEDI in their team who can support, advise and contribute ideas on how this might be achieved.

In 2003, we put in place a range of initiatives to support the implementation of the policy for annual, triennial and septennial curriculum reviews, drawing on our experiences in facilitating graduate attributes to inform us of how best to do this. This approach enables us to position TEDI within the university community in both a top-down and bottom-up approach to facilitating, supporting and managing a university-wide change.

Investigating, articulating and disseminating scholarship in (and on) teaching, learning and education development

The development and enhancement of quality teaching and learning practice continues to be a concern to government and the higher education sector across the world. The Australian higher education sector is currently experiencing a renewed interest in university teaching. With distinct echoes of the United Kingdom's reform in the 1990s, the recently released Nelson Report (DEST, 2003) makes recommendations that include the establishment of a National Institute for Teaching and Learning, and a range of initiatives directed at the provision of support for, and recognition of, excellence and quality in university teaching. EDUs are thus currently poised to consider (or reconsider) their role and the extent to which they participate in, and contribute to, the emerging emphasis on quality in university teaching and learning.

The practice and dissemination of quality teaching has traditionally been the basis for education development work. This has been addressed through workshops, learning-circles and a range of consultancy activities for many years. However, the emerging emphasis on scholarly teaching and learning brings with it a shifting point of reference for scholarship. University teachers themselves are increasingly actively engaged in the scholarly development of their own teaching. In part, the structure of university appointments and promotions processes has elicited a greater interest in evidencing teaching practice. However, it is also the case that many academics willingly embrace their role as university teachers as an essential part of their professional identities. As a result, education developers have noted an increasing interest in the evaluation and research of academics' own teaching and learning, with many EDU staff maintaining active and ongoing research collaborations across a range of discipline areas (Brew, 2003a). This trend has also been apparent at our university, and TEDI staff sustain a healthy research profile that has been strongly oriented towards collaboration and scholarship in teaching, curriculum development and learning design.

Such a trend is notable not simply for its potential to enhance the learning community. EDU academics are often cast in the role of 'educational expert' or 'education theorist' within these collaborations, while discipline-based colleagues bring 'content knowledge' or 'teaching experience' to the task. In many instances, it is not uncommon for teacher/researchers to rely upon the educational perspective and experience of their EDU colleagues. Moreover, education developers generally bring with them an implicit aim to improve practice, as well as an opportunity to 'illuminate' an area of inquiry (Brew, 2003a). An educational perspective is not without its philosophy and values. As we continue to encourage greater depth of scholarship within university teaching, we are mindful of the potentially political functions and pedagogical positioning such collaborations may yield (Brew, 2003a; Gosling, 2003). As Barnett has argued (1997), the contemporary university sets out to privilege preferred models of teaching and learning in order to achieve desired learning outcomes. EDUs, through carrying out their education development work and their research, become an integral part of that process.

While many of our research collaborations have been based upon small action research-style projects, some of our activities have been on a larger national scale with international implications. Most recently, TEDI was project leader in two Australian University Teaching Committee projects. The first project, 'Teaching Large Classes' (Chalmers *et al.*, 2002b) involved 24 universities from around Australia and resulted in significant resources being developed, and with 24 different university-based initiatives being undertaken. Many of the university-based initiatives have continued well beyond the 12-month duration of the project itself. The second initiative, 'Managing, Supporting and Training Sessional Teachers' (Chalmers *et al.*, 2002a) attended to a long-acknowledged need to provide support and resources towards the growing trend for sessional and short-term teaching positions. The resources on the website continue to be regularly updated, particularly through adding new case studies of good practice. TEDI has optimised the benefits of these projects for the University of Queensland, as we continue to draw education development outcomes and resources from them for the teachers and academic managers within our own community. However, it is the breadth of the initial project teams that have proved the most valuable benefit. Drawn from universities across the country, the projects allowed for greater sharing of excellence in practice, and the chance to develop and engage a network of colleagues similarly engrossed in addressing the challenges of university teaching and large class issues. The principles identified in the two projects of engaging and sharing practice across universities have been successfully adapted in a new national AUTC project on the teaching of psychology to take place in 2004–5. We see a greater role for EDUs in the design and facilitation of such projects in the future in light of the growing interest in excellence in university teaching at the federal level.

The increasing responsibilities and areas of development undertaken by academics within education development units rely upon an expanding suite of knowledge, experience, expertise and understanding. As the debate continues about the professionalisation of roles in higher education (Macdonald, 2003; see also Fraser and Ryan, this volume), it falls upon education developers to continually review our role and reconstruct our identity accordingly (Brew, 2003a; Rowland, 2003). To do so requires a commitment to negotiating our positions within university contexts, and persistence in the development of our own practice. As Candy (1994) points out, education developers could be considered 'meta-professionals' whose 'area of research and teaching happens to be higher education itself' (in Macdonald, 2003: 6).

This meta-perspective requires a depth of knowledge and understanding in teaching and learning as it is applied mindfully to a range of university contexts. It also brings obligations of scholarship and critique, in which to ground and validate our own work. The model we have presented here draws upon Rowland's notion of academic development as critical practice (2003), and originally, Habermas's conception of communicative action (1991). We seek to elicit an inquiry approach to the task of education development, wherein all participants question and explore the connection between theory and practice, the purposes of higher education, and the nature of student learning in relation to the wider social context.

We have established a programmatic research agenda in TEDI for the academic staff and others who are interested in research in the field of higher education. We believe that it is important to contribute to the understanding of teaching and learning in higher education and are committed to supporting our own staff to achieve this. Two recent programmes have included an evaluation on flexible learning at the Ipswich campus, and our current research focuses on quality teaching and quality enhancement in teaching, particularly the role of education development and the process of peer review. Such a programmatic approach provides TEDI staff with a research focus: a community of scholars investigating a field of mutual interest in a way that allows them to adopt different perspectives and utilise different methodologies. Such an approach supports the career development of staff working in EDUs who can find it difficult to undertake independent research, as well as providing the opportunity of making a contribution to new understanding and knowledge in the work of EDUs and teaching and learning in higher education.

CONCLUSION

Education development as a vehicle for the enhancement of university teaching must be well positioned for both 'point-of-need' management of the constantly shifting dilemmas our teachers and students face, as well as preparing for the future demands of an ever-changing socio-economic and political context. Education development units play a highly participative role in managing a suite of challenges that encompass current issues as well as a futures orientation, for which we envisage education development in a participative and highly active role within the university community.

We have outlined those challenges as comprising four overarching concerns, specifically: maintaining a corporate memory of, and sustained engagement in, the issues, initiatives and innovations in teaching in higher education; engaging in comprehensive and systematic implementation of teaching and learning initiatives; creating and facilitating communities of learning involved in the iterative and dynamic top-down/bottom-up engagement and management of educational initiatives; and investigating and disseminating scholarship in (and on) teaching, learning and education development.

As interest in the quality of teaching and learning in higher education continues to grow, universities will need to consider a range of options for acting mindfully to the challenges this brings. We have argued that education development units play a central role in this future. In this paper we have presented a case for the articulation of EDU engagement within the university community in a way that offers a strategic and outward looking approach to the many roles of education development, in a reflexive community of practice model. Boud captures these sentiments with the claim that 'staff development must be at the heart of the creative and responsive institutions ... in order to ensure the health and vitality of higher education' (Boud, 1995: 213).

In conclusion, while our focus in this chapter has been on teaching and learning, we do not suggest that this is the only focus with which an EDU should engage. Many EDUs are actively involved in policy development and implementation, quality processes and auditing, research and research training, leadership and human resource development, and community service roles that are not specifically related to teaching and learning.

We propose that the conceptual model and framework outlined in this chapter facilitate flexibility, reflexivity and continuity of education development within the complex and multilayered environment of higher education, and that as such, has greater potential for achieving authentic and sustained enhancement of quality in university teaching and learning. In addition, we contend that the principles of the conceptual model and framework can be usefully applied to additional roles an EDU might be engaged in as an effective model of engagement, support and change within a university.

NOTES

1   The University of Queensland Strategic Plan: http://www.uq.edu.au/about/index.html?page=4235; UQ Teaching and Learning Enhancement Plan: http://www.uq.edu.au/about/index.html? page=1037.
2   TEDI Staff Development Programme: http://www.tedi.uq.edu.au/sdh.

5

Decentralised approaches to education development: supporting quality teaching and learning from within a faculty

Alex Radloff

This chapter identifies education development issues that need to be addressed in order to enhance the quality of teaching and learning within an academic unit, in this case in a Faculty of Life Sciences. The focus of education development is programme development and renewal in the context of a programme quality assurance framework guided by an institutional teaching and learning strategy emphasising a capability-driven, learner-centred curriculum with a strong emphasis on the use of emerging technologies to enrich learning.

BACKGROUND

Universities are having to meet increasing expectations from a range of stakeholders for the quality of the teaching and learning that they provide. Students, employers, governments and taxpayers are all seeking assurances that the education they are contributing towards is of a high standard and that universities have in place processes to assure and – where necessary – improve the quality of teaching and learning. At the same time, as outlined in Chapter 1, the massification of higher education and the related changes in student demographics have created a growing need for flexible learner-centred approaches to teaching. The rapid growth of information and communication technologies has prompted universities to look to technology for ways of extending student access, supporting flexible learning and improving teaching efficiencies; and all of this is happening in a market place where universities are competing with one another and alternative higher education providers for domestic and international students in an effort to broaden their funding sources and assure their financial futures.

What does the emphasis on quality and accountability within a financially stretched and competitive university system mean for decision makers? How do they meet the challenges of both proving and improving the quality of teaching and learning in institutions with increasing student–staff ratios, reduced budgets and declining staff morale? In this chapter, these questions are considered from the perspective of someone who is responsible for the quality of teaching and learning within a faculty and where a decentralised approach to education development has been taken to address some of these issues.

THE CONTEXT

The context is the Faculty of Life Sciences at the Royal Melbourne Institute of Technology (RMIT) University, a large, dual-sector institution providing educational programmes at both certificate and degree level. The faculty has approximately 3,000 full-time equivalent students and approximately 300 staff in four departments and a school. The faculty is responsible for approximately 40 educational programmes in biomedical, biotechnical, environmental and health sciences leading to accredited awards from certificate level to doctorates. Each programme has a programme team consisting of staff responsible for the management and teaching of the programme, and a programme leader responsible for the co-ordination of the team and reporting to the head of department or school. Educational activities for all programmes are supported by the Office of Programme Quality located centrally in the faculty and responsible for supporting programme development and renewal, programme quality assurance and improvement, staff capability building and the scholarship of teaching and learning in line with university strategic directions, the university's teaching and learning strategy, and related policies and processes.

The faculty is committed to ensuring that its programmes are high quality in terms of student satisfaction especially with regard to teaching, relevant in terms of community and industry needs and graduate employability, and viable in terms of student demand for places and cost-effectiveness of the programme.

The university's teaching and learning strategy incorporates the Boyer Scholarships of discovery, integration, application and teaching, and a commitment to quality processes including a programme quality assurance system. Following a review in 2000 of its quality processes related to educational programmes, the university introduced the new quality system as the overarching quality framework for all educational programmes offered by the university. Programme quality assurance is framed by a set of guiding principles, the key being an evidence-based approach to continuous quality improvement using a set of criteria. The criteria were

identified through a process of consultation and incorporate the requirements of the Australian Universities Quality Agency, which audits
universities on a five-year cycle and the Australian Qualification Training
Framework, which audits technical and further education programmes, as
well as those of a range of professional accrediting bodies that accredit
university programmes. The programme quality assurance criteria are:

- *need for the programme*, including industry and community need for
  graduates;

- *educational design*, including graduate capabilities and alignment between
  objectives, learning experiences and assessment;

- *equity*, including access to programmes and student support;

- *management*, including processes and documentation;

- *resources*, including staff capabilities and facilities;

- *evaluation* and maintenance, including ongoing review of programme;
  and

- *stakeholder requirements*, including the needs of professional accrediting
  bodies.

Additional guiding principles include a holistic review of programme
performance using a critical approach, regular reporting against the criteria,
external validation, alignment between accreditation, ongoing programme
improvement and re-accreditation, maximising return on effort, and
commitment to the Boyer Scholarships (Boyer, 1990).

Using programme quality assurance as the framework, the university is
engaged in a systematic process of programme development and renewal
with an emphasis on developing flexible student-centred, capability-driven
curricula with a strong international emphasis and positive vocational
outcomes. In addition, there is an institutional commitment to developing
learning online using a central distributed learning system. Drivers for
educational change and quality include stakeholder needs and demands,
government accountability and audit requirements, and financial
constraints.

In order to facilitate and support quality teaching and learning, each
faculty has an associate dean (academic)/director of teaching quality or
equivalent position. These are senior academic positions with responsibility
for leading educational change, and enhancing and assuring the quality of
teaching and learning across all programmes within a faculty.

The university also has a number of centrally situated groups such as
Learning Technology Services, Learning Support Unit, Planning and

Quality, etc. which have the capacity to support teaching and learning activities. However, given the size of the university and its decentralised organisational structure, and the fact that most of the programmes in the Faculty of Life Sciences are taught on a campus some 17 km from the main university campus, while much of the impetus for quality improvement comes from the centre, the main work to support quality processes and outcomes occurs primarily at the faculty level.

This chapter outlines my experiences during a two-year period as Associate Dean (Academic) in making decisions about ways to support and enhance quality teaching and learning through education development from within the faculty. Specifically, I outline the issues that I have confronted in trying to support and enhance the quality of teaching and learning and describe my responses. These include determining what capabilities staff need in order to meet university expectations for quality educational programmes, what education development approaches might be effective in supporting such capability building in the faculty, how such education development may be provided, and how best to evaluate the outcomes of such efforts.

THE ISSUES

The issues that I have considered in my role as Associate Dean (Academic) have revolved around my main objective and role, namely to improve the quality of teaching and learning in all life sciences programmes in line with university vision, values, goals, quality systems, and policies and practices.

In order to achieve this objective, a number of issues have had to be addressed, including:

- how to motivate staff to engage with the task of continuous quality improvement;

- how to facilitate and support staff capability building in teaching and learning to allow them to engage effectively in quality improvement activities;

- how to support improvement activities as part of continuous quality improvement including the resourcing of such activities;

- how to evaluate the effectiveness of improvement activities;

- how to recognise and reward positive outcomes;

- how to support the Boyer Scholarships especially the scholarship of teaching and learning; and

- how to maintain a cycle of continuous quality improvement (amongst other priorities) with limited resources.

The programme quality assurance system provides the framework for these tasks with programme annual reporting against the quality criteria being the key strategy adopted by the Faculty to manage programme quality improvement and assurance (Wahr *et al.*, 2002). Programme annual reports included a 'stocktake' against the quality criteria using a number of sources of evidence, some mandated such as student demand for the programme and graduate feedback from the national course experience questionnaire, and others less formal such as feedback from employers and external examiners. Reports also identify areas for improvement, provide improvement plans and identify any additional resources required to achieve outcomes.

CAPABILITIES NEEDED FOR QUALITY TEACHING AND LEARNING

The task of continuous quality improvement of educational programmes raises questions about the kinds of capabilities staff need to be able to engage in and contribute meaningfully to the quality improvement process in teaching and learning. Indeed, the university as a whole has been considering this question in its efforts to establish a professional development and qualifications framework for the university (Taylor, 2003).

Taylor analysed key University documents including the university's strategic directions, *Dissolving the Boundaries: Towards a Sustainable RMIT* to identify what capabilities staff need in order to meet the university's goals for teaching and learning. Table 5.1 presents a summary of the capabilities needed for quality teaching and learning.

Table 5.1 *Capabilities needed for quality teaching and learning*

Capability	Description
1. Engagement locally and globally	Able to develop and nurture partnerships with individuals, enterprises and communities, both globally and locally, to enable learning, innovation and change.
2. Engagement with peers and colleagues	Able to foster and maintain collaborative, creative and open working relationships across the boundaries of academic, administrative and support services.
3. Equity and pathways	Able to provide opportunities and pathways for increased participation and achievement of equity groups in education and training.

Table 5.1 *continued*

Capability	Description
4. Leadership	Able to provide leadership and vision at all levels within the organisation.
5. Engagement with learners	Able to engage with learners respectfully and openly to support life-long learning and productive citizenship.
6. Entrepreneurship	Able to design and implement commercially viable, innovative products and services in education, training, research and consultancy for local and global markets.
7. Designing for learning	Able to design and tailor internationalised and work-integrated programmes of learning for diverse learner groups within a quality assurance framework.
8. Teaching for learning	Able to implement appropriate, flexible and cost-effective learning strategies to enable skills development, enhance knowledge and encourage active engagement in and reflection on learning.
9. Assessing for learning	Able to design and conduct assessment that is integrated with learning; valid, reliable, fair, flexible and considerate of diverse needs.
10. Evaluation of teaching and learning	Able to collect and analyse data from a range of sources to assess performance against outcome measures and inform improvements to the quality of teaching and learning.
11. Reflective practice and professional development	Able to reflect critically on and engage with peers and learners to scrutinise one's own performance and engage in activities to enhance the quality of teaching practice. Able to continually enhance and update knowledge and skills within a professional or academic field through research, consultancy and/or active engagement with industry and community.
12. Personal management	Able to develop strategies to maintain personal resilience, confidence and commitment within a challenging, complex and rapidly changing environment.
13. Management of teaching and learning	Able to manage systems and resources to support efficient and sustainable educational programmes and services within a framework of organisational policies and procedures and legislative requirements.

Source: Table created from data in an unpublished RMIT report (Taylor 2003).

This list highlights two issues related to capabilities. First, quality teaching and learning as envisaged by the university requires a broad range of capabilities encompassing not only traditional discipline and pedagogical knowledge and skills but also an understanding of the global and connected nature of education and skills in leadership and management. Second, given the breadth of capabilities identified, it is unrealistic to expect that every member of staff would possess all the capabilities needed. Rather, taking an organisational perspective, the goal is to have capabilities spread across teams including both academic and administrative staff. It is also important to recognise the need for and role of education development in supporting the development of the broad range of capabilities needed.

WHAT SHOULD BE THE FOCUS OF EDUCATION DEVELOPMENT EFFORTS?

At the faculty level, given the broad range of capabilities needed to achieve improvement in the quality of teaching and learning in all programmes and the relatively limited resources available for education development, the challenge has been to determine the focus of education development efforts. The decision was made to focus effort two ways. First, education development has to be aligned to our goal of improving the quality of all educational programmes in life sciences using the programme quality assurance system. Second, education development activities have to be both effective and efficient – they have to work (and to be seen to work), and they have to be sustainable.

In order to improve the quality of our programmes, education development has to focus on 'normalising' quality activities, with an emphasis on improving rather than on proving quality; on enhancement rather than merely on compliance. It also needs to reinforce the notion of professional responsibility and self-management among staff including strengthening an inner locus of control and engagement in reflective practice as an integral part of academic work. And, finally, it needs to contribute to the development of a culture that values and requires evidence in teaching and learning; a culture of engagement in the scholarship of teaching and learning. Thus, the focus of education development should be to help staff to develop and enhance the capabilities that will allow them to manage and improve their programmes within a continuous quality-improvement cycle. In order to do this, they need not only pedagogical knowledge and skills but also an understanding of quality processes and a commitment to evidence-based practice.

In terms of effectiveness and efficiency of education development, three sources of information have helped to shape our thinking about, and planning for, education development efforts in the faculty. These sources have included research on teaching and learning, education development and change management, lessons learned from my previous experiences in education development, and knowledge of the contextual factors including the professional backgrounds, roles and responsibilities, and experiences of staff in the faculty.

Based on the research literature, there is evidence that education development is most likely to be effective when it acknowledges current activities and capabilities of staff and builds on those (Martin, 1999); takes a collegial approach that involves '... exchange of ideas ... [and] links among colleagues within and across departments' (Austin, 1998: 1); focuses on programme renewal through curriculum development including focus on approaches to teaching and teaching and learning strategies (Zuber-Skerritt, 1992); involves planning and carrying out classroom research or action learning projects (Cross and Steadman, 1996; Kember and Associates, 2000; Kember and McKay, 1996); and encourages reflective practice (Brookfield, 1995) and the scholarship of teaching (Bass, 1999; Bender and Gray, 1999; Hutchings and Shulman, 1999). Education development also needs the support of those in leadership positions such as deans and heads department/school (Kotter, 1996; Ramsden, 1998b; Wergin, 2003).

There is also evidence that education development efforts need to be ongoing since they may require quite profound changes in approaches to teaching and learning and associated conceptions of teaching and learning that are unlikely to occur as a result of one-off and *ad hoc* attendance at seminars and workshops (Gibbs and Coffey, 2001; Kember, 1998; Rust, 1998; Trigwell *et al.*, 1999b).

My previous experience in education development to support curriculum development and teaching and learning has also provided insights into the factors that impact on the effectiveness of education development. In addition to reinforcing the validity of research-based findings, it has also highlighted the importance of having clear goals and expectations for education development activities, articulating what educational principles underpin and guide education development activities, ensuring that staff involved in supporting education development have appropriate expertise and skills, and providing targeted funding (de la Harpe and Radloff, 2000, 2001, 2002; Parker *et al.*, 1998; Radloff *et al.*, 2001).

Finally, we have had to consider the characteristics of staff in Life Sciences when deciding on the focus and form of education development efforts. Staff have a range of science backgrounds, many also have clinical experience, and all teach into programmes with strong vocational outcomes. In addition, most staff, in line with university imperatives, have incorporated aspects of online learning in their approaches to teaching. Some have had to develop strategies for teaching students at a distance and teaching a growing number of international students.

Staff have experienced a considerable degree of change in the past few years including changes to organisational structures and in senior leadership, and a move for many of them from the main university campus to a smaller outer-metropolitan campus. These changes have been accompanied by increased job uncertainty, stress and financial constraints, all of which have impacted negatively on staff morale and motivation. Moreover, the faculty is part of a large university that is evolving models for education development and currently relies to a large extent on local support provided within faculties. This reliance on local support is especially pronounced where staff are situated at a smaller campus with fewer centrally provided facilities, as is the case with the majority of staff in Life Sciences. To have any chance of success, education development activities have to take into account these contextual factors and work within their constraints.

PROVIDING EDUCATION DEVELOPMENT SUPPORT WITHIN THE FACULTY

Given the above considerations and evidence about effective approaches to education development, we have, over time, evolved a model for supporting quality teaching and learning within the faculty. The model is based on the assumption that quality teaching and learning requires staff to be self-managing professionals engaged in reflective practice, with the scholarship of teaching and learning as an integral part of their work. Education development provides support for staff to develop and refine the capabilities they need to meet university expectations. The model also recognises the importance of aligning institutional values, goals, policies, practices and resources to achieve desired education development outcomes. Further, in line with the programme quality assurance system adopted by the university, the model stresses the importance of evidence-based practice, with the use of data such as student demand for programmes, student performance and student and employer feedback, and research-based information such as on the design of assessment tasks and the effectiveness of different online learning activities. Finally, the model recognises the value of having a range of education development supports to meet the diverse needs of staff.

In late 2001, the Office of Programme Quality was set up within the faculty centre to bring together and co-ordinate work around programme development and renewal, programme quality assurance, and staff capability building (see http://www.life.rmit.edu.au/tl/opq/ for details). The Office of Programme Quality consists of the associate dean (academic) / director of teaching quality, the education development manager, the educational enhancement co-ordinator, and the personal assistant to the

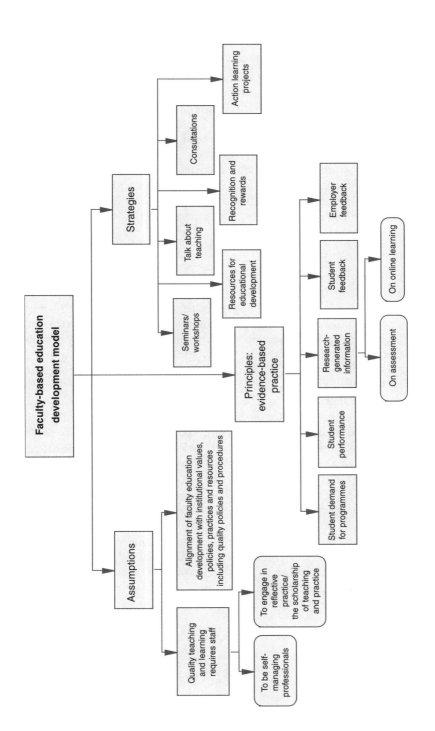

Figure 5.1 *Faculty-based education development model*

associate dean who also provides administrative support to the office. Depending on budget, Office of Programme Quality work has also been supported by one or more project officers.

Using the model described above as the basis, the Office of Programme Quality has established a series of education development activities aimed at developing staff capability to support quality teaching and learning. These include seminars and workshops, consultations at programme team and individual staff level, action learning projects, development of resources to support staff capability building, and recognition and reward for teaching. Each of these is described below. More detail of current and past activities supported by the Office of Programme Quality can be found at http://www.life.rmit.edu.au/tl/academic-development.html.

Seminars/workshops

The Office of Programme Quality arranges regular seminars and workshops open to all faculty staff and designed to model good practice in facilitation of active learning and appropriate use of technology. *Teaching and Learning Seminars* usually presented over lunchtime and lasting two hours, address 'hot topics' related to teaching and learning and provide opportunities for visiting experts to introduce new ideas. Topics have included 'Selecting the right assessment tools', 'Identifying and embedding graduate capabilities for Life Sciences', 'Undertaking classroom research', 'Developing a professional portfolio' and 'Clinical reasoning and peer coaching'.

Talking about Teaching (TaT) are one-hour sessions followed by drinks that encourage discussion about teaching issues across the faculty and provide an opportunity for staff to share their experiences and views about the changing role of university teachers. Each issue is introduced using as a trigger a quote or brief extract from an article. TaT topics have included 'University teacher: a crisis of professional identity?', 'Achieving quality programmes – the leadership challenge', and 'Academic and general staff – a partnership?'

Workshops tailored to specific groups such as sessional staff, programme leaders and staff developing online learning materials focus on topics of significance to the particular group. Examples of workshops include 'Supporting active student learning; why you should and how you can', 'Programme Leaders' 2003 planning day', and 'Designing criterion-based assessment'.

Consultations

Consultations with programme teams and individual staff are provided on a needs basis, mainly around policy implementation and advice on faculty and university requirements for programme development and programme renewal. Consultations are also used to support programme leaders in preparing programme annual reports and developing programme logs, which form an auditable document repository for each programme. Finally, consultations with teams and individual staff have involved providing advice on developing online materials and building confidence in working with technology. Staff consultations have also been provided by a staff member from the Programme Renewal Group (a central university group) to support staff to develop graduate capability curricula for new and renewed programmes.

Action learning projects

The Office of Programme Quality supports staff to undertake strategic initiative projects aimed at improving student learning experiences and programme quality. Funding is offered on a competitive basis and provides staff, usually working in small teams, with the opportunity to undertake a project that addresses a need in a particular programme. Projects must have the potential to improve programme quality in more than one programme and to develop graduate capabilities in students through changed teaching practices. Project outcomes are disseminated through a seminar or forum and must include a scholarly product, such as a paper or conference presentation. Part of the funding can be used for conference attendance to present a paper. A project officer provides ongoing support for staff undertaking projects, including help with locating resources, design of evaluation activities and preparation of final reports. To date, 13 projects have been completed and outcomes disseminated. Project titles have included 'Who assesses who? Development of a self-assessment tool for nursing students on clinical placements', 'Enrichment of a web portal for Chinese Medicine', 'Development of student e-portfolios' and 'The use of asynchronous e-communication in journal club'.

Resources for education development

A number of resources have been developed to support staff capability building. A refurbished Life Sciences teaching and learning website provides information about events and projects, and links to useful resources to support teaching and learning. A services directory outlines the different services that the Office of Programme Quality and the university offer to support programme and teaching and learning quality. Weekly email programme team updates (PTUs) are sent to programme leaders and heads to share with programme teams and other interested staff. PTUs typically consist of brief news items, and information and advice related to teaching and learning. Staff may submit items to be included in the PTU. Another source is a set of guidelines including useful references on developing portfolios, for publication of staff profiles on the Life Sciences website with a view to encouraging reflection and a scholarly approach to teaching. Another form of resource development has been contribution to the review of university-level policies and practices related to teaching and learning with a view to having them better align with programme, staff and student needs.

Recognition and reward

In 2001 the faculty instituted Teaching Quality Awards, the aim of which is to:

- recognise and reward staff who have made a significant contribution to the faculty goals in teaching and learning;
- raise the profile and status of teaching and learning in the faculty;
- provide an opportunity for staff to share their knowledge and skills about teaching and learning across the faculty; and
- encourage and support staff to nominate for the University Teaching Awards.

Teaching Quality Awards are awarded annually to individuals and teams in recognition of excellence in supporting student-centred learning, the scholarship of teaching and research supervision. Staff are nominated by students and peers and their applications include a teaching portfolio and supporting statements from students and peers, and endorsement by heads. Award recipients are asked to provide advice on good teaching in the form of a letter to a new colleague, which has been posted on the faculty teaching and learning website. Award money can be used to support further professional development through participation at a conference or staff development activity and/or through the purchase of resources for teaching and learning.

EVALUATING OUTCOMES OF EDUCATION DEVELOPMENT EFFORTS

The main focus of recent activity has been in establishing the Office of Programme Quality and putting in place processes to support educational programmes and teaching and learning, including staff capability building, through the education development activities described in this chapter.

However, in line with our commitment to evidence-based continuous quality improvement and the need to be accountable for the resources we use, we have also been considering how to evaluate the effectiveness of our efforts. This is always a major challenge given the complexity of teaching and learning and the many variables involved in determining teaching and learning outcomes, in addition to education development efforts such as, for example, administrative support, physical resources and student–staff ratios.

Donald Kirkpatrick's widely used approach to evaluating development and training activities in business (Kirkpatrick, 1998) provides a useful starting point for identifying what evidence we might need to collect to help us determine the effectiveness of our approach to education development. Using his four-step evaluation strategy – satisfaction, learning, application and impact – we can begin to map out what might constitute useful evidence for the effectiveness of education development efforts:

- positive staff reaction to support and professional development opportunities in the form of feedback surveys, informal comments, participation in activities and 'return business' (satisfaction);

- increased staff confidence and competence in teaching and learning through self, peer and student evaluation (learning);

- improved teaching and learning practices at programme and course (subject) levels as evidenced in the design of learning activities and assessment tasks, self reflection and peer review (application);

- improving student performance as evidence by reduced attrition rates, increased progression rates, and enhanced learning outcomes (impact);

- increasing student, graduate and employer satisfaction with learning and learning outcomes (impact); and

- improving programme performance in terms of the university's 'business rules', namely quality (student and graduate satisfaction), relevance (employability of graduates) and viability (demand for the programme and cost-effectiveness) (impact).

It is relatively easy to gather evidence related to the first level, that is, staff reactions (satisfaction), and we do so routinely and have used such feedback to review and modify our education development activities. It is much more difficult to determine what might constitute valid evidence for the other three levels – learning, application and impact – with impact being the most problematic given the many variables that may intervene between education development and improving student performance, increasing student satisfaction and improving programme performance. Moreover, systematic evaluation requires a level of resourcing and staff commitment that is not typically available and is certainly not currently available within the faculty. At present, within the programme quality assurance framework, we are gathering evidence relating to a number of the variables related to impact including student attrition and progression rates, student, graduate and employer satisfaction and programme performance. The challenge is how to relate any trends in these indicators to the range of education development activities we presently have within the faculty in a systematic way.

Nevertheless, with the increased imperative for universities to meet targets related to quality teaching and learning and to use limited resources effectively, we will have to devise ways of evidencing the effectiveness of education development efforts that are both rigorous and perceived to be so by key stakeholders such as university staff in decision-making positions, governments and funding agencies. Failure to do so will put education development activities under increasing pressure as budgets tighten and staff workloads increase. In our experience, this is already happening as heads of department/school argue for more of the budget to be allocated to teaching and research at departmental and school levels with less available at faculty level to support education development.

FUTURE PLANS

As a result of recent university-wide restructuring, the faculty, together with two other faculties, has become part of the Science, Engineering and Technology (SET) Portfolio, one of three academic portfolios within the university. The work of the academic portfolios will be supported by other portfolios including Teaching and Learning, and Students. The restructure is providing an opportunity to consider how some of the ideas we have been developing within the faculty might be used to build SET Portfolio education development activities, including:

- cross-faculty projects to address key issues such as access and equity, assessment practices and student learning experiences;
- support for sessional/casual teaching staff – on and off campus;
- development of staff professional portfolios including e-portfolios;
- strengthening of evidence-based practice as the basis for programme and teaching quality; and
- cross-disciplinary collaboration around the scholarship of teaching and learning.

Whether and how the model we have developed in one faculty might be adapted across a much larger and more diverse group is something we have only recently begun to explore.

Meanwhile, we need to consider the longer-term implications of the restructure for education development. In particular, given that the new structure aims to locate as much as possible of academic work within schools, it may be at this level – rather than at the SET Portfolio level – that education development will be situated, signifying a further step in decentralisation. Thus, the head's attitude to education development becomes pivotal in determining what support will be provided at school level. Further, the question of what role the academic portfolio leadership may assume in relation to education development remains to be answered. And beyond that, the role of the Teaching and Learning and Students portfolios in leading and providing education development is still being clarified.

CONCLUSION

In this chapter, I have described a model of decentralised education development within a faculty. The model has evolved over two years and has focused on building staff capability around programme development and renewal using an evidence-based continuous quality improvement approach in line with the university's programme quality assurance framework. Decisions about the kind of education support to provide have been made using evidence from research and past practice and taking into account the context and staff background. We are now seeking ways to evaluate our efforts in terms of the impact on teaching and learning. Over time, as we refine our targets and the sources of evidence we need to use, we will be in a better position to judge how well this decentralised approach to education development is working.

Given the current university restructure, the issue of where best to locate education development efforts is still very much on the agenda. Some combination of centralised and decentralised approaches will be the most likely outcome but what and how each area may contribute will need to be carefully considered. Perhaps, even more importantly, we need to work out how all levels – school, academic portfolios and other portfolios such as Teaching and Learning and Students – can work together to achieve our goals. A good decision depends very much on how well the senior leadership understand the kinds of capabilities staff need to support quality teaching and learning and operate as self-managing professionals, and the role that education development can play in this process. It may be that it is at this group that our future education development efforts are best directed.

6

Alignment and synergy: leadership and education development

Margot Pearson and Chris Trevitt

INTRODUCTION

Much of the discussion about management and leadership in universities in Australia, the USA and the UK has focused on meeting pressures from government for expanded access and participation in higher education, more efficient and effective governance and administration, more accountability, and resource constraints (Scott 1995; Gumport and Sporn 1999; Marginson 1997). A common response to these pressures for change has been to focus on management structures and the restructuring of administration and academic areas (e.g. McNay 1995; Yetton 1997). It is not surprising in this policy environment that within universities and in the literature the focus, even in education development, has been on managing change at the institutional level leading to a prevailing top-down perspective as concluded by Trowler (1998). Even in education development, while there has been a range of initiatives for new activity addressing institutionally derived goals in areas such as improving student access, student support, IT literacy, and career development, many such programmes take place, or are initiated, outside mainstream academic departments (e.g. Slowey 1995; Pitkethley and Prosser 2001; Pearson *et al.* 2002). The overall effect is to create an impression that significant sustainable innovation and 're-invention' of teaching and learning practice in higher education is more widespread than is necessarily the case.

Encouraging systemic change in the culture of teaching practice so that successful adaptation and innovation is sustained from within academic departments (or schools, henceforth referred to as academic organisational units (AOUs)) is of a different order as argued by Massy and Zemsky (1995), Pearson (1998) and Trowler (1998). The variable success of funded innovation projects and programmes (Weimer and Leinze 1991; Hayden and Speedy 1995; Alexander *et al.* 1998; Mathew and Land, Chapter 10) is instructive in this regard. The experience of such programmes over time has been to establish the now well-known difficulties such as: the fragmentation of effort and lack of sustainability where 'lone rangers' follow their own interests in isolation from others and without organisational support; and the lack of scholarly input leading to re-inventions of the wheel, or innovation that is of limited value in advancing student learning. Additionally, as individuals and departments react to perceived opportunity and create their own agendas, they can make changes that are not necessarily aligned with institutional goals and directions. These directions, in a competitive educational market, increasingly include developing a high-quality student learning environment, and teaching programmes and courses that are responsive to changing student, industry and community expectations.

One response to complexities and difficulties of this kind is to call for stronger leadership by AOU heads as well as by senior management (e.g. Ramsden 1998a). Another is to seek to improve internal and external organisational alignment by developing institutional strategic plans and changed staffing policies and strategies to suit changing conditions (e.g. Coaldrake and Stedman 1999). However such responses assume top-down linear change processes that are of questionable value in education development that seeks adaptive and sustainable changes in teaching programmes and teaching practice. This is especially the case in higher education systems where the impact of organisational diversity and complexity is compounded by the constant pressure for change from different and, at times, conflicting sources (Clark 1996a; McNay 1995; Gumport and Puser 1999).

In contrast, drawing on the experience of school reform, Fullan (1993) argues for a multifaceted, multi-level approach that allows for, and co-ordinates, both top-down and bottom-up strategies for educational reform, an approach for higher education supported by Johnston (1997) and Trowler (1998). Taking Fullan's approach to the change process suggests the need to rethink the role and work of leadership in education development. Likewise, it suggests a reassessment of the potential and limitations of leadership power and influence. The way leadership is enacted is critical to a process that involves working with people, fostering group and individual synergies, and seeking alignment with institutional directions.

In this chapter we argue that leadership is more than directing and mobilising resources; that education development can itself be a strategy and vehicle for change; and that alignment is best conceived as a goal following the approach of Senge (1990). Senge uses the metaphor of a jazz group to illustrate how the alignment process can combine both spontaneity and co-ordination. Key issues for leaders, especially heads of AOUs, in achieving alignment and synergy through education development discussed in this chapter and explored in a case study are:

1   the nature of the work of leadership for education development;

2   the significance of people and process in change management and education development;

3   the potential of a multifaceted approach to education development;

4   the importance of capacity building for adaptive change, and

5   ways to share leadership and work collaboratively to effect change.

LEADERSHIP AND CHANGE MANAGEMENT – WHAT'S AT ISSUE FOR EDUCATION DEVELOPMENT?

Accepting the need for a multi-level and multifaceted approach to change management does not mean rejecting the need for senior leaders to set directions and develop policy frameworks. It does however suggest the need for a particular focus on leadership at the level of the AOU head and on the engagement of academic teaching staff with their institutional change agendas for effective education development. It is at this level that policy and plans are enacted. Critical to such enactment being generative, sustainable and aligned with institutional goals are two important issues: how departmental (AOU) leadership is carried out; and how teaching staff are involved in the change process.

The impact of heads of AOUs on departmental climate and commitment to change in teaching programmes and practice has been widely recognised (Middlehurst 1993; Hayden and Speedy 1995; Ramsden 1998a; 1998b; Knight and Trowler 2001) and has led to continued calls for heads to strengthen their leadership and management practice (Sarros *et al.* 1997; Ramsden 1998a; Knight and Trowler 2001; Winter and Sarros 2002). Advice on leadership practice has varied, drawing on a range of models as to what constitutes leadership and management in general, and in higher education in particular. Where models have been imported into academia there has been a tendency to position the head as a type of middle manager (Tucker 1984; Moses and Roe 1990; Pearson 1996; Ramsden 1998b; Knight and Trowler 2001) and focus on the functional responsibilities or 'job' of the head managing staffing, research, teaching and so on. However, as noted by Tan (1995: 86–7) a focus on the functional responsibilities of a head can lead to job descriptions that omit the dynamic elements of their role in adapting and improving teaching and research. Nor does such a focus fully identify the potential of the institutional position of the head as the nexus where top-down directions and local initiatives meet (Moodie 2002). In this position the head is a key figure in achieving the co-ordination, alignment and synergy required for effective education development.

Where there is a focus on change some would look to transformational leadership of the kind proposed by Kotter (1990). He argues that leaders cope with change by setting directions, devising a vision and strategies, aligning people (communicating directions) and motivating and inspiring people. In contrast he describes management as dealing with complexity and involving planning, budgeting, organising staff, controlling and problem solving. His model has been elaborated for an academic setting by Ramsden (1998b) who, as with Kotter, argues for the complementarity of management and leadership and the need for both to be carried out effectively. Ramsden identifies as problems those situations where there is 'strong management without strong leadership' which leads to 'a sense of dis-empowerment and irritation ...', as well as those situations where strong leadership is not coupled with strong management, which he suggests contributes to the 'failing of innovative courses in traditional academic contexts ...' (Ramsden 1998b: 107–9).

An alternative to stressing complementarity is to focus on the integration of leadership and management roles. This has been studied in detail by Mintzberg (1980) drawing on observational research into what managers do on a daily basis. He developed an integrated model in which the manager/leader carries out three sets of roles that flow from their formal institutional position and authority. These roles together form a gestalt, and include:

- interpersonal roles – figurehead, leader, liaison;
- information roles – monitor, disseminator, spokesman (sic); and
- decisional roles – entrepreneur, disturbance handler, resource allocator, negotiator.

Mintzberg's leader/manager is more a facilitator than a heroic figure, entrepreneurial rather than charismatic, and one who seeks to find resources, including people, to do what has to be done. As entrepreneur, Mintzberg's leader/manager monitors problems and opportunities within and external to the unit and then, as he puts it, 'initiates and designs much of the controlled change' through 'improvement projects'. Informational roles are important as the leader/manager acquires information from a variety of sources, many informal, and some arising from her position and formal contacts. According to Mintzberg the informational roles 'tie all managerial work together – linking status and the interpersonal roles with the decisional roles' (p. 71). The applicability of this approach to the academic setting is supported by the findings of Middlehurst (1993) who reported that a cybernetic and entrepreneurial perspective was evident in discussions of the day-to-day tasks of leadership and management with academic leaders. Similarly, Marshall *et al.* (2000) in their study of academic perceptions of leadership state that the majority of their academic respondents endorsed the importance of the operational dimension of leadership. In particular they identified as significant the capacity 'to co-ordinate the full range of complex and inter-related tasks and activities associated with change' (p. 47).

A situational perspective presented by Heifetz and Laurie (1997) further elaborates the nature of the work of leadership in implementing change. They juxtapose two contrasting scenarios, one that represents 'an adaptive challenge' where there are 'often systemic problems with no ready answers' (p. 124) and one demanding technical routine solutions. Where leaders face an adaptive challenge, these authors argue against the notion of leadership consisting of having a vision and aligning people to it (p. 134). Instead they position leadership as a form of learning. Leaders they argue (p. 124): '... do not need to know all the answers. They do need to ask the right questions.' Faced with an adaptive challenge, it is the people in an organisation who constitute the locus of responsibility for problem solving – 'giving work to the people' as they put it. Asking the right questions then helps provide staff with an appropriate direction or framing. Getting people to do adaptive work is difficult, however, not only because it breaks the pattern of expecting the leader to give solutions (even if these solutions are then subsequently dismissed or contested, we would add) but because adaptive change is distressing for people experiencing it (Heifetz and Laurie 1997). Leaders have to 'engage people in confronting the challenges, adjusting their values, changing perspectives, and learning new habits' (p. 134).

How teaching staff are involved in the change process is the second significant issue for leadership, change management and education development – what Heifetz and Laurie termed giving 'the work to the people'. While organising action and mobilising resources will require institutional policy frameworks and plans, by their very generic nature such frameworks and plans ignore the particularities of context that will affect the implementation process and the lives of those who have to carry out the work of change. Institutional policies and plans with strategies and targets do not connect effectively with many academic teaching staff who, as professionals and discipline specialists are concerned with context-specific priorities and issues in their teaching practice. Debate about plans and strategies for changes in teaching and teaching infrastructure is further hampered by the lack of both a sufficiently detailed knowledge and a shared understanding of the teaching and learning process (Massy and Zemsky 1995). In the absence of such understanding, staff are being asked to accept or make decisions under circumstances where they cannot work out the significance and implications for their own practice in advance. This is obviously the case where new technologies are involved, but can be so where new approaches to course management and teaching are involved such as semesterisation and classroom collaboration (Trowler 1998).

It follows that any framing of the issue of participation in change by academics primarily as a people management issue misses the point. That framing positions academics as passive recipients of policies and procedures rather than as key actors in the change process (Trowler 1998). Teaching as a professional activity cannot be scripted in advance, nor mandated (Fullan 1993). Even where teachers are willing participants in change they must have sufficient understanding of the principles, components and theoretical framework of an innovation if they are to adapt it effectively into their practice (Pearson 1983). The leadership challenge is to create an environment in which teachers can engage actively with the change process, adapting their practices, innovating and interacting with the policy environment to contribute to the shaping of change agendas.

Creating a climate that fosters free-flowing and open-ended engagement demands first acknowledging and respecting the different positions, values, conceptual frameworks and world views that teaching staff bring to bear on their practice. Such views form part of differing stances or ideologies as to the nature and purpose of education (Millar 1991; Trowler 1998). In higher education, difference has most often been read as difference in disciplinary identities (Becher 1989). However academics are members of diverse communities and can bring many perspectives to bear from reference groups inside and outside the university, such as national and international colleagues, professional communities, colleagues from other departments, and friends and relatives (Välimaa 1998). These influences are similar to what Trowler (1998) calls 'cultural traffic'. The value of such diversity is argued by Tierney (1997: 15) who calls for different ways of diagnosing organisational action, culture and socialisation. He argues that learning organisations or knowledge-creating companies are ones that 'work from frameworks that accept difference and discontinuity, rather than similarity and continuity'.

In this context the conclusions about innovation of Somekh (1998) provide a guide to what leaders and decision-makers at all levels might expect or foster for any change programme, and for education development. She gives five key concepts as central to successful innovation:

- *messiness*, the acceptance of situational complexities, and the recognition that different motivations prevail from different points of view within an organisation;

- the *power of individuals* to make a positive contribution to bringing about change;

- *partnership*, and creating a 'critical mass' of 'shared meanings' and understanding;

- *professional development* as central to the process of planning and implementing change; and

- the need for the *integration of theory and practice*, for example, by the use of action learning approaches.[1]

ACHIEVING ALIGNMENT AND SYNERGIES – A CASE STUDY OF MULTIFACETED EDUCATION DEVELOPMENT

To ground these ideas we draw on a case study of a small AOU – the Legal Workshop (LW). The LW is an organisational entity within the Faculty of Law which administers and teaches a Graduate Diploma in Legal Practice (GDLP). This study programme is taken by many hundreds of students every year from all over Australia as well as overseas, many of whom are in full- or part-time work. It is typically completed in less than a year, but some students may take up to three years. There are some 15 separate courses of study, involving a comparable number of instructors and half as many support staff.

In the late 1990s the LW was faced with an urgent need to move to flexible delivery to maintain its market position. The LW director proved both entrepreneurial and inventive in seeking the necessary resources for educational and technical support. He had recognised the potential for web-supported courses to enhance the options for students to mix and match work, study and other commitments. At the same time he was aware too of the need to encourage his colleagues to develop the skills to use IT appropriately, and was alert to the possibility that this might also lead to their adoption of alternative or creation of new teaching approaches. Among other resources, he negotiated a cooperative project with the institutional academic development unit (the Centre for Education Development and Academic Methods, CEDAM). Drawing on a history of collaboration between the two areas, the project involved the creation and appointment to an experimental staff position within CEDAM designated as a learning design support trainee consultant (consultant coach). A senior educational consultant, also located in CEDAM, supervised this new position.

The project centred on the use of one-to-one coaching as a way to support and skill staff (Trevitt 2003), and sought to link them to other emerging technical support and educational infrastructure coming on stream centrally. An iterative process of course design and evaluation was orchestrated by the CEDAM educational consultants, who worked closely with all staff individually and in groups and with the director. As elaborated below, further professional and teaching development – such as enrolling in formal study and working in self-managing subgroups – is now being undertaken by the teaching staff. The unit climate is positive towards such development activity, and to working with other groups in the university and externally, and to change as a way of life. Leadership is increasingly distributed amongst the academic staff, who are developing a collaborative culture focused on the overall department teaching programme.

Table 6.1 summarises the activities engaged in by all the key players (see headings in the second, third, fourth and fifth columns). The first column indicates the sequence of events with five phases from the pre-project phase to the post-project phase. The total duration amounts to 24–30 months. The sixth column illustrates the relevant changes occurring in the broader university environment over the same period.

Key features of the overall approach to education development that evolved in the case study were:

- the leadership approach of the LW director;

- education development centred on professional growth through action learning; and

- the emergence of collaborative education developments and shared leadership.

THE LEADERSHIP APPROACH OF THE DIRECTOR

The actions of the LW director combined elements of both the Mintzberg and Heifetz models. He was entrepreneurial, and used his information roles to foster an open dialogue within his AOU and to keep himself well informed about institutional directions. He constantly scanned the horizon reaching out from the group, linking to institutional information and emerging university policy directions, and linking to the wider profession at large taking up-to-date soundings of the nature of emerging niche markets. A natural outcome of this environmental scanning was the opportunity to locate and secure sources of funds and other resources, and to set up partnerships internally (for example, with the CEDAM) and externally (for example, with law firms).

The director attended to both the management tasks of resourcing the project and monitoring its progress as shown in Table 6.1, while interacting

Table 6.1 A multifaceted approach to education development

	Academic staff	Consultant coach	Senior education consultant	Director	University environment
Pre-project	Heightened awareness of market trends. Exposure to new technologies. Desire to strengthen own skills.	In part-time employment at CEDAM already. Attracted by novelty of the job description. Developing own familiarity with relevant literature.	Canvas technologies and commercial products for LW. Confirm university backing. Frame project outcomes, boundaries. Determine approaches to be taken and expected project activities. Craft job description.	Liaise with range of senior university/ faculty managers. Locate and secure funding. Clarify group expectations and roles. Locate and secure arrangements with external provider for WebCT.	On-going policy discussions on shape of new technology systems to support teaching and learning preparatory to re-structuring initiatives.
Set up	Clarify: • project expectations and possibilities; • broader university infrastructure; • role of each of the educational consultants.	Clarify job duties and role expectations. Commitment to the position.	Liaise with director LW re project. Conduct orientation for LW staff. Introduce LW staff to new appointee.	Liaise with senior education consultant re project. Arrange for staff induction into project. Keep LW committee of management informed of project plans and initiatives.	Significant re-structuring of major information services providers on the campus.
During	Invent new teaching strategies. Iterative rethinking and rebuilding of curricula.	Consult with LW staff. Adopt a just-in-time (JIT) one-to-one approach.	Brief and debrief junior consultant, especially regarding specific curriculum	Monitor project activities. Fine-tune activities.	

continued...

Table 6.1 *continued*

	Academic staff	*Consultant coach*	*Senior education consultant*	*Director*	*University environment*
	Maintain existing teaching, and day-to-day professional commitments.	Cross-fertilise useful ideas. Do brief/debrief with senior consultant, especially with a focus on separating out course and programme-level issues.	innovations and consulting strategies. Engage in own JIT consulting with some LW staff. Liaise with director and senior staff.	Initiate new administrative arrangements. Adjust support staff roles and activities. Maintain routine management commitments.	Establish institutional teaching information management structures, and set up WebCT technical infrastructure.
Shut down	3–4 iterations of curriculum change required for complete transformation. Reflect on nature of curriculum change. Set up embryonic self-organising staff support structures, e.g. peer-coaching.	Begin phased disengagement. Assist LW staff to 'go it alone'.	Contribute to review and future strategy planning. Reflect strengths of project experience back to LW staff. Draft project report. Locate in broader research-base context.	Conceive, plan and arrange major review workshop. Carry out forward planning post-project activities.	
Post-project	Pro-active role as 'peer leaders' for forward strategy planning.	Increase 'distance' from LW staff and their 'day-to-day' work.	Write project report. Liase with senior staff.	Conduct review workshop. Share leadership responsibilities for post-project activities with range of LW staff. Move LW courses onto own institutional WebCT.	

with his colleagues and negotiating the shape of developments being pursued. These tasks included routine and day-to-day requirements within the group, ensuring that current cohorts of students were not compromised by disruptions due to implementation of new systems and approaches; identifying and acting to implement opportunities for technological stream-lining of routine communications with students; and ensuring the provision of support for staff to harness new technologies in timely and thoughtful ways. In all of this his style was flexible, more hands-on for the routine tasks, more hands-off for the adaptive work. In some circumstances he would display a 'command and control' style (or at least project himself this way), in others he would take on more of a listening, nurturing and motivating approach.

Particularly significant was the director's approach to goal setting and project management. Although he had a clear focus on moving the LW programme towards flexible course provision, he provided a loose framing of this objective. The project needed to be framed at the programme, not course, level as the multiple courses together formed the curriculum and the basis of the student learning environment. But programme change was approached in the beginning in a sufficiently open-ended way so that an ethos compatible with the existing individual course ownership culture was maintained.

The project itself was informed by a vision of education development/ consulting that the director was prepared to work with even though he was not sure just what it entailed and where it might lead teaching practice. He was attracted to the appointment of a consultant to work directly with his staff as they engaged with the technology, but he was also prepared to have that assistance provided within an education trainee framework, not through the more usual appointment of a technical IT assistant in his AOU. This open-endedness was itself possible because both levels of other staff involved had sufficient confidence and trust in the value of such an experiment and in the LW director and senior education consultant. This open-endedness made constructive risk taking possible. It offered an 'evolu-tionary space' – one that fostered both creative advancement by individuals working at their own pace, and that permitted the project itself to evolve within relatively flexible parameters with limited constraints. As the project advanced, the comfort with 'risk taking ' among the teaching staff in their teaching practice grew (Trevitt 2003).

Important too was the director's attention to infrastructure issues and communications. With an increasing number of LW students being located off campus, and often geographically remote, a number of infrastructure and administration issues became pressing, particularly since the institution had no history of catering for such student cohorts. The director did not wait for institutional policy and plans for central IT systems to be implemented; rather, his approach was to find an interim solution so that the LW could continue to develop its programme in a timely way. Prior to this project he had introduced a number of local initiatives, including the development of substantial print-based resources; a duplication, distribution and mailing system; and, as the distributed programme grew, a telephone booking system for courses. In preparation for the project outlined here, access to the WebCT facility at an adjoining institution was negotiated, ensuring that the LW was well set up to take advantage of local institutional systems when they subsequently came on stream.

At the same time, the director kept himself informed more broadly about infrastructure and communications developments that might impact on developments within the LW. He liaised with the senior education consultant who was involved with policy development for flexible learning and the institutional introduction of WebCT. The director made a point of joining various working parties and taking part in relevant meetings. In this way he engaged with the policy agendas and contributed to their shaping.

EDUCATION DEVELOPMENT AS PROFESSIONAL GROWTH

At the beginning of the project some LW staff were open to using new technology, and others were apprehensive. There was minimal realisation that profound change in teaching and emphasis in curriculum might be implied by serious engagement with the new WebCT system. In anticipation of just such an eventuality, however, the education consultant's approach to the project centred on an agenda of professional growth focused on curriculum, not just skill development for use of new technology. In the job description prepared for the consultant coach attached to the project, the approach to instructional design was couched in the following terms:

> The intention is not so much to provide an instructional design service for areas, rather it is to facilitate areas' capacities to re-think teaching practice and re-invigorate course provision in ways which draw on instructional design concepts and reinforce the ethos of a research-led institution. The aim is to move beyond classical instructional design models and exploit opportunities opened up by new technologies.

In other words, the purpose was not only to ensure that successful redevelopment of curricula occurred during the project but, at the same time, to aspire to the development of in-house capacity within the LW group to continue to mount and manage such course redevelopment activities into the future. The project was envisaged as an exercise in local growth and capacity building, and there was an express intention to avoid creating dependency on 'outsider' educational consultants.

Three features informed the education development framework. First, the principle of curriculum *alignment* explained by Biggs (1999) was adopted, whereby curriculum goals, student activities and assessment are devised in such a way that they reinforce one another. Second, an action learning approach was encouraged at the level of the individual course and instructor. Third, a simple, practical and rapid means for soliciting formative student feedback comprising four open-ended questions administered by email was used to ensure the action learning activity was grounded in student perspectives of the curriculum. Thus, while much of the initial education consulting contact with academics was triggered by technology issues, these three features lay at the heart of the educational principles that were fostered using a just-in-time (JIT) one-on-one coaching process rather than scheduled training programmes or courses (Trevitt, 2003).

Coaching sessions usually lasted up to one hour, but some were shorter and many longer. The education consultants usually initiated the first contact with an academic. As rapport, trust and mutual respect built up, so it became feasible to elicit greater contextual detail and explore increasingly abstract and nuanced educational advice. Once an understanding had been developed between the relevant individuals, either party called meetings. Often an exchange of emails or a telephone discussion sufficed. At other times working side-by-side at a keyboard was called for. Repeat sessions with a given academic occurred at different intensities. Sometimes multiple sessions each week were required; at other times contact did not occur for upwards of a number of weeks. In the lead up to a teaching period, it was urgent that preparations met required deadlines, and this could result in frequent interactions. Corridor exchanges also proved important.

Overall monitoring and feedback of the process occurred formally and informally. Given that the education consultants had offices located remote from the LW group, at least one consulting session was usually arranged back-to-back with weekly LW staff meetings with a view to 'hanging around', being seen and enabling 'chance' encounters with others. Additionally, at the beginning of the project, most coaching sessions were 'sandwiched' between a 'briefing' and 'debriefing' meeting involving the senior and junior education consultants. The meetings were used as a means for monitoring and for improving the consultancy process itself (Trevitt 2003). In these ways rapid and extensive information flow, and targeted professional development was sustained involving both individual academics in LW and the two education consultants from CEDAM.

COLLABORATIVE EDUCATION DEVELOPMENT AND SHARED LEADERSHIP

Another feature critical to staff engaging with the process of change was the openness on the part of the LW director to sharing of responsibilities and roles. The LW director openly accepted the need for a distributed approach to leadership. While he was always responsible for a substantive teaching workload of his own, and had prior experience of education development, the director took care not to try and do everything himself. He was open and receptive to educational advice and support for curriculum and programme change from both his own staff and the two education consultants located 'outside' LW, but still assumed all operational responsibility for staff and programme decisions.

Ongoing project leadership and co-ordination centred on an informal steering group. Membership of this group varied from meeting to meeting but was based on a core comprising the LW director and the senior education consultant. This group met periodically in order to review progress and develop plans for next steps. A range of responsibilities and tasks were involved. Periodic 'championing' of the project and its underlying strategic purposes was carried out in various faculty and university fora, as required, and opportunities arose. Identifying development directions and needs, and clarifying tasks, emerging issues and opportunities happened in an adaptive fashion as issues were encountered. Emphasis was given to 'just-in-time' (JIT) rather than 'just-in-case' (JIC) approaches to change and development.

As with the one-on-one coaching and consulting relationship with individual academics, similar JIT approaches were employed at the project management level. For example periodic project review and priority setting was undertaken at both programme and course levels. This was undertaken at special staff meetings arranged separately from the regular weekly staff meetings. (Nevertheless, these regular staff meetings frequently featured teaching and curriculum issues as a significant proportion of the agenda.) The 'special' staff meetings provided an opportunity for periodic updating of the LW group's 'common perspective' on programme curriculum and change. Even the to-ing and fro-ing involved in determining the agenda for each such session contributed to the development of shared perspectives and priorities. These meetings usually lasted for upwards of half a day, and sometimes involved going for a meal together afterwards. Four such substantive meetings were held over an 18-month period, interspersed with additional group meetings of a less formal or extensive nature.

Further, as those staff most heavily involved in the project developed their experience and insights, so leadership responsibilities were increasingly devolved, with the director assuming a co-ordinating role. For example, in the immediate wake of the project, a strategy meeting saw six senior staff take responsibility for further development in: marketing; course costings; course review and further curriculum change; arranging a strategic planning retreat; student internship arrangements; and IT management matters. This was a substantive demonstration of a self-organising and self-coaching outcome achieved over a 12- to 18-month time scale.

Periodic clarification of the role and expectations of the two main support staff in LW was also undertaken. Broadly, these positions provided support for desktop IT and WebCT functions, and compiling and printing print-based study materials. As these roles evolved, so the education and curriculum development consulting undertaken by CEDAM staff was adjusted accordingly.

Overall the case study demonstrates how a multifaceted approach was 'messy' (Somekh 1998) and yet achieved sustained change in the LW teaching programmes and teaching practice. The education development activity strengthened individual academics' capacities to inform their own curriculum development through a process of evidence-based reflection, and strengthened the departmental (and hence the programme) capacity to diagnose and inform its own development agenda in an analogous fashion. These processes were embedded through a distributed approach to leadership. Initiative was exercised on the part of many individuals, only some of whom are represented in Table 6.1. The importance of preparatory activities, and making opportunities to develop shared under-standings of one another's points of view, as suggested by the entries in the 'pre-project phase' (the first row in Table 6.1) should not be underestimated. Inevitably, these activities depended for their success on high levels of information flow: information that was substantially accurate. In this way changes in educational practices were achieved that were aligned with evolving institutional policy directions and infrastructure developments.

EDUCATION DEVELOPMENT FOR LEADERS – WHAT LEADERS NEED TO KNOW AND WHAT THEY CAN DO

What can be drawn from the case study experience? Leaders concerned with education development and responsible for innovation in teaching programmes and practice are facing adaptive challenges and need to work on a number of levels and in a number of ways. They need to ensure that teaching programmes are well managed in the interests of both students and staff, but leave curriculum and associated teaching and student adminis-trative processes open to evolutionary development in response to adaptive challenges. While keeping the 'bigger picture' of institutional frameworks and their own goals in mind and maintaining focus, they must create the necessary space, information flow and impetus for their colleagues to engage with the change process.

For this reason it is critical that the leader knows enough to identify promising directions, resources and expertise, but does not fall into the trap of presenting solutions, whether it be a vision for innovation, or a prescription, or even a set of propositions for 'good' learning. As argued in Kayrooz *et al.* (1997) there is a tension pervading all education development activity that is aligned to some framework establishing what is 'good practice' or desirable practice, with a commitment to acknowledging the complexity of situated practice and the agency of academic practitioners. The difference in underlying approaches is summed up by Webb (1996). Webb contrasts the developmental paradigm, analogous to a process of biological maturation and moving along a predetermined course, with an evolutionary model of change, one for which there is no predetermined course and which unfolds according to changing environmental conditions.

One productive frame for opening up debate is the curriculum. The significance of curriculum change has recently received more attention in higher education (Boyer Commission on Educating Undergraduates in the Research University 1998; Barnett *et al.* 2001). Curriculum design and review processes are potential vehicles for looking critically at educational issues of significance to a workgroup. Where curriculum review involves more than 'horsetrading' of speciality subjects, it opens up issues, and allows critical review of goals against evidence in the form of outcomes. It induces a more focused analysis in discussion and planning centred on goals and outcomes without prescribing the means in advance. A focus on the curriculum, its learning outcomes and student audience, prevents premature or unexamined foreclosure on known teaching strategies while lessening any perceived threat to professional autonomy.

Important here is to distinguish between programme-level curriculum design issues (affecting overall student experience, and usually involving all members of the workgroup) and course-level design, generally the province of just one or two staff members. Course-level curriculum design is where individuals in the workgroup exercise a leadership role. As can be seen from Table 6.1, a major focus within the briefing and debriefing sessions conducted by the trainee and senior consultants in the case study involved separating out those curriculum issues related to the overall programme from those associated with individual courses. Subsequent individual coaching sessions were then focused on the course-level issues, while programme-level issues informed discussions with the director and other senior members of staff as well as staff-meeting agendas. These communication strategies thus explicitly countered the general trend toward an information-depleted decision-making setting that was noted by Massy and Zemsky (1995) (and discussed earlier). They also served as a catalyst, helping generate more extensive as well as wider ranging discussions about teaching within the workgroup – a role that necessarily became part of the repertoire of the director in the longer term (see further discussion below).

Action learning and experimental project approaches, along with curriculum debate and planning, provide another powerful means for learning about teaching and dealing systematically with adaptive challenges. They enable reflection and creative adaptation at many levels (McGill and Beaty, 1995; Gibbs, 1995). They lead to a sense of individual 'ownership' of changes 'based on participation and involvement of people, as well as mutual understanding and open discussion of different points of view' according to Somekh and Thaler (1997). These authors argue that an action inquiry approach offers two very powerful features, which support individual commitment and foster personal professional growth. First, it 'accepts and values individuals' own knowledge about the organisation' and encourages them to use this in planning their teaching and 'implementing development' of novel curriculum. Second it is 'grounded in strategies which improve communication'. Action learning offers a powerful way to *integrate theory and practice*, accommodate the *messiness* of situations, and harness the *power of individuals*: three of Somekh's five key factors for achieving successful innovation discussed earlier.

For action learning to be optimally productive, encouraging both formal and informal communications and access to a wider range of ideas about teaching is essential (an explicit role that needs to be acknowledged and addressed by the group leader, as noted above). This demands that time and opportunity be set aside (and, where necessary, structured appropriately) for individual and group learning to occur. Enhancing communications through such internal and external information flows at least partly addresses the *professional development* requirements that Somekh (1998) noted were central to the change process. Where there is a very limited view which is unchallenged of 'how we do things around here', and what is possible and knowable, learning and growth will require more information flows and exchanges during conversations about teaching of any kind, rather than focusing on unidirectional dissemination encouraging emulation and adoption. The 'central importance of invisible … tacit knowledge in the socialisation process' of staff is discussed by Trowler and Knight (1999), and they go on to consider 'socialisation as an example of professional development' that goes to the heart of 'the way in which departments operate' (p. 188–90). For these reasons, exchanges, visits, face-to-face and e-conferences and all such forms of collegial activity will generate constructive ferment where they are connected to everyday teaching practice (Pearson 1998; Boud 1999) and help promote a dynamic rather than moribund social milieu.

Recognition of the importance of shared responsibility for adaptive change in education development raises the issue of the nature of academic collaboration and work patterns in teaching. For many, teaching is still a very individual activity with the potential to produce curricular fragmentation and variable quality in teaching programmes (Dill 1993). However, it is not uncommon for the range of leadership and management responsibilities associated with teaching and teaching programmes within an AOU to be distributed among academic staff. Roles and functions include: committee work (teaching and learning, or curriculum committees, for example), project co-ordination, management of teaching laboratories, holding positions such as subdeans, course/programme leaders, honours co-ordinators, first-year co-ordinators, etc. This sharing of responsibilities can include formal delegation, or dispersal as part of established collegial governance (Birnbaum 1992; Knight and Trowler 2001).

Recently group teaching has become more common, and the use of the term 'team' often appears in this context, but that use is problematic in academic, and other, settings. Benjamin (1997) found a range of approaches to 'team teaching' reported by teachers: a delegation model, co-operative sharing, co-ordination through an agreed framework, and building the curriculum around existing strengths so that each teacher operates independently were some of the approaches identified. A comparable variety of approaches was found by Akerlind *et al.* (1993), with some so-called 'team teaching' comprising a form of serial teaching by individuals without any collaborative interaction.

These findings suggest that the capacity for collaboration cannot be assumed among academic workgroups. They also call in question the use of the term 'team' in academic settings if teams are defined as groups committed 'to a common purpose, set of performance goals, and approach for which they have made themselves mutually accountable' (quoted in Wergin 1994: 112). Nor need 'teamwork' be seen as the goal. As argued by Sinclair (1992) there are difficulties with group operations in dealing with power, emotion and conflict, issues that she states are inevitable aspects of group work. She therefore suggests a flexible contingency approach for deciding when team-based structures are appropriate. Within any workgroup there will be times when individual activity is appropriate and times when collaboration is likely to be more effective. This approach is supported by Fullan (1993) who concludes that both collective and individual action are necessary, an excess of either, he states, is what is dysfunctional. More important than size and type of grouping is the opportunity for interaction and engagement during which meanings are negotiated, and which leads to the shared ownership and collective alignment that Wenger (1998) contrasts with alignment achieved through compliance (see also the later work of Wergen, 2003).

CONCLUSION

We have argued that the work of leadership for education development involves a multifaceted and collaborative approach. It entails capacity building for adaptive change, drawing in all relevant people at the local level while taking account of broader institutional and environmental concerns. As Senge's jazz metaphor nicely makes visible, the reality of development in a university is that it is untidy, uneven, and driven by various players, and yet can be productive. For education development can encompass modest solo improvement initiatives and outstanding performances by star players, variations on a theme as ideas spread, new renditions of old favourites and altogether new songs. But as with a jazz group, sensitivity to the audience and context shapes direction. The case study illustrates the reality and the potential of an effective change process that combines individual spontaneity and group co-ordination to create synergies and alignment of activity and goals in teaching practice, teaching programmes and institutional directions.

Working effectively with the grain of academic and professional processes requires an openness to the unexpected, a willingness to take risks, and a willingness to share ownership of ideas and initiatives. For what is at issue for leadership and adaptive change through education development is not primarily organisational structures or policies, nor clearly identified goals. It is the need to build the capacity for collaboration in an AOU or workgroup that ensures organisational learning through continuous improvement and problem solving (Dill 1999). Building this capacity demands active engagement in activities of consequence to all. Such activity is doing the work of change – changing the curriculum, changing the teaching methods and the learning environment, working individually or collaboratively as appropriate.

The challenge facing leaders and decision-makers is how to balance their priorities and manage the environment and policy pressures for education development. Too loose an institutional framing can lead to costly fragmentation in services, infrastructure and the curriculum, leading to an adverse effect on the quality of the learning environment and of the student experience. Too tight a framing for change from the top will discourage local initiative, and constrain the growth of adaptive teaching cultures.

ACKNOWLEDGEMENTS

We are grateful to Gary Tamsitt and Aliya Steed for their thoughtful, professional and constructive engagement both in the case study experience cited here, and in the debriefing and documentation activities that made it possible to write this chapter in the first place.

NOTE

1   Action learning is taken to mean 'a continuous process of learning and reflection, supported by colleagues with the intention of getting things done' (McGill and Beaty 1995: 21).

7

Integrating teaching and learning principles with IT infrastructure and policy

Carmel McNaught

This chapter explores some issues that arise for education development staff who provide advice relating to decision-making about IT infrastructure and policy in their institutions. The chapter begins by exploring the nature of the modern university, contrasting especially the characteristics of corporate universities and those based on a collegial model. Some broad implications of these models for planning IT infrastructure and policy are outlined.

All modern universities, no matter what their character, have growing diversity and complexity. This is described and examples of how technology might either inhibit or facilitate effective educational practice are given.

There are two case studies in this chapter, one following on from the other. The lessons learnt from a large education development exercise in an Australian corporate university have been considered carefully and have been useful in framing an approach to working in the very different context of a much smaller collegial university in Hong Kong.

THE NATURE OF MODERN UNIVERSITIES

Universities worldwide are currently in an environment of intense change. In this environment, universities have had to reassess their fundamental business and the way they go about it. Information technology (IT) is viewed as an important factor in streamlining their operations.

One way in which the importance of IT can be seen is the increasing trans-national character of university teaching. For example, there was a three-fold increase in overseas student enrolments in Australian higher education institutions during the period 1997–2002, and these enrolments are now 10 per cent of the total higher education student population.

Further, off-shore enrolments increased from 22 per cent to 37 per cent of total overseas student enrolments during this time period (DEST, 2003). A snapshot from the other side shows that, in 2001, Hong Kong hosted more than 150 overseas higher education providers. The teaching in these transnational programmes usually has a significant face-to-face component with home institution staff travelling offshore, sometimes partnering with local teachers. However, the majority of such programmes also use IT in some way or another. This mirrors what is happening in university programmes which are based largely in one country; for example, in 2002, 54 per cent of university courses in Australia used the Web in some way or another for teaching and learning, though only 1.4 per cent of courses were fully online (Bell *et al.*, 2002).

Furthermore, there are now new competitors in the higher education market. The three reports (Cunningham *et al.*, 1998, 2000; Ryan and Stedman, 2002) explore the nature and potential impact of a plethora of new models for higher education provision. The models they identify are: 1) for-profit universities (of which the University of Phoenix is a well-known example); 2) corporate universities (McDonalds is an often cited one here); 3) virtual universities (for example, the underperformance of the Western Governors University in terms of attracting a sufficient number of students highlights the fragility of the business models in this area); 4) public corporate universities (the US Department of Defense is an active example); and 5) service companies (a range of companies selling technical platforms, consultancy services and courseware; an interesting example is Thompson Learning which is now linked to a consortium of traditional universities through the Universitas21 global partnership).

I have listed these examples, mainly to illustrate just how complex the higher education terrain has become. Ling, in Chapter 1, also emphasises this complexity. It is almost an apology in advance for the relatively simple model that I will explore below. I think it is still useful but it must be seen as needing other layers and nuances when applied to actual contexts.

There are several ways in which the diversity of models for the modern university can be described. One is McNay's (1995) four-fold classification of universities with orthogonal axes of policy definition and control of implementation: collegium (loose policy definition and loose control); bureaucracy (loose policy definition and tight control); corporation (tight policy definition and tight control); and enterprise (tight policy definition and loose control). The two universities described in this chapter broadly fit the corporation (RMIT University in Australia) and the collegium (The Chinese University of Hong Kong).

The model described by Downey (1995) helps us to focus more closely on the differences between a corporate university and a collegial one. Rather than defining axes of policy and control, Downey discusses the changing nature of the communities in the two different organisational models. He defines community as 'a culture in which things grow' (p. 8). The important differences between the two types of university are not structural ones but relate more to relationships and values. The structural differences are consequences of, and not determiners of, differing community values. Universities do not fit neatly into one mode or other and all have aspects of both corporate and collegial systems. Downey describes a modern university as a 'trinity' of corporation, collegium and community.

The growth in size of the modern university has resulted in a growing emphasis on systems of budgeting and resource allocation, financial accounting, personnel management, infrastructure planning, etc. – all characteristics we associate with corporate institutions. The collegium, on the other hand, handles the decisions about who works and studies at the university, what areas shall be taught and researched, and what standards will be adopted. It is a 'complex network of assumptions, traditions, protocols, relations, and structures within the university which permit the professoriate to control and conduct the academic affairs of the institution' (Downey, 1995: 6). The nature of the community determines whether corporate accountability dominates academic standards or whether academic decisions drive the design of management systems. This tension is becoming more apparent in our universities.

CENTRAL VERSUS DEVOLVED FUNDING

Mechanisms of funding are often clear ways in which we can see this corporation–collegium tension. Universities with a more corporate orientation tend to adopt centralised models of funding and those with a greater collegial character tend to support more localised control.

Let's consider two examples. The first is the debate about whether university funding for courseware design and production (both online and print) should be through central or faculty-based processes. Teaching staff want the skills and expertise that exist in central units, but wish to have it provided without reduction in funding to faculties. The requirement to pay for services from central units can set up resistances. Most universities use both approaches (McNaught *et al.*, 2000). It is finding the appropriate balance point that is the challenge. Table 7.1 summarises the arguments for, and issues associated with, each approach.

The second example is the consideration of the costs of facilities; these include computer laboratories, space, furniture, as well as the number and level of staff computers. Huge investments into IT facilities are a major item in all university budgets. Using student computer laboratories as an example, Table 7.2 summarises the arguments for and issues associated

Table 7.1 *Pros and cons for centralized and devolved funding*

Centralised funding	Devolved funding
Points in favour of:	
Can reduce duplication of expensive services by funding a range of projects, the design ideas and products of which can be used in other faculties.	Can fund projects based on local knowledge of curricula and faculty culture.
Can foster cross-faculty collaboration and communication.	Can develop stabl.e ongoing teams for future developments
Can allow university strategic priorities to be enacted.	Can allow local ownership and commitment to grow.
Can foster the integration of outside funding with university priorities.	Can source funding from discipline and industry-related bodies.
Issues associated with:	
If the funding committee is not broadly constituted, this can result in a restricted range of models being favoured.	Traditional practices in the discipline can dominate, and it may be difficult for some innovative projects to be funded.
Can be dominated by a few strong university personalities; this may disadvantage certain faculties.	Can be dominated by a few strong faculty personalities; this may disadvantage certain departments/schools.

Source: McNaught *et al.*, 2000: 113.

Table 7.2 *Pros and cons for centralized and devolved management of student computer laboratories*

Central university control	Faculty control	Department/school control
Points in favour of:		
Supports equity principles in that all students can access.	Provides access for the entire faculty.	Special needs of students can be known and accommodated more readily.
University standards for level of machine can be adhered to.	Some overall discipline customisation in choice of machine and software possible.	Machines can be customised to suit individual subject needs.
University bulk purchasing or leasing easier.	Machines can be ordered to suit discipline needs but this may be more costly.	Machines can be ordered to suit discipline needs but this may be more costly.
Development of policy about 24-hour access (e.g. through a smart card) may be easier.	Local laboratories can foster student work in teams on projects.	Local laboratories can foster student work in teams on projects.
Issues associated with:		
The software and configurations cannot be specialised at all for particular disciplines.	Expense of customisation and maintenance.	Expense of customisation and maintenance.

Source: McNaught *et al.*, 2000: 114.

with focusing the management of student computer laboratories at university or local level.

Tables 7.1 and 7.2 make it clear that the decisions are not clear-cut. These decisions involve considering the pros and cons of the two approaches and how they can be balanced within a specific context. Whatever model is adopted, better co-ordination between central and local facilities needs to occur.

TECHNOLOGY AS A FACILITATOR OR INHIBITOR OF EFFECTIVE EDUCATIONAL PRACTICE?

No matter what the nature of the university, every modern university is engaged in monitoring, developing and reworking their IT policies. In doing so, the tension between the productive possibilities and the potential disasters must be recognised. Technology can operate as both an inhibitor and a facilitator of change. It is an *inhibitor* if institutions become locked into heavy investments in the belief that they will get a return on those investments. However, it can be a *facilitator* of change if it is used to provide more options in the teaching and learning space. Let's examine each option in turn.

Technology as an inhibitor of effective teaching and learning

Here an example will make the potential dangers inherent in the relationship between technology and teaching and learning clear. The story of RMIT University's investment in technology is one which illustrates a clear vision of the desire for streamlined corporate management. RMIT University is an 'old' (in Australian terms – RMIT began in 1887) technological university. It is highly diverse – it is a cross-sectoral (i.e. includes a vocational or polytechnic sector) university and has the largest number of overseas students enrolments of any Australian university. RMIT has had a clearly defined central teaching and learning policy since 1995. This strong central policy is in keeping with the character of RMIT as a corporate university.

During the early and mid 1990s there was an increasing use of information and communication technologies (ICTs) in individual courses which increased students' flexible access to RMIT courses in several ways. However, it became increasingly clear that a sustained approach to developing flexible courses for both on- and off-campus students required a more focused university-wide approach. In 1998, the university embarked on a comprehensive and ambitious project to align the information technology systems to the principles and goals of the teaching and learning strategy. This was to be a AUD50 million investment by RMIT over the four years 1999–2002. It was formulated after an extensive report, the Information Technology Alignment Program (ITAP) Report, which had 113 specific recommendations relating to the following six areas of work:

- a strengthened IT infrastructure;

- an online learning management system;

- an Academic Management System (AMS), fully integrated with the online learning management system to provide enrolment and subject and course progress records, electronically accessible to academics and students;

- an extensive review of all academic processes within the university in a business process re-engineering project;

- a strong commitment to a digital library; and

- extensive staff development in the use of technology for teaching and learning.

Prior to the ITAP Report, there had already been substantial investment by RMIT to promote quality learning outcomes. The investment was quite considerable, with approximately 5 per cent of each faculty budget being set aside, along with central money, to fund a programme and course renewal process. Also, major upgrading of the RMIT network, and student and staff computer facilities had taken place. The university tried to move on several fronts at once and many policies and processes were being formulated quite quickly. Many of us involved in education development and infrastructure renewal in the late 1990s at RMIT had a sense of trying to juggle several balls at once, and we tried hard to develop the art of keeping them all in the air and in relation to each other. It was a time of learning and growth; overall, a positive time for the university. Writing in 2000 I commented: 'Have we reached critical mass yet, where the appropriate use of technology for networked learning will roll out across the university? Probably not, but we feel we are on the right track' (McNaught, 2001a: 123). Certainly, many of the components of the ITAP plan have stabilised and there is some evidence that the quality of the online courseware has improved (McNaught, 2001b).

However, the implementation of RMIT University's Academic Management System (AMS) has dealt a crushing blow to the vision of a centralised, integrated set of IT systems supporting teaching and learning functions. The following extracts from the Victorian Auditor-General's Office (2003) report on RMIT tell the story clearly (sums in Australian dollars). The AMS is not functional and this disaster is crippling RMIT's financial fluidity.

- The anticipated cost of implementation of the AMS to the end of 2003 of AUD47.2 million represents 3.7 times the original implementation budget. RMIT, as part of the original budget, also allocated a further AUD6 million per annum for three years for licence fees, additional implementation work, consultancies and software upgrades.

- The current system has not provided the functionality originally planned and RMIT faces significant challenges in transitioning to a high-quality student administration system that is sustainable in the medium to long term, as well as funding the activities necessary to achieve this outcome.

Further, there has been a large amount of adverse media attention on RMIT, its management and prospects. Some of this is particularly feisty, such as the several articles about RMIT on the www.crikey.com.au website. It is not my intention to argue about how much of the allegations, comments and predictions about RMIT are based on evidence, and what the future is for this large technological university. What I want to point out is that this story clearly demonstrates that caution is needed in adopting the notion that a university can invest in large IT systems in the hope that there will be a return on that investment in terms of improved teaching and learning quality, which will then result in improved prestige and greater marketability for the university's programmes. It is just not that simple.

Technology as a facilitator of effective teaching and learning

Higher education rests on the premise that student learning can be facilitated by operating in a planned environment. If we don't believe that, we should return to the days of unstructured discovery learning that many of us tried in the 1960s and 1970s (either as learners or teachers) and found very unsatisfying. Basically, not only does the curriculum need to be planned, but also the nature of the total student experience over, usually, a period of years needs to be considered if curriculum alignment is to occur and result in demonstrable benefits for students. Educational design is essential for facilitating effective learning. However, what about the 'online' or 'e' aspect? The key thing here is not to think of online learning as being totally different from learning which occurs in traditional face-to-face education. The learning process is not different (after all, students are still people with the same neural pathways), but several significant aspects are different in electronically mediated environments. Also, the role of technology depends on a wide variety of other new factors in higher education.

First, the global partnerships in higher education mean that various perspectives on knowledge need to be negotiated. Second, there is an increasing diversity in the students who enter post-secondary education.

This diversity covers academic motivation and orientation, linguistic and cultural background, prior educational experiences, and approaches to learning. These students interact with teachers who have diverse approaches to and beliefs about teaching and learning. Third, there is increasing diversity in the learning contexts students enrol in; these might be workplace learning, studio-centred learning, programmes with intensive block teaching (often across national borders), cross-sectoral programmes and tailored industry-related programmes. Finally, the technology itself means that there is an increasing range of tools and strategies for us to use in designing programmes and courses. All this diversity is summarised in Figure 7.1. The important thing to note is that unless technology does support this fragile and complicated set of relationships, it is not likely to be a facilitator.

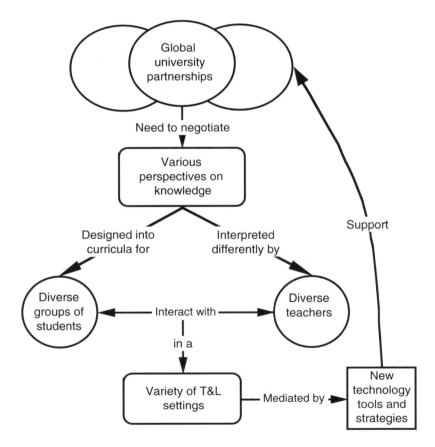

Figure 7.1 *Diversity in higher education supported and mediated by technology*
Source: After McNaught, 2003a: 290.

MODEL(S) OF EDUCATION DEVELOPMENT TO STRENGTHEN THE IT/T&L RELATIONSHIP

The number of players in the education development area is large, including:

- more 'traditional' education development units, concentrating on general teaching and learning support; these can be centrally located or within faculties;

- units where the key focus is the use of information and communication technologies in teaching and learning; these can be centrally located or within faculties; often they are called flexible learning units and may or may not be integrated with education development units;

- units which focus on courseware production using technology; these can be centrally located or within faculties; some of these units have evolved from print-based distance education units;

- centrally-based information technology services units which focus on the technology alone with very little reference to pedagogy; such units often manage the infrastructure of the online learning systems; and

- university libraries.

Hughes *et al.* (1997) in a study of 20 Australian universities describe three approaches to support the use of information technology in teaching – integrated, parallel and distributed. These approaches are defined, and the discussion in Hughes *et al.* is summarised, in Table 7.3. In reality, universities use a combination of approaches, though with a trend in one direction. The table is a useful tool for assessing the potential strengths and weaknesses of the combination of any particular set of support units in a given university.

Two cases will be described and analysed below. They will focus on the challenge of how best to support university teachers in renewing their educational programmes in ways that enable the potential of online technology to be utilised. The two cases are sequential and so the second builds on the lessons learnt in the former. This strategy has been chosen so that other education developers may be able to see that there is no 'one size fits all' method for education development. The work we do is crafted as a response to a perceived need and, in my own case, strongly influenced by previous experiences. Education development work is thus iterative and evolving.

Table 7.3 *Integrated, parallel and distributed approaches to staff development for the use of information technology in teaching*

Integrated approach (eggs in one basket!)
Strong structural links between units or section of the one unit that provide general T&L support, support for using IT in T&L, and production support for courseware. Essentially top-down.

Benefits:	*Issues raised:*
Coherent policy framework. Efficient planning of resources and avoidance of duplication.	Ease of access by all staff limited. Individual approaches less likely to be recognised. An emphasis on one technological solution may emerge and overwhelm educational design.

Parallel approach (never the twain shall meet?)
Separate units for general T&L support and support for using IT in T&L

Benefits:	*Issues raised:*
Allows due recognition to be given to a wide range of T&L issues (e.g. internationalisation) and not just educational design associated with the use of IT.	Co-operation between the various units may be difficult to achieve. There is a potential for confusion and competition to emerge.
Allows the development of expertise relating to the new technologies.	May result in a narrow range of educational issues being addressed in the IT in T&L units.

Distributed approach (organic sprouting)
More bottom-up than the other two approaches. A range of units, centrally located and in faculties which are not tightly co-ordinated. Project management remains with local projects.

Benefits:	*Issues raised:*
An 'organic' solution where unnecessary controls do not hamper innovation.	Can result in weak project management where there may be insufficient educational expertise.
Can be economical as skills are sought when they are needed.	Potential for innovations to falter without visible institutional support.
Can have more local ownership and stronger interpersonal relationships.	Can result in waste and duplication of effort and resources, including equipment.

Source: After Hughes *et al.* 1997.

A CORPORATE UNIVERSITY WORKING WITHIN A LARGELY INTEGRATED APPROACH

The first case is within the context of RMIT University, a corporate university in Australia. The university has an applied focus and interdisciplinary study is common. The challenges of diversity are substantial.

(Table 7.5 describes this diversity as a contrast to the more homogeneous nature of The Chinese University of Hong Kong.)

The model of education development adopted in the late 1990s was largely an integrated approach but there were aspects of distributed support as well. The education development initiative I will describe ran from mid-1999 to the early part of 2001. It was called the Learning Technology Mentor (LTM) programme. It was a university-funded initiative which provided for 140+ academic staff to have one day per week release over one semester, in order to:

- learn how to use the university's recently established online education system;

- design and implement online learning in their faculty's education programmes, and

- promote and support similar activities among colleagues in their departments.

There were two LTMs in most departments of the university and some in central areas such as the Library. Each LTM was funded for 26 days release, and some for longer periods.

The aim of making a significant investment in learning technology mentoring by academic staff – rather than establishing a specialist online design and production unit to service them, for example – was to achieve widespread adoption of online learning as part of effecting a change in the culture of academic work. Extended time release of more than one semester was required to achieve useful outcomes in some cases; these academic teachers were called Experienced Learning Technology Mentors (ELTMs). Many ELTMs engaged in more strategic roles in their faculties, such as quality assurance of online subjects, development and implementation of online publishing standards, etc.

All LTMs undertook an extensive staff development programme for about a week. Some of the key topics related to RMIT's vision with respect to the university's position as a major international technological university. The Boyer (1990) Scholarship model, which emphasises that teaching should be a scholarly activity, has been used for some time as an integrating model for all RMIT work. Within this framework, the evolution of the teaching and learning strategy over the last few years and the structure and function of the IT alignment programme were discussed. There were also sessions covering a range of practical 'hands-on' sessions with online learning tools, as well as workshops in areas such as assessment and evaluation strategies for online learning, student induction methods, managing digital resources, project management, etc.

Over the two years of the programme, a network of individuals developed in several faculties that remained after the formal end of the programme (Gray and McNaught, 2001).

Many lessons were learnt from the RMIT experience of the LTM programme. There was a good measure of success (McNaught, 2003) but further issues emerged during the process of the LTM programme. How can another university benefit from the story of this mentoring scheme set in the context of one particular university? In Table 7.4 I have tried to sum up the positive aspects of the learning technology mentoring scheme as well as the issues and challenges which were not solved satisfactorily. Moving at once on several fronts – policy, infrastructure and support – is absolutely essential. Working across the university in all faculties and departments is also essential, so as to develop local ownership, build generalised capability and maintain productivity in a shared context.

This experience led me to develop a model of two-way integration of education development initiatives. There is a need to *horizontally integrate* initiatives so that staff development is integrated with curriculum reviews and key strategic courseware renewal projects. There is also a need to *vertically integrate* staff development activities, so that discussions with heads of department and for programme co-ordinators are seen as essential to ensure support for teaching staff as they explore technology in their own teaching and learning. The need for the involvement of university leaders is emphasised by Pearson and Trevitt in Chapter 6. The RMIT experience strengthened my conviction that education development cannot be an isolated activity.

How can these two principles of vertical and horizontal integration be applied in another context?

A COLLEGIAL UNIVERSITY WORKING WITHIN A LARGELY DISTRIBUTED APPROACH

The second case is The Chinese University of Hong Kong (CUHK), an essentially collegial university. In Hong Kong there are eight higher education institutions (University Grants Committee, undated a), each with a distinctive character. None of the Hong Kong universities is large, all having undergraduate populations of less than 10,000 students. There are three research-intensive universities, with CUHK being the one with the strongest Chinese cultural ethos. The vision of the university is stated to be 'acknowledged locally, nationally and internationally as a first-class research university whose bilingual and bicultural dimensions of student education, scholarly output and contribution to the community consistently meet standards of excellence'. This combination of the maintenance of

Table 7.4 Successes and remaining challenges of the LTM *programme*

Factor	Key successes	Remaining challenges
Emphasis on local support	The ability to cater for varying contexts. Some departments were building sophisticated online environments for whole programmes; some were focusing on developing teachers' basic computer skills.	In departments where there were organisational problems (e.g. restructuring, unclear or overbearing management, rapid turnover of staff), no progress was made and keen individuals suffered. Implementation of the LTM programme was uneven and resulted in widening of divisions. The organised and innovative departments ended up with more funding than the departments which actually needed most help.
Culture of the department and faculty	Several faculties perceived benefits and thus were willing to collaborate in the broad processes, and to commit a significant level of specific co-ordination effort, to achieve outcomes for their departments.	Putting content online is faster and easier to achieve than thoughtful and innovative renewal of courses and programmes. Learning technology mentoring is not a quick fix. Building a culture of excellent process and practice in online teaching and learning takes longer, but may lead ultimately to greater competitive advantage. This perspective was not universally shared. Where organisational restructuring was occurring, this occupied most of the creative energies of the staff and there was little interest in any teaching innovation.
Workload	The LTM programme was premised on funded time release for academic staff to be mentors. This created genuine amounts of time for several mentors.	Finding suitable short-term replacement staff was an ongoing difficulty. There was no time release for those being mentored.

Table 7.4 *continued*

Factor	Key successes	Remaining challenges
Reward structure	Those staff who participated certainly added substance to their teaching portfolios, and thus enhanced their prospects for academic promotion on this ground. Participants had to have a desire to move themselves professionally into an area of continuous change and challenge; if so, they were able to derive considerable personal satisfaction from this opportunity.	There was an insufficient incentive compared to research rewards. Most participants weren't likely to find time to pursue qualifications in staff development or courseware production, and so could not take advantage of accreditation programmes that would formally recognise their expertise as LTMs.
Scale of programme	The legacy of this project was two or three academics (about 10 per cent of academic staff) in each department who had actively taken part, whose academic practices were influenced by the experience, and who remained as models and a point of reference for their colleagues.	Sustained funding for follow-on activities of the network of LTMs, or for adequate growth of other support structures, only occurred in some faculties.

Source: After McNaught, 2003: 42.

Table 7.5 *Comparison between RMIT University and The Chinese University of Hong Kong*

Characteristic	The Chinese University of Hong Kong	RMIT University
Establishment date	1962	1887, but full university status in 1992.
Nature of the faculties	Seven faculties. Comprehensive, including traditional humanities and medicine. A relatively small number of interdisciplinary programmes.	Seven faculties. Applied focus. Cover the discipline areas across art, architecture, business, design, education, engineering, sciences (physical, life and social). The university has an applied focus and interdisciplinary study is common.
Number of students	9,500 undergraduate, 5,500 postgraduate.	Close to 60,000 students, approximately 25,000 undergraduate higher education and nearly the same number of vocational sector students, 10,000 postgraduate.
Style	Collegial	Corporate
Diversity of student background	Chinese	30 per cent born overseas.
Diversity of student ages	Almost all undergraduates are straight from school.	45–50 per cent are mature (25+ years).
Part-time and full-time student numbers	Only 3 per cent undergraduates are part-time.	40 per cent of students are part-time across the whole university.

Chinese cultural values together with an active outreach to the world is an intriguing challenge.

There is no doubt that CUHK is very different from RMIT. Table 7.5 clearly illustrates this. Both IT and T&L policies are much more devolved at CUHK than at RMIT. Funding is not largely internal funding and external government funding is necessary. The education development work here has been designed to build on the lessons learnt from the RMIT experience but is also designed to be situated within a university with a very different cultural context.

The Centre for Learning Enhancement And Research (CLEAR) (http://www.cuhk.edu.hk/clear/) is a new education development unit. It is centrally located for the reasons cogently argued by Chalmers and O'Brien in Chapter 4. It is an academic unit, rather than an administrative one and there is a clear expectation that research is an essential aspect of education development. Hence, evaluation is an integral part of our activities. When a new unit begins with academic staff who come from a variety of backgrounds and experience, the process of utilising that rich set of prior knowledge occurs both informally and formally. Informally, we often say, 'well, we tried … and it seemed to work'. Formally, we developed a strategic plan. The principles of horizontal and vertical integration were enacted through the decisions we made about our preferred mode of working. These are described in Table 7.6.

In Table 7.6, I have italicised two strategies, one for horizontal integration and one for vertical integration. These two were chosen just to give variety to the discussion. Let's see how, just over one year after the articulation of these principles, these two strategies are working.

FORMAL LIAISON BETWEEN CENTRAL UNITS WITH IT AND WITH T&L SUPPORT FUNCTIONS

At RMIT, the main support for IT in T&L was centralized. In addition, there were general links between other support units, such as the Library, but they were not very strong and were not formalized in any way. This is not surprising in a very large organisation, even one which adopts a corporate approach. I had a feeling that there were lost opportunities at RMIT and I wished to avoid this at CUHK, where I knew that I would have the additional challenge of services being distributed.

In a highly distributed environment, such as exists at CUHK, liaison often relies on incidentally meeting and finding common ground with colleagues. While this can be very effective, it can also mean lost opportunities, especially in a bilingual environment. The map described in Figure 7.2 has been developed as an iterative exercise involving several meetings

Table 7.6 *Enactment of the principles of horizontal and vertical integration*

	Horizontal integration of education development with curriculum renewal	Vertical integration within faculties
Enactment	*Formal liaison between central units with IT and with T&L support functions*	Maintaining connections at all levels in each faculty. This was begun with formal meetings with Deans, followed by contact with Chairpersons of all departments
	Less emphasis on open university-wide activities, such as generic workshops, and more on project-based work where outcomes can be achieved and then shared. This can result in the development of exemplars for dissemination of good practice across departments. There is a clear synergy between this focus on working with specific projects and the strategy of focusing on several levels of responsibility of programmes.	*An emphasis on working at programme level (which, in many cases, means working at departmental level) rather than just with individual teachers. This strategy means that, while we work with any individual teachers who request assistance, the majority of our time is spent on projects where departmental chairs and programme co-ordinators are involved, alongside other teaching staff*

with both the Information Technology Services Centre (ITSC) and the Library. There were also several more informal meetings with teachers and IT staff in faculties. Initially, I suspect that these meetings occurred because people were being polite to the new professor who liked drawing *Inspiration* diagrams! (http: www.inspiration.com). But interest grew and the increasing clarity of the relationships between the roles of the central units in supporting teaching and learning, as well as a clearer understanding of the relationships between the central units and small faculty-based support groups (often just a technical officer) has had significant benefits. For example, a joint CLEAR/ ITSC/ Library seminar series has been run; CLEAR has input to the design of technical platforms; a joint ITSC/ CLEAR project to begin evaluating the effectiveness of the online learning system has begun. There is potential for this evaluation to impact on IT infrastructure policy.

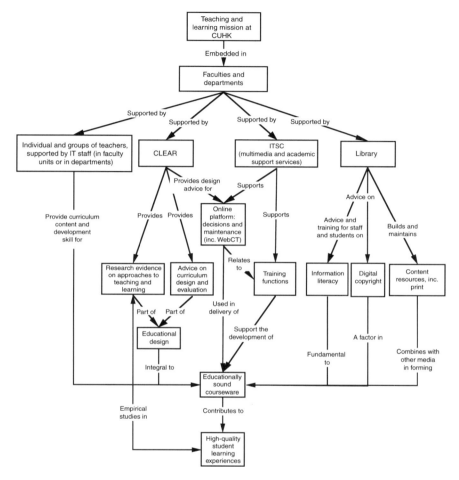

Figure 7.2 *Map of relationships between faculty staff, ITSC, CLEAR and the Library at CUHK*

WORKING AT PROGRAMME LEVEL RATHER THAN WITH INDIVIDUAL TEACHERS

Just how has CLEAR tried to achieve vertical integration within faculties? Much education development work in Hong Kong is funded by the Hong Kong government through the University Grants Committee (undated b). As in Australia, many of these government grants have been for individual projects, which have not resulted in university-wide benefits, let alone system-wide ones. These projects, devised by enthusiastic individuals, often working in isolation from their colleagues usually receive funding for short-term products and so evaluation is limited to the requirements of a project report produced in a relatively short time-frame. In Australia, Alexander *et al.* (1998) reviewed 104 of the 173 IT projects which received funding from the Committee for the Advancement of University Teaching (CAUT) in 1994 or 1995. One major concern was that many IT projects were not owned locally and so there was little institutional leverage from the work of individual developers. One recommendation was that: 'Priority in funding be given to projects which are linked to the strategic plans of the faculty or institution' (p. xiv). This study supports our principle of looking at the context of the whole programme. So, in applying for a major grant, CLEAR staff focused attention on programme-level work. We were successful.

The approach we have taken involves working with all undergraduate programmes in the university. In many programmes, profiles are being developed of students' experience on three main themes: 1) personal development of various capabilities such as critical thinking, problem solving and interpersonal skills; 2) their perceptions of the teaching and learning environment such as level of interactivity with teachers and with other students, whether the assessment and curriculum were relevant; and 3) engagement in various types of learning activities such as individual and/or group projects.

Based on the findings in the three main themes, areas of strength within programmes can thus be identified. Then the teaching staff involved are being invited to assist in the development of guidelines and resources about how to engage students in active learning. The exemplary work of successful programmes will assist in the support for other programmes where curriculum and teaching challenges exist. Thus, cycles of student feedback and learning enhancement projects can be established. CLEAR staff are available to act as facilitators for the overall process. Through this process it is anticipated that the teaching and learning quality of the programmes within the university will be demonstrably enhanced. This work has implications for university policy; it is a form of grounded quality assurance that suits a collegial university where responsibility and support for teaching and learning is distributed. Figure 7.3 illustrates the design of our approach.

The student experience profiles are initially discussed with department chairs and programme co-ordinators, so that broad parameters of what we are calling learning enhancement projects can be established. Then a tailored set of education development activities and courseware development projects are set in place in individual departments. In this way the design of the educational programme is placed at the centre of the initiative, and technology is called into service to that end. This is congruent with

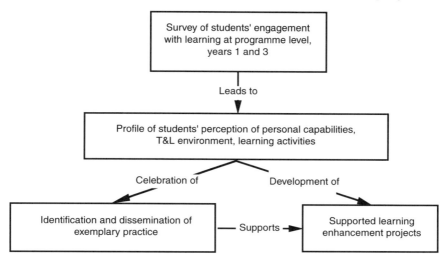

Figure 7.3 *Education development at a programme level*

the model of a distributed approach to quality assurance outlined by Patrick and Lines in Chapter 3. At the time of publication, consultations have taken place with all 50 undergraduate programmes, with follow-up activity in many of them.

CO-ORDINATION AND INTEGRATION ARE THE KEYS TO SUCCESS

The relationship building we have undertaken between the various support units at The Chinese University of Hong Kong enhances our work with particular programmes in individual departments. This is probably the main message of this chapter. Whether one works in a corporate or collegial university environment, co-ordination and integration are essential between:

- service units, be they IT, education development, central or faculty-based;
- courses within a programme;
- levels of authority in a department; and
- teaching and learning experience across departments.

The form that this co-ordination and integration might take will differ but the need is universal.

In order to ensure that technology is a facilitator of effective educational practice, it is vital to avoid the 'techies and the teachers: them and us' mentality. Good education development work places pedagogy firmly at the centre. In my view the technology is interesting and useful enough to slot in where and when it is needed.

Further, this chapter illustrates that lessons from one context can be applied to another if core principles are extracted. Indeed, it is the hope of the authors of this book that readers will be able to apply what we have learnt to their own contexts.

8

Educating university teachers: participation and access issues for students who have a disability

Kym Fraser and Ellen Sanders

DISABILITY TRENDS

At this moment in time there are more people in the community identifying that they have a disability than at any other point in history. This fact is due mainly to:

- an ageing population and people developing disabilities as they age;
- people with pre-existing disabilities living longer, mainly as a result of significant improvements in diagnosis, medicine and medical technology; and
- changes in social attitudes meaning that more people are comfortable about identifying as having a disability.

A survey undertaken in the UK between 1985 and 1988 was the latest that specifically attempted to determine the number of adults with a disability in the UK population. It was estimated at that time that 6.2 million adults in the UK had a disability, which, at the time of the survey, represented 14.2 per cent of the adult population. Surveys undertaken by the Australian Bureau of Statistics estimate that the percentage of Australians who have a disability rose from 15 per cent in 1981 to 19 per cent in 1998.

DRIVERS FOR INCLUSIVE EDUCATION

Historically in education, students who have a disability were often placed in segregated settings, if they received an education at all. There has been a clear shift in attitude towards education in integrated or mainstream settings and now there is a drive towards inclusive education. This is where the total environment is such that the majority of students who have a disability are accommodated most of the time without anything 'additional' or 'special' being done 'for' them.

There have been a number of drivers for this including:

- A move over the last 20 years from a medical model of disability to a social model. In the social model, barriers are perceived to exist in society and not rest with the individual. Many so-called barriers can be overcome with creative thinking!

- Developments and improvements in the range of assistive devices available.

- Expectations of the student.

- Anti-discrimination legislation.

In the UK drivers also include:

- The Quality Assurance Agency's (QAA 1999) 'Code of Practice: Section 3 on Students with Disabilities'.

- HEFCE's Widening Participation agenda (HEFCE undated).

- The Department for Education and Skills White Paper *The Future of Higher Education* (DfES 2003).

In Australia drivers also include:

- Student equity programmes that have been in place for many years.

As an increasing number of students who have a disability enrol in higher education institutions, the onus is on the university to create inclusive environments in every area, i.e. built, web, IT, learning, teaching and assessment. Figures from the Higher Education Statistics Agency (HESA undated) in the UK show that from 1994 to 2001 the number of students with a disability in UK higher education institutions rose from 2.6 per cent to 4.1 per cent. In Australia, figures from the Department for Education, Science and Training show an increase of non-overseas students from 1.9 per cent in 1996 to 3.0 per cent in 2000. This has enormous implications for decision makers and education developers who must ensure that all members of staff are aware of their responsibilities under legislation and are able to deliver programmes that follow best practice. There are also resource implications although these may not be as onerous as one may first be led to believe. The key is 'universal design', i.e. if all environments are designed/ built in such a way that the majority of people are catered for most of the time, immediately an inclusive environment is created. For example:

- use of access consultants to check plans for new buildings and refurbishments;

- ensuring that staff developing websites and online teaching materials are educated about accessibility issues;

- writing teaching and promotional materials in such a way that they can be easily transcribed into the required alternative format on request, i.e. electronic material on disk;

- sub-titling all videos as a matter of course. This also assists students whose first language is not English. The education of international students from non-English speaking backgrounds is a significant industry in western countries such as the UK, USA and Australia; and

- ensuring course curricula incorporate sessions on inclusivity where appropriate. For example university courses on the built environment should include lectures on how to design environments that are inclusive.

DISABILITY DISCRIMINATION LEGISLATION

The Disability Discrimination Act (DDA) exists in both Australia and the UK but was introduced at different times and in different ways. In Australia, the Federal DDA came into force in 1992 and is encompassing of all areas, i.e. education, employment, goods and services and so on.

In the UK, however, it was introduced in 1995 and will encompass different areas at different stages. The legislation applying to education, the Special Educational Needs and Disability Act (SENDA 2001) came into force in September 2002. It is being rolled out in three key stages. After each stage it would be possible for a student or potential student to legally challenge a university's position and provision. This legislation is designed to ensure that a proactive, not reactive, approach is taken to accommodating students who have a disability and that changes in the environment will be anticipated, and made, before the arrival of an individual.

THE DISABILITY DISCRIMINATION ACT IN AUSTRALIA

The Federal Disability Discrimination Act (DDA) 1992 in relation to education

The Federal Disability Discrimination Act (DDA) 1992, which came into effect in March 1993, has meant that rights of people who have a disability are now legally protected.

The legislation aims to:

a) eliminate, as far as possible, discrimination against persons on the ground of disability in the areas of:

- work, accommodation, education, clubs, sport;

- the provision of goods, facilities, services and land;

- existing laws; and

- the administration of Commonwealth laws and programmes; and

b) to ensure, as far as practicable, that people with disabilities have the same rights to equality before the law as their fellow citizens; and

c) to promote recognition and acceptance within the community of the principle that people with disabilities have the same fundamental rights as their fellow citizens.

(Section 3, Federal Disability Discrimination Act 1992)

In practical terms, the Federal DDA means that students who have a disability have the right to request and receive 'reasonable' accommodations or adjustments in relation to the way courses are delivered and assessed, unless the university can demonstrate that to do so constitutes 'unjustifiable hardship'. For example, the Federal DDA means that:

- students with a mobility impairment have a right to expect, within reason, that lectures, practical classes, and tutorials will be in accessible locations;

- students who are deaf or hearing impaired have a right to expect, within reason, that alternative means are available to access audio information which is made available to other students;

- students who are blind or vision impaired have a right to expect, within reason, that alternative means are available to access printed information which is made available to other students; and

- students with dyslexia have the right to be assessed, within reason, in ways that do not disadvantage them on the basis of their disability.

However, the Federal DDA is complaints-driven legislation which relies on people who have a disability being aware of their rights, being prepared to identify and request these rights, and pursuing the relevant procedures to address any discriminatory processes.

Defining disability

Under the Federal DDA, a disability is defined as the condition that arises when a person, because of an impairment, is unable to perform a task or function. Such a person may be disadvantaged if goods, services, and facilities do not exist or are not changed to eliminate or markedly reduce the impact of their disability. For example, a person may have a congenital heart condition and therefore, be disadvantaged because they are unable to climb four flights of stairs to sit for an examination in a building which has no lift.

Generally, accommodations can be put in place which will prevent, minimise, or overcome barriers which create or contribute to a disabling condition. These barriers or disadvantages can be viewed as discriminatory situations, circumstances, or practices. Policy and legislation exists to encourage people and organisations to overcome discrimination on the basis of disability.

The Federal Disability Discrimination Act (DDA) defines disability as follows (http://scaleplus.law.gov.au/html/pasteact/0/311/top.htm):

'Disability', in relation to a person, means:

a. total or partial loss of the person's bodily or mental functions; or

b. total or partial loss of a part of the body; or

c. the presence in the body of organisms causing disease or illness; or

d. the presence in the body of organisms capable of causing disease or illness; or

e. the malfunction, malformation or disfigurement of a part of the person's body; or

f. a disorder or malfunction that results in the person learning differently from a person without the disorder or malfunction: or

g. a disorder, illness or disease that affects a person's thought processes, perception of reality, emotions or judgement or that results in disturbed behaviour; and includes a disability that:

- presently exists; or

- previously existed but no longer exists; or

- may exist in the future; or

- is imputed to a person; (refer to the Disability Discrimination Act (DDA) 1992).

Disability in education

In education, the term 'impairment' refers to any permanent or temporary condition that reduces a person's ability to undertake their studies. An impairment can create a situation of inequality. According to the Federal DDA, a disability can arise from any sensory, physical, psychiatric, medical or neurological condition. A student may experience disadvantage or discrimination if a disability, directly or indirectly, results in:

- a significant increase in time (e.g. students requiring materials in alternative formats may not receive textbooks in their preferred format until after the semester has commenced);

- a significant increase in difficulty; and

- making necessary the use of human or technical assistance.

These results would not apply to a student without a disability wanting to access and process information, prepare and present information, carry out personal care and functions, or undertake any activity, which would reasonably be expected of a student.

Discrimination and harassment based on a person's disability can diminish the level at which that person can operate. A person would be likely to be a more successful student or employee if they were not subject to discrimination. Discrimination occurs when policies or practices result in restricting access to services or educational or employment opportunities on the basis of stereotyping people who have a disability.

Discrimination can have the following effects:

- creating an intimidating, hostile, offensive or distressing work or study environment; and

- adversely affecting an individual's access to participate in a range of educational opportunities, support services, social and recreational facilities provided by the university.

Defining discrimination in relation to education

Section 4 (1) of the Federal Disability Discrimination Act 1992 (DDA) states:

> Direct discrimination refers to less favourable treatment in the same or similar circumstances for a person with a disability than for those without a disability.
>
> Indirect discrimination can occur when a condition or requirement is imposed, which may be the same for everyone but which unfairly excludes or disadvantages people with a disability.

Section 22 (1) states:

> It is unlawful for an educational authority to discriminate against a person on the ground of the person's disability or a disability of any of the person's other associates:
>
> 1. by refusing or failing to accept the person's application for admission as a student; or
> 2. in the terms or conditions on which it is prepared to admit the person as a student.

Section 22 (2) states:

> It is unlawful for an educational authority to discriminate against a student on the ground of the student's disability or a disability of any of the student's associates:
>
> 1. by denying the student access, or limiting the student's access, to any benefit provided by the educational authority; or
> 2. by expelling the student; or
> 3. by subjecting the student to any other detriment.

Section 22(4):

> This section does not render it unlawful to refuse or fail to accept a person's application for admission as a student at an educational institution where the person, if admitted as a student by the educational authority, would require services or facilities that are not required by students who do not have a disability and the provision of which would impose unjustifiable hardship on the educational authority.

THE DISABILITY DISCRIMINATION ACT IN THE UK

The Special Educational Needs and Disability Act 2001

The Special Educational Needs and Disability Act (SENDA 2001) added a new Part IV to the Disability Discrimination Act (DDA) 1995. Under this section, it became unlawful for universities to treat students who have a disability, or applicants, less favourably for a reason connected with their disability, unless it can be justified. Universities also have a duty to make reasonable adjustments to ensure that people who are disabled are not placed at a substantial disadvantage, compared to people who are not disabled, in accessing education. It applies to overseas or EU students as well as to British students, and to those who are only taking part of a course. Accommodation and leisure services which the university provides mainly for students, as well as education, are covered. Under this legislation, higher education institutions are required to be proactive rather than reactive in meeting the requirements of students.

The key dates for rolling out SENDA were and are:

- From 1 September 2002 – the introduction of the Act and notions of 'anticipatory duty' and 'reasonable adjustment'.

- From 1 September 2003 – the adjustments that the university will have to make will include supplying auxiliary aids and services.

- From 1 September 2005 – the adjustments will include physical provision and access.

Defining disability

This definition differs from that used in Australia.

The definition is:

A person with a physical or mental impairment which has a

- substantial;

- adverse; and

- long term (can be intermittent or fluctuating but lasting or expected to last for at least 12 months) effect on his or her ability to carry out 'normal' day-to-day activities'.

Physical or mental impairment includes mobility, sensory disabilities, medical conditions, specific learning difficulties (e.g. dyslexia) and mental health issues. Progressive illnesses are covered, even those in remission.

Past conditions are also covered. The conditions must be 'clinically well recognised'.

What is discrimination?

Under SENDA, it is:

- treating someone *less favourably* than someone else for a reason related to his/her disability without *justification*; and

- failing to make a *reasonable adjustment* placing a student at a *substantial disadvantage* in comparison to someone who is not disabled.

Knowledge and less favourable treatment
BEING UNAWARE THAT THE STUDENT HAS A DISABILITY   Not knowing that a student has a disability is only an excuse for less favourable treatment if the university has taken reasonable steps to find out, and has actively encouraged disclosure. If the student has told someone in the university about the disability, or declared it on the application form, the university may not be able to claim that it did not know, unless the student has requested strict confidentiality. Students retain the right not to disclose a disability.

Courts will ask what steps were taken to find out about a disability. Did the responsible body know, or could it reasonably have known, that a person had a disability? Claiming lack of knowledge will not necessarily be a defence. Institutions must demonstrate they have taken reasonable steps to find out whether a student has a disability by creating an open culture which will encourage students to disclose and by asking at critical points in a student's lifecycle at a university, e.g. on application, when applying for access to different services, modules or courses, for accommodation or a field trip, or for attendance on a conference. Universities are also advised to let the student know why this information is being sought and assure confidentiality for the student.

Universities must ensure they have systems in place to deal with these issues. Systems such as internal communication mechanisms and confidentiality policies must be robust and both staff and students need to be aware of these. Staff need to ensure their actions are within the Data Protection Act which precludes the release of any written or electronic 'sensitive personal' data without the individual's explicit permission.

JUSTIFICATIONS FOR LESS FAVOURABLE TREATMENT   The justifications for less favourable treatment must be reasonable and substantial. They must be related to the circumstances of the individual situation. They will only apply where reasonable adjustments cannot be made such as :

- the maintenance of academic standards;
- reasons that are material and substantial;
- other 'prescribed' standards, e.g. that prescribed by the body regulating entry into a profession; and
- treatment of a 'prescribed' type, or in 'prescribed' circumstances.

The onus is on the institution to show that an action was justified and that the justification would still be valid even after a reasonable adjustment was made. It therefore becomes more vital than ever before to keep good records.

Reasonable adjustments
A responsible body must take *reasonable steps* to ensure that disabled people or students are not placed at a *'substantial disadvantage'* in comparison to someone who is not disabled. When making reasonable adjustments an institution needs to consider:

- maintenance of academic standards;
- financial resources of the institution;
- grants/loans available to the student (some students are eligible for a Disabled Students' Allowance);
- practicality;
- other aids or services available;
- health and safety requirements. Health and safety legislation takes precedence over SENDA but must not be used spuriously to exclude a student; and
- relevant interests of other people including other students.

Issues affecting adjustments include:

- anticipation;
- knowledge; and
- confidentiality requests.

Universities have an anticipatory duty to review their arrangements so that they will be ready to accommodate students with different requirements. The review should be continuous, so that account can be taken of changing circumstances and of developments in technology. If a student requesting adjustments approaches the institution at or after commencement of his/ her studies, it may be too late to make adjustments unless some planning has been done in advance. Failure to plan in advance will not be a justification.

To *anticipate* will entail considering the likelihood of people who have a disability using a service and making adjustments in advance to improve access. It is likely to be particularly important to make anticipatory adjustments in areas where it is difficult to make adjustments at short notice – such as physical access, curriculum design issues or e-learning materials or where permission is needed from leaseholders. When improvements are made in anticipation, fewer adjustments have to be made for individuals leading to a more inclusive environment. It is likely to be important to plan and to budget for making such changes.

If a student requests that the existence of their disability remains confidential then this takes precedence over the duty to make adjustments. It is important to document this request and explain to the student that *different adjustments* may have to be made, or in some cases *lesser adjustments* will be the only option. It would be necessary to explain that their request might limit what can be done for them whilst still trying to make adjustments. For example, it may be that a student would be provided with handouts after class rather than a notetaker in class.

It may mean that adjustments are made but that the staff members making those adjustments are not fully informed of the reasons for those adjustments. For example, it may be that a lecturer is asked by a disability adviser to provide a particular student with extra time in a class exam, but is not told the details of the individual student's disability. If a lecturer requests information on a student, sometimes it may be appropriate to talk generally about the impact of some disability on study – the emphasis being the impact of the disability and accommodations required as opposed to the actual diagnosis.

Disability Rights Commission Code of Practice

The Disability Rights Commission (DRC) has developed a Code of Practice to assist higher education institutions to implement the duties of SENDA. Whilst the code is not in itself a legal document, courts are expected to refer to it when hearing complaints of discrimination. It came into force in September 2002 and deals with education after the age of sixteen. The code provides examples of reasonable adjustments and can be viewed at: http://www.drc.org.uk/thelaw/practice.asp. The DRC has also produced a range of good practice guides including 'Teaching and Learning', 'Examinations and Assessment', and 'Marketing and Admissions'. The guides can be viewed at: http://www.skill.org.uk/info/drc-guides/index.asp.

While not all students who declare a disability may satisfy the strict definition under the Act, the only safe way to proceed is to assume that the disability in question (including mental health conditions) has a substantial long-term adverse effect on the student's ability to carry out normal day-to-day activities. The university will have a responsibility to make every effort to ensure that organisations with which it arranges placements, including universities in other countries, are not treating students who have a disability less favourably than they would treat students who do not have a disability.

While the Statutory Code of Practice will be legally enforceable, the Quality Assurance Agency's Code for Students with Disabilities remains a source of guidance on good practice, and is not superseded.

IMPLICATIONS OF THE LEGISLATION FOR LEARNING AND TEACHING DECISION MAKERS

Inclusive practices – a university-wide responsibility

In order for practices to become truly inclusive in higher education settings, many areas of the university need to be addressed. *All* staff have a responsibility for ensuring this environment is created.

Appropriate committees need to be established at university and faculty level and disability issues should be a standing item on the agenda of the latter. As the notion of inclusive practices implies a culture shift, 'champions' need to be identified at senior levels who will review progress in the area on an annual basis to ensure barriers and 'gaps' in provision are identified and issues are addressed within an appropriate time frame.

Key policies and plans must be integrated and need to complement each other. Implementation strategies must be devised which are cohesive and consistent across the university structure. Faculties and central services need to collaborate and co-ordinate for purposes such as ensuring standards for teaching rooms are appropriate and referring students who have issues with timetabling. Robust referral and communication mechanisms must be devised while bearing in mind the issue of confidentiality for students.

In Australia, it is recommended that institutions develop a disability action plan (DAP) which is lodged with the Human Rights and Equal Opportunity Commission. In the development of this plan, the views of key stakeholders should be canvassed so that these people have ownership and feel a responsibility in progressing the objectives and strategies identified. Courts refer to these plans when hearing cases of discrimination. Developing a DAP is the best approach for institutions who seek to comply with the Federal DDA in Australia and a valuable process in the UK. The

DAP also allows for an organisation to more adequately address its responsibilities under the Act and develop strategies to eliminate discrimination.

Innovative programmes to promote and progress inclusion and, ultimately student retention, need to be developed. These could include:

- a dedicated unit with appropriately qualified staff to provide advice and support for students who have a disability, dyslexia or a long-term medical condition;

- flexible admission policies;

- transition programmes;

- bridging courses;

- mentoring schemes;

- adaptive technology rooms in central locations such as libraries;

- a network of disability contact officers in faculties; and

- equality/equity and diversity scholarships.

Developing inclusive teaching practices

Developing an awareness of inclusive teaching practices and diversity that exists in how students learn is crucial to a student's achievements. It is clear that adjusting methods of teaching and assessment benefits all students and not only this cohort.

Professional development (PD) is thus essential in contributing to the successful participation and retention of students who have a disability. Traditionally such PD has been implemented via the conduct of workshops and information sessions that are often optional. Below we suggest a broad range of ways in which PD can be implemented:

1   Induction sessions and materials:

- ensure that information is available, e.g. leaflets about the services provided;

- ensure that new staff undertake relevant disability awareness professional development; and

- for new academics include inclusive teaching practices (refer to the case study in the second half of this chapter).

2   Continuing professional development:

- provides educational opportunities to explore the implications of specific disabilities for teaching, learning and assessment. For example, what are the teaching, learning and assessment implications for someone who is blind and uses braille or for someone who is deaf and uses sign language to communicate? The University of Nottingham website has useful information for teaching higher education students who have a disability: http://www.nottingham. ac.uk/disability/ITS%20leaflets.htm;

- discusses Federal DDA/SENDA information and implications in the HE environment. Often this information is offered through stand-alone workshops and information sessions, either centrally or in faculties; e.g. http://www.nottingham.ac.uk/sedu/courses/ EO_courses.php;

- target staff in particular services such as the library, estates or halls who deal with specific issues arising in these areas;

- supports the design of accessible websites in order to meet W3C worldwide accessibility standards; and

- includes general disability awareness programmes.

Some universities are currently developing online equality/equity and diversity training programmes that would be made compulsory for new staff.

3   University provision:

- includes institution-specific resources and materials; e.g. develop and disseminate documents on support available at the institution for a range of disabilities; and

- develops selection and promotion criteria that include demonstration of inclusive practices.

To make it more attractive to attend face-to-face sessions, it may be wise to market sessions as pertaining to the entire student cohort (e.g. as 'teaching skills for a diverse environment' or 'student-focused teaching to increase retention rates'), rather than isolating a specific group of students such as those who have a disability. Sessions could then be combined with other equality/equity and diversity issues such as gender and race.

Building in accountability

- university quality audits need to take into account issues related to learning, teaching and assessment for students who have a disability;

- academic staff must be clear that a particular mode of teaching or assessment is essential to the achievement of the learning outcomes or to the intellectual integrity of the course if these modes substantially disadvantage certain students;

- disability action plans (DAPs) which are monitored, evaluated and reviewed regularly by senior committees are a crucial tool which need to have documented timelines; and

- student feedback on a range of issues should be regularly sought via formal means such as questionnaires and focus groups. The student union has a role to play here also.

Diversity is 'normal' and in order to ensure that the greatest number of people have access to the most number of facilities, the principles of 'universal design' should be adopted as a matter of course. This will reduce the time and resources required to support students on an individual basis as the environment in general becomes more inclusive.

ENGAGING ACADEMICS

Universities are now required by law to provide access to their courses to an increasingly diverse student population. To achieve this access, universities worldwide are tackling the issues at many different levels and in different ways. For instance many have introduced policy on disability and equality/equity issues and developed central offices to provide assistance to staff across the university. Such central offices frequently develop written guidance and conduct workshops and seminars for both staff and students. While staff members of these offices do a great deal of work and provide invaluable assistance to other members of the university, anecdotal evidence suggests that the vast majority of university staff, especially academics, remain unaware and unengaged with the ideas and issues.

One approach that has been used to introduce academics to the concepts and issues of teaching students who have a disability is discussed below. While the authors recognise that this approach will take many years to result in the majority of academics having engaged with the concepts, the recent move in both the UK and Australia towards requiring all academics new to teaching to undertake teaching professional development, provides the opportunity to use this approach nationally. In fact, in Australia, the new draft of the Disability Education Standards (formulated under the Federal DDA) now states that institutions have an obligation to provide staff with 'training'. In the case study below we describe a particularly effective way to teach academics about teaching students who have a disability.

CASE STUDY

As described by Fraser in Chapter 9, Monash University, a large Australian university, introduced a part-time Graduate Certificate in Higher Education (GCHE) in 1999 for academic members of staff. The GCHE was taught by the central Higher Education Development Unit and accredited by the Faculty of Education. In 2000 the programme, was made compulsory for inexperienced teaching members of staff who joined the university. In 2001 a module that focused on the teaching of students who have a disability was incorporated into the 'Teaching for Learning' subject of the GCHE. This module was jointly developed by the authors of this chapter.

Subject 2: Teaching for Learning

The subject HED5002 'Teaching for Learning' focused on the teaching approaches typically used in universities, and participants were required to demonstrate competence in lecturing, small group teaching and working with individual students. Face-to-face and mediated approaches to teaching were discussed in the subject. In 2001 the subject consisted of seven modules of varying lengths. The modules were called 'Principles of good teaching', 'Teaching students who have a disability', 'Lecturing', 'Tutoring', 'Flexible Teaching', 'Working with individuals' and 'Practicum'. The focus of this case study is the second module, 'Teaching students who have a disability'.

Module 2: Teaching students who have a disability

This module discussed the challenges that students who have a disability face at university and asked participants to think about how they might make their classes more inclusive and accessible for these students. Inclusive teaching practices cater for the diversity that exists across a 'classroom' and therefore it was recognised that changes made for the benefit of students with a disability would benefit all students.

The learning outcomes for the module were that upon completion of the module, participants would be able to:

- discuss the characteristics of several disabilities;

- discuss the impact of a specific disability on a student's ability to study; and

- describe some accommodations or adjustments that can be made to provide a more inclusive environment.

The design of the module was underpinned by principles of learning, two of which are particularly relevant for this chapter. The authors believe that learning is enhanced when individuals engage with information in a context of experience and application. The module was designed to introduce the participants to the disability discrimination legislation and resources (information). This information was coupled with the experience of interviewing students and, in light of those interviews, determining accommodations or adjustments the participant could make to two of their learning environments for that student (experience and application). Peer assessment was used in the module to enhance learning from peers. Participants interviewed one student and therefore learnt from that student about the specific disability the student experienced (not always but usually just the one disability). By assessing their peer's work, participants were introduced not only to information about another disability, but also to the approach the peer would take to adjust his/her teaching environments.

The 37 participants taking the module were provided with brochures from the University Disability Liaison Unit (DLU) that provided information on the federal legislation, DLU services, the need for alternative arrangements for assessment, web accessibility, an overview of issues and considerations for six of the more common disabilities (vision impairment, hearing impairment, learning disability (called dyslexia in the UK), mental illness, mobility impairment, epilepsy), and general advice. This written material was supplemented by devoting 80 minutes in one of the two, three-hour, face-to-face sessions in the subject, to discussing this information, providing examples of student requirements and teaching accommodations, providing a statistical student disability profile of each of the faculties in the university, suggesting possible ways to start the interview with a student who has a disability (see the next paragraph) and taking questions from the participants. During that time, most of the participants were clearly engaged with the topic as evidenced by the many questions asked and the attention given to the second author who conducted that part of the session.

The DLU had contacted students registered with them and asked if they would be willing to be interviewed by academics taking this subject. Participants were provided with the contact details of a student who had agreed to be contacted. Efforts were made to match participants with a student from their own campus. In all but three cases the participants talked face-to-face with the students. The two Monash Malaysia participants communicated with their students over the internet.[1] Seven participants asked if they could interview a student in their own classes whom they knew to have a disability. These participants were advised to ask their student in a way that explicitly allowed the student to decline the offer of the interview.

Participants were required to write and submit online up to 800 words on their interview with the student. They were specifically asked to indicate in their reflective report:

- the barriers to learning the student faces; and

- the accommodations or adjustments the participant could make to two of their learning environments (e.g. lectures, tutorials, laboratories, field trips, clinical settings) to assist that student to overcome the barriers identified.

Participants were also required to read and assess the reflective report of one of their peers. It was agreed with participants that both assessor and assessee would be known to each other. The assessment criteria for the report were that the work must:

- list the implications of the particular disability for the student's learning; and

- list and explain possible accommodations or adjustments that the participant could make to two of their learning environments which would assist the student to learn.

The subject co-ordinator chose the reports participants assessed. The sole criteria for this choice was that participants would peer-assess a reflective report that discussed a disability that was different from the disability of the student whom the participant had interviewed.

Evaluation of the module: participant feedback

At the end of the semester we were particularly interested to seek the advice and opinion of the participants in order to inform decisions about the value and place of the module in the GCHE. We wanted to know if the module enhanced participant understanding, if it changed their practice, if they thought that it was worth keeping in the GCHE, if the design of the module was useful, etc. The evaluation specifically focused on the participant perceptions of the module at the end of the subject. This evaluation was intended to determine whether or not to keep the module in the GCHE, where to locate it, and if it was to remain, how to improve it. If the participants supported the future inclusion of the module in the GCHE the authors intended doing follow-up evaluation work to determine the actual impact of the module on participant teaching practice and seek peer review of the module. Before the subject was offered again, both authors moved to take up positions in the UK and so this follow-up evaluation was not carried out by the authors.

In the development of the evaluation, the first author drafted a set of questions and the second author reviewed them, providing feedback and adding questions. The resulting questionnaire is provided at the end of the chapter. The comments on questionnaires were analysed for patterns of responses across participants. Quotes provided illustrate such patterns and are representative of the comments made by participants. The comments were also analysed for quotes that countered the patterns of responses. The results reported here are drawn from questions 1–7 and question 11 of the 14-question survey.

Results

Background
Of the 37 participants 30 responded to the questionnaire that was handed out at the second face-to-face workshop held at the end of the subject and also sent to participants who did not attend the session. As indicated in Tables 8.1 and 8.2, the gender distribution of the respondents was approximately even and the cohort was approximately evenly divided

Table 8.1 *Gender of respondents*

Male		Female	
No.	%	No.	%
16	53	14	47

Table 8.2 *Teaching experience of respondents*

	First year	Two–five years	Six–ten years	More than 10 years
Total (% is of all 30 respondents)	10 (33%)	9 (30%)	8 (27%)	3 (10%)
Female (% is of the 14 female respondents)	3 (21%)	4 (29%)	5 (36%)	2 (14%)
Male (% is of the 16 male respondents)	7 (44%)	5 (31%)	3 (19%)	1 (6%)

between those new to teaching, those with two–five years' experience and experienced teachers who had taught for more than six years.

Of the 30 respondents 57 per cent had taught a student who had a disability (Tables 8.3 and 8.4). Interestingly 87 per cent of the female participants had taught a student who had a disability compared with only 31 per cent of the male participants. It may be possible to account for some of this difference in that more male respondents than females were in their first year of teaching. To their knowledge, five of the seven male respondents in their first year of teaching had not taught students who had a disability, while one of the three females teaching in their first year had not.

The specific accommodations/adjustments the respondents reported making previously for their students can be categorised as changes to:

- communication – e.g. taping lectures, use of special microphones, leaving the lights on in the lecture theatre so that a signing deaf student could see an interpreter;

- resources – e.g. provision of detailed lecture notes, provision of lecture notes prior to the lecture, increased consultation time; and

- alternative assessment arrangements – e.g. providing extra time during examinations and in the submission of assessable tasks during term

Table 8.3 *To your knowledge, have you taught a student(s) who has a disability in any of your university classes?*

	Have taught a student who has a disability	Have not taught a student who has a disability
Total (% is of all 30 respondents)	17 (57%)	13 (43%)
Female (% is of the 14 female respondents)	12 (87%)	2 (13%)
Male (% is of the 16 male respondents)	5 (31%)	11 (69%)

Table 8.4 *Distribution of those who had and had not taught a student(s) who has a disability with teaching experience*

	First year (% is of 10 first-year respondents)	Two–five years (% is of 9 respondents in this category)	Six–ten years (% is of 8 respondents in this category)	More than ten years (% is of 3 respondents in this category)
Yes	4 (40%)	7 (78%)	5 (62.5%)	1 (33.3%)
No	6 (60%)	2 (22%)	3 (37.5%)	2 (66.6%)
Total respondents	10	9	8	3

time, student's use of a 'writer'/scribe/amanuensis during exams, verbal responses to examination questions rather than written answers.

Confidence

Of the respondents 80 per cent reported that having done the module they had more confidence in relating to students who have a disability. These respondents commented that they found it easier to approach the student than they had expected, and that having talked to a student about his/her disability they expected to have increased confidence in approaching others. They also reported that having a better understanding of student requirements and awareness of the support services provided by the university helped their confidence. Two of the respondents who said 'no' to the question 'Do you have more confidence in relating to students who have a disability? Please comment' said that they did not feel confronted by talking with students who have a disability and so their confidence did not need to improve.

> Yes. I have learnt that it is easier to approach [a student and] discuss their disability than I expected.

> No. I didn't really have a problem relating to a student who has a disability – this module gave me an excuse to interact with a student who has a disability.

> Yes. The student I interviewed was so open to talking about the issues related to her disability. I felt comfortable with her – and then that [means that] I would be comfortable with approaching others.

Learning

Of the respondents 90 per cent reported having learnt something from doing the module (Table 8.5). Those who responded 'no' were all female. One of the 'no' respondents had taught for more than ten years and had reported that, to her knowledge, she had not previously taught a student who had a disability. The other 'no' respondent had taught for two–five years, had taught four students who had a disability and had instituted

Table 8.5 *From doing module 2 in HED5002 have you learnt anything that you did not previously know?*

Yes	No	No response
27 (90%)	2 (6.6%)	1 (3.4%)

changes to her teaching to assist them with their learning. The non-respondent had more than 10 years of experience and had taught more than 20 students who had a disability and had made changes to her teaching.

Each of the 27 respondents who said that they had learnt from the module provided examples. They can be summarised as:

- information about disabilities – the wide range of disabilities, the impact of specific disabilities on student learning, etc;

- disabilities can be invisible and that many students who have a disability are reluctant to inform their teachers;

- knowledge about resources and specific strategies that can assist students and that many of those strategies are also of value to students without disabilities;

- the existence of the Monash University Disability Liaison Unit and its role. The issues associated with having note takers, signing interpreters, etc. in your classroom; and

- empathy.

Probably not that I didn't know. However, my previous knowledge was fairly narrow and vague. It made me more aware of the issue and to look beyond what I see.

Simple strategies that would benefit all students are of particular benefit to students with a variety of disabilities, e.g. having lecture notes available prior to the lecture.

Yes, not to judge some student's ability too quickly.

Certainly about the nature of dyslexia and related specific learning disabilities. Many of the required teaching accommodations would fall under the heading of 'general good teaching practices' which is good to reinforce. Good to know of DLU [Disability Liaison Unit] also and of how invisible disabilities can be.

Yes I did. I learnt that there are disabled students [in] the class, disableness [sic] is not always visible and I need to understand barriers faced by disabled student[s] and accordingly, I need to make changes to my teaching style.

Table 8.6 *Was doing the peer assessment for activity 2 of any value to you?*

Yes	No	No response	Peer assessment not completed at that stage
23 (76.6%)	2 (6.7%)	3 (10%)	2 (6.7%)

Peer assessment

Almost 80 per cent of respondents reported that doing the peer assessment in the module was of value to them (Table 8.6). Interestingly, one respondent reported specifically that she was going to use peer assessment in one of her subjects[2] in the following semester. Thirteen respondents reported that they learnt about a different disability and nine reported that they valued and learnt from reading a peer's response. The quotes below provide insights into the things that the participants gained from peer-assessing other participants' work.

> Yes, because my student had a visible disability so it broadened my awareness of non-visible disabilities.

> Found the peer assessment very good as I found out about a student with a different disability (by peer assessing) and another person's view on how to handle the disability.

> It gave me a second perspective on the situation and also reinforced my self-evaluation of my performance in the task.

> Yes. I picked up some of the strategies she would adapt differently in response to the situation which I would not have thought of before.

Changes to teaching practice

Participants were asked if they had introduced or were considering introducing changes to their teaching practice as a consequence of doing the module (Table 8.7). The types of changes the 'yes' respondents reported as intending or having implemented as a consequence of doing the module can be characterised as:

- encouraging students to disclose their disability to them; and

- changes to communication, e.g. changes to presentation, modification of speech, taping of lectures, the use of more diagrams, and the development of written notes.

The comments below indicate the different ways that participants responded to this question.

Table 8.7 *Are there any changes that you have introduced/are considering introducing to your teaching as a consequence of doing this module?*

Yes	No	No response
20 (66.6%)	6* (20%)	4 (13.4%)

* Two of these respondents reported that they would make changes if they had students who had a disability in their classes and one said that there was nothing that s/he hadn't already done.

Attempting to identify students with disabilities at the earliest time.

No. In some ways I will wait until I have to because [of the] large effort involved in changing material, etc.

… looking at ways in which material can be adapted for the specific student.

No, but I would adjust my teaching if the situation required it. Most of my teaching is to smaller groups – disabilities would be known to me or divulged to me, so wouldn't be 'missed' (hopefully!!!)

Making lecture notes available before the lecture – WebCT could facilitate this! I have not really been in favour of this before.

CONCLUSIONS

Awareness of disability discrimination legislation is the responsibility of all university academics. Providing 'modules' such as the one outlined above is one way of ensuring academics are cognisant of the law and what they need to do to comply. This case study provides encouragement to those interested in integrating professional development about teaching students who have a disability into teaching graduate certificates and diplomas. Participants taking the Monash University GCHE in 2001 were a mix of experienced and new teachers. Of the respondents, regardless of whether or not they had previously knowingly taught students who have a disability, 90 per cent reported that they had learnt something from taking the module and 80 per cent reported that, as a result of taking the module, they had more confidence in relating to students who have a disability. Over 60 per cent of the respondents reported either having made changes to their teaching as a result of taking the module or they intended to make changes.

Respondents reported learning from the module things including an increased understanding about different types of disabilities, that many disabilities are invisible, and about the services provided by the university and adjustments that can be made. Over 70 per cent of respondents reported that their involvement in peer assessment of reports had been a valuable experience to them, primarily because it provided them with the opportunity to learn about another disability and to consider a peer's approach to making adjustments for a student who had a specific disability.

While two- to three-hour, 'one size fits all' compulsory workshops may raise awareness of the issues, one of the strengths of integrating education development about student disabilities into a graduate certificate is that academics engage with the concepts and issues over a period of time, and they engage with them in relation to their own disciplinary context. In doing so, we can hypothesise that the impact on teaching practice may be greater over time when compared with academics engaging with two- to three-hour workshops. A suitable evaluation of the impact of the module on participant teaching practice is timely.

While complying with legislation is necessary, there is a also a moral component to be considered: it is morally right to engender an environment that includes all people, to recognise that 'diversity is normal' and to create environments that are universally accessible. The approach outlined in the case study is one effective way of achieving this.

OTHER USEFUL REFERENCES

Accessible curricula. Available online at http://www.techdis.ac.uk/pdf/ curricula.pdf (accessed 11 February 2004).

Health Records Act 2001(Victoria) Data. Available online at http://www.dms.dpc. vic.gov.au/sb/2001_Act/A00824.html (accessed 11 February 2004).

Higher Education Funding Council for England (2002) HEFCE publication 02/48 'Successful student diversity – Case studies of practice in learning and teaching and widening participation'. Available online at http://www.hefce. ac.uk/pubs/ hefce/2002/02_48.htm (accessed 11 February 2004).

Monash University 'Monash University Web Accessibility Policy'. Available online at http://www.its.monash.edu.au/web/policy/accessibility.html (accessed 11 February 2004).

Online materials for staff disability awareness. Available online at http: // jarmin.com/demos/ (accessed 11 February 2004).

SKILL National Bureau of Students with Disabilities. Available online at http:// www.skill.org.uk (accessed 11 February 2004).

The University of Nottingham's Office for Disability Issues. Available online at http://www.nottingham.ac.uk/disability (accessed 11 February 2004).

The University of Melbourne's Disability Liaison Unit. Available online at http: //www.services.unimelb.edu.au/disability/ (accessed 11 February 2004).

APPENDIX 1: MODULE 2 (TEACHING STUDENTS WHO HAVE A DISABILITY) QUESTIONNAIRE

Question 1. What is your gender?

Question 2. How many years experience do you have as an academic with responsibility for teaching student groups (not only at Monash University)?

Question 3. To your knowledge, have you taught a student(s) with a disability in any of your university classes?

Question 4. If you have done anything specifically to assist students who have a disability to access your teaching please indicate the things that you have done.

Question 5. From doing module 2 in HED5002:

a) have you learnt anything that you didn't previously know? Please elaborate.

b) do you have more confidence in relating to students who have a disability? Please comment.

    A) Yes   B) No

Question 6. Are there any changes that you have introduced/are considering introducing to your teaching as a consequence of doing this module?

Question 7. 'The types of changes that I can make to my classes for students with disabilities are changes that would assist all students'. Please comment.

    A) True   B) False

Question 8. 'Having done this module I am now more aware that student disabilities are not necessarily visible'. Please comment.

    A) True   B) False

Question 9. Was the student you interviewed allocated to you by the subject co-ordinator or did you locate the student yourself?

    A) Allocated by co-ordinator   B) Found myself

Question 10. In your interview, was the student willing to disclose their barriers to learning? Please comment.

A) Yes   B) No

Question 11. Was doing the peer assessment for activity 2 of any value to you? Please comment.

Question 12. I am interested to know your opinion of peer review by an **identified peer** and being an **identified** peer assessor.

a)   Did knowing the peer and being a known assessor introduce particular difficulties for you?

   A) Yes   B) No

b)   Would you prefer to conduct peer review of an unidentified peer?

   A) Yes   B) No

c)   If you passed the work, would you have asked for the work to be redone if you had not known the peer?

   A) Yes   B) No

Question 13. Would you recommend keeping this module in the Graduate Certificate in Higher Education?

   A) Yes   B) No

Question 14. If you answered YES to question 13 in which subject do you think this module would be most usefully located? Please comment.

   A) HED5001   B) HED5002

Other comments
        Thank you very much for your insights.

NOTES

1   The Monash University Malaysia (MUM) campus did not have any students who have a disability registered and so we could not provide MUM participants with students to interview from their own campus.
2   At Monash University, a subject is a 'unit' of work, generally completed during a 13-week semester.

9

Education development: the role of graduate university teaching programmes

Kym Fraser

INTRODUCTION

As Ling discusses in Chapter 1, in the past decade the changes that have taken place in higher education have had a significant impact on teaching across the higher education sector. Helping to drive these changes are increasing student numbers and student diversity, an increasing emphasis on student-centred teaching and flexible learning, and the use of educational media, in particular online environments. Education development units are positioned to build on some of these changes through award-bearing university programmes that focus on teaching in higher education. These programmes can be used to introduce staff to what is already known about the facilitation of student learning through good teaching and to encourage staff to take a scholarly approach to their teaching. Programmes of this nature are also one way to begin the professionalisation of university teaching.

While graduate university teaching programmes have existed for several decades, the current climate requires today's programmes to be quite different from those developed in the 1980s and early to mid-1990s. Today's programmes need to: be more accessible to academics; model the learning environments in which we teach; enrol participants who are at a stage in their academic career at which they can cope with the scholarly nature of the discipline of teaching/student learning in higher education; take into account the different disciplinary and local contexts of academics; be articulated with higher degrees and be linked to institutional structures that promote teaching.

GRADUATE UNIVERSITY TEACHING PROGRAMMES: THE ISSUES FOR DECISION MAKERS

The last decade has seen increasing government investment in the improvement of university teaching in many countries. In part this investment has been in response to the increasing requirement for university accountability for the quality of teaching and student learning. In 1995 the government of the Netherlands provided $240 million over three years for the improvement of teaching programmes in the 13 Dutch universities. Schreurs *et al.* (1999) report that the development of teacher training programmes was one of the most popular uses of the funding. In South Africa the national Standards Generating Body for Higher Education and Training developed a set of 'unit standards for a competency-based national qualification for lecturers in higher education, called the Post Graduate Certificate in Higher Education' (Quinn, 2003: 1).

Following the quality teaching reviews of the mid-1990s, many Australian universities developed graduate certificates in university teaching and a study of this provision in 2002 (Dearn *et al.*) reported that 21 of the 38 Australian universities provided award-bearing programmes, with two programmes being compulsory for probationary staff. In the UK, most universities also provide such programmes, in part in response to the Dearing Report of 1997 (Bamber, 2002). The Standing Conference on Academic Practice (SCAP) overview of teaching/academic practice provision 2002 reported that of 27 responding universities, (out of 28 contacted), 18 (66 per cent) had award-bearing programmes, with 14 (51 per cent) of those programmes being compulsory for probationary academics. For ease of writing, I will refer to these award-bearing programmes as Graduate Certificates in Higher Education (GCHEs), while acknowledging that there are different awards and that the programmes are called many different things. Dearn *et al.* (2002) report 11 different names for 21 Australian graduate certificates of this nature.

GCHEs differ in very many respects (Partington and Stainton, 2003). Dearn *et al.* (2002), established that the requirements for the 21 existing Australian graduate certificate programmes varied '... between 200 and 660 hours of work with staff taking between two and four subjects over one or two years' (p. 25). GCHEs also vary in terms of who takes them (full-time, part-time, graduates), how they are taught and assessed, and their aims and purposes. Gibbs and Coffey (2000) in their survey of 23 programmes in eight countries report that programmes appear to promote five different types of goals: behavioural change; conceptual change; reflective practice; improvement in student learning; and teacher efficacy. Many different factors determine the goals and philosophical framework that underpin a GCHE, including the goals of the university, the needs of the academics, and the beliefs of those who teach the programme. Anecdotal evidence and the increasing literature on the impact of these GCHEs, suggest that regardless of which of these goals programmes set out to achieve, the goals are achieved by some, but not all, of their participants (Ho *et al.*, 2001). Particular goals and the underlying philosophies appear to make sense to and are taken on by particular academics and usually not all academics in the programme. While it is not clear that at this stage it is useful or helpful to prescribe a particular underlying philosophical framework or set of goals for all GCHEs, there are a number of factors that are important for programme teams to consider in the development and renewal of their programmes, and for national agencies to consider in developing national guidelines for these programmes. The rest of this chapter is devoted to exploring each of these factors.

Award-bearing programmes need to:

1. explore the discipline of teaching in higher education (i.e. to focus on more than teaching skills);

2. be appropriate for academics[1] at different stages of their teaching career;

3. be appropriate for academics in terms of accessibility and their disciplinary and local contexts;

4. be linked with institutional structures.

The discipline of teaching in higher education.

Traditionally teaching has been viewed as a role that anyone can do as long as they have the substantive disciplinary knowledge. In the twentieth century the disciplinary doctorate was the proxy for teaching quality. Knowledge of teaching and learning as a discipline in its own right has, until recently, not been recognised as useful or important. In truth, academics have taught for years without substantive professional development or qualifications associated with this aspect of their multifaceted role. Little wonder that it has long been assumed that anyone can teach as long as they have the knowledge of their discipline. However, with an increasingly diverse student body, the move to online learning and a host of other changes in the sector, the sector is being called to account for the quality of teaching and student learning and is being asked to demonstrate and improve both.

Central education development units have existed for over 30 years[2] and in that time, teaching was often conceptualised as a generic set of skills that could, as Rowland (2001) says 'be learnt through familiarity without undue intellectual or theoretical efforts' (p. 163). He refers to this as the 'atheoretical perspective' and likens education developers to trainers in the craft of teaching. The focus of education development in past decades was often on strategies and tips, related to things such as the conduct of lectures, small group teaching, practical classes, curriculum design and assessment strategies.

During the last 20 years the discipline of teaching and learning in higher education has developed and there is a growing consensus as to what constitutes effective teaching in higher education, how students learn, and how to improve teaching through both professional development and the scholarship of teaching (Andresen, 1995; Biggs, 1999; Boyer, 1990; Elton, 1987; Huber and Morreale, 2002; Johnston 1996; Kember 1997; Land, 2001; Ramsden, 1992; Zuber-Skerrit, 1992). Rowland's (2001) 'educational expertise perspective' refers to the growth of the discipline of teaching and learning in higher education. From this perspective, Rowland argues that academics who aren't in that discipline should be guided by the experts and the experts' '... findings should be applied by the non-educationalist academics in their discipline' (p. 163). Today's GCHE needs to introduce academics to more than teaching tips and strategies. They need to introduce academics to the discipline of teaching and learning in higher education; and to higher education research and scholarship.

In spite of this growing expertise, it is clear that education developers differ in our opinion as to what best underpins a GCHE. This is reflected in the variety of different frameworks that underpin programmes. For instance, Ecclestone (1996) reported on the prevalence of references to the reflective practitioner framework (Schon, 1987) in GCHEs. The 'conceptions of learning' framework is used by many programmes. This framework proposes that there are a number of clearly defined conceptions of learning and of teaching and that students and teachers are able to move through these conceptions (Marton and Saljo, 1976; Gow and Kember, 1993). Other programmes introduce academics to different epistemological perspectives. Quinn's (2003) programme introduced four ontological/epistemological 'orientations': traditional (positivist or scientific); interpretive (hermeneutic); critical, and postmodern and asked academics not to adopt one of the orientations but to 'see where their belief systems are in relation to these ...' and to 'use these orientations to explore how knowledge is created in their disciplines, to question their assumptions about teaching, learning, assessment and evaluation and to inform their curriculum development processes' (p. 5). Some programmes exhibit combinations of the five underpinning frameworks articulated by Gibbs and Coffey (2000).

Education developers value these frameworks differently. Knight (2002), summarises the critiques of the notion of the 'reflective practitioner'. It 'is unwise to praise reflection indiscriminately, and that it is not unchallenged as a way of conceptualising the conversion of some tacit knowing into explicit knowledge' (p. 29). Ho *et al.* (2001) point out that 'Empirical evidence relating to the effectiveness of the conceptual change approach to staff development in higher education is very limited in the literature ...' (p. 145). Anecdotal evidence and some research (Quinn, 2003; Ho *et al.*, 2001) suggest that academics who enrol in our programmes have mixed responses to them and report varying degrees of value to their teaching from the programmes.

The discipline of teaching and learning in higher education is a much-contested one. 'In order to develop a critical discourse of professional practice in higher education we must learn to speak across the divides *within* the field of education as well as between the different disciplines' (Rowland, 2001: 165). It is imperative that in our programmes we represent that contestation. Murphy *et al.* (2000) report on what they perceive to be a highly successful team approach to developing a programme in the late 1990s.

> Inevitably, given the academic staff's [education developers] varied professional backgrounds, there was some initial tension due to alternative visions of how to teach the program ... [Given that diversity of backgrounds] reaching agreement on what 'learning theory' meant, and how far we could implicate students at this introductory level in the argument of learning theory, was a real challenge. Through many meetings and discussion, the position was arrived at that we would give an authentic appreciation of the highly contested area of learning theory and consider positivist, humanistic and critical perspectives ... we had to engage with each other's beliefs and values and concluded that healthy disagreement is more productive than convergence on a particular theory or model (p. 7).

> Such a process was costly in time but has resulted in a much deeper understanding of what 'normal' academic departments need in [order to be] able to achieve in this area (p. 6).

It is worth pointing out that as a member of that team, I concur with the above quote. After four years of teaching on that programme it became apparent that that sense of a team began to break down as education developers left the Centre to take up new positions and new education developers joined the Centre. This phenomenon is not atypical of education development teams and it would suggest the usefulness of going through such a team and programme-building process every three to five years.

It is important for each team of education developers to negotiate and determine the philosophical framework for and goals of their GCHE. The

GCHE needs to introduce (and we must accept that often it is only an introduction) academics to the highly contested domain of higher education research, albeit in ways that reduce the almost inevitable confusion that comes from introducing those new to higher education research to the conflicting theories. As we will explore in the next section, academics at different stages of their career may be more or less able to engage with that research.

Academics at different stages of their career

One of the difficulties facing education developers is that of designing a GCHE that suits academics who are at very different stages of their careers. It is extremely useful to have experienced and not-so-experienced academics included in a cohort and to have university-wide programmes in which there exists an interdisciplinary mix. This mix has the potential, as Rowland (2001) describes, for the professional development to become a 'critical interdisciplinary field' for the cross-fertilisation of ideas, for questioning and learning about different ways of teaching in different contexts. However, depending on what you are trying to achieve with that cohort, it can be exceedingly difficult for academics who are very new to teaching, to get the most out of a GCHE that is not focused on teaching tips and strategies.

Inexperienced teachers
Teaching for the first time is demanding, intellectually and emotionally. Before engaging in a programme that seeks to introduce education theories, critical reflection, etc., academics who are new to teaching need to learn some practical skills and strategies relevant to their discipline and mode[3] of teaching (Walker, 1993; Ho *et al.*, 2001). For example, if we haven't lectured before, we need to know about the structuring of a lecture, strategies for engaging students, the important things to do in a first lecture, use of a microphone and voice, how to operate the lecture theatre, etc. Eventually these skills and strategies become automatic, but initially, they take time, thought and energy. A priority for new teachers in higher education is to know how to conduct tomorrow's class in a way that instils confidence in their students and themselves. They want to appear competent in front of their students (McKeachie, 1997).

I believe that it can be a mistake to encourage or require academics who are very new to teaching to take a GCHE of the nature described in the first section of this chapter, when what they really need is something designed specifically to help them 'survive' their everyday teaching and to grow in confidence. After they have achieved a degree of confidence in their teaching and an understanding of the teaching of their discipline, they will be in a better cognitive space to engage with education theories and understand the complexities of the discipline.

The type of 'non-GCHE preparation for teaching' programme that will be appropriate and relevant will depend upon the university and departmental context. It may be that a university-wide programme, which has the advantages of cross-disciplinary discussion and comparisons is most appropriate in one context, while a departmental programme will be most appropriate in another. It may be that the programme focuses on different types of teaching modes in different departments/universities. Online teaching, distance education, laboratories, Oxford tutorials, etc. will be relevant in some contexts and not in others. The mix of full-time, part-time, graduate students, etc. will vary depending on a number of things, including the financial position of, and the resources available to, the institution/department. Similarly the length of time devoted to the programmes will vary. Two things are, I believe, critical for initial teacher preparation programmes: 1) as Ryan *et al.* argue in Chapter 11, for the professionalisation of university teaching, preparation programmes must be a compulsory part of probation for academics new to teaching; and 2) the rationale and the aims of the programme need to be made explicit to participants and the link and the differences between the preparation programme and the GCHE need to be made explicit. Having completed the preparation programme, new teachers then need time to learn and think about their teaching and perhaps 12 to 18 months after beginning to teach, enrol in the GCHE.

After completing the GCHE, some participants will value the opportunity to take their study of higher education further. GCHEs that are explicitly linked to a diploma, which in turn leads to a masters programme, which in turn leads to a doctorate, provides participants with a structured opportunity to pursue qualifications and interest in university teaching/student learning. It makes a great deal of sense for GCHEs to be structured with this type of progression in mind.

Experienced teachers

Clearly the provision of award programmes does not meet the needs of the vast majority of experienced academics. Dearn *et al.* (2002: 25) determined that in 21 such programmes in Australia in 2001, a total of 300 individuals were enrolled '... representing less than [0].5 per cent of the total of Full-Time Equivalence (FTE) of 82,233 academic staff in all Australian universities'. Granted some experienced teachers will enrol in GCHEs and perceive the programme to be part of their continuing professional development as a teacher. The vast majority of academics will not.

Partington and Stainton (2003) suggest that staff development needs to be life-long, that certificates need to be updated and that experienced staff need to refresh their skills. While most experienced academics do not engage in teaching programmes and seminars, academics can be encouraged to engage in continuing education development in a number of ways including: through teaching development projects and collaborative research; team teaching, especially if it incorporates peer observation and discussion of teaching; curriculum design; attendance at discipline specific teaching conferences; and taking teaching-related sabbaticals. As outlined by Smith in Chapter 2, the Learning and Teaching Support Network (LTSN) has been developed along disciplinary lines and provides a range of opportunities of this nature for both beginning and experienced academics to engage in disciplinary-focused continuing professional development of their teaching. Academics can also be encouraged to engage with some of the ideas of the GCHE by being mentors for academics taking the programme. Of course, if institutional incentives relate only or primarily to research, many academics will be strategic in the use of their limited time, and education development will not feature in their professional development plans. This will be explored further in the final section of this chapter and in Chapter 11.

Programme accessibility and academic disciplinary and local contexts.

Two reasons that academics give to explain not engaging in education development are 1) their exceedingly heavy workload coupled with a perceived lack of reward for education development and 2) that GCHEs don't reflect the teaching of their discipline (Dearn *et al.*, 2002). It is therefore essential that GCHEs fit as closely as possible with the current workload of academics, and model the types of teaching in which the academic engages. This can be achieved in a number of ways. The following are examples.

In the last 10 years undergraduate and postgraduate university courses/ programmes/subjects in many universities have increasingly moved from print and face-to-face contact to incorporate online activity. The online activity varies from the provision of information and course administration (submission of assignments, etc.) to the use of interactive facilities, such as online discussions, chat groups and online group work. Changes of this nature can provide education developers with the opportunity to introduce staff to what is already known about good teaching and the facilitation of student learning, and to encourage staff to take a scholarly approach to their teaching. As academics are increasingly teaching in an online environment, it makes sense for GCHEs to model this type of teaching by incorporating a mix of environments in which the participant may learn (face-to-face workshops, online discussions/activities/access to information, printed study materials, etc.). Online activities can be designed to represent typical face-to-face workshop experiences (Murphy *et al.*, 2000). They can also encourage participants to learn from each other, which is a useful aspect for a GCHE to model. As well as modelling and reflecting the types of learning environments in which the academic teaches, the use of online environments allows academics to learn and interact with each other asynchronously at a time and place of their choosing. Hence the ability to take part in a GCHE can be co-ordinated with other commitments.

Because their discipline is the source of most academics' professional identity, Jenkins (1996) argues 'the way education developers should seek to work with the vast majority of staff is to recognise, value and build on staff's concerns for their discipline' (p. 15). Chalmers and O'Brien (Chapter 4) echo this argument by emphasising the importance of '… recognising and affirming the integrity and authenticity of the various disciplinary fields' (Chapter 4: 52). Many if not most GCHEs are offered to academics university-wide. Financial and logistical reasons support this approach. Such programmes also provide an environment in which the cross fertilization of ideas from different disciplines can be supported. Anecdotally this is often one of the key aspects that many academics value in GCHEs; the opportunity to discuss with other academics approaches to teaching and conceptions that aren't held in their own discipline. How do we structure our university-wide GCHEs to recognise and build on disciplinary teaching? There are a range of ways in which we can achieve this. The provision of a disciplinary mentor who supports the discussion and possible application of ideas developed in the GCHE in their discipline complements the interdisciplinary environment. It is not clear whether it is necessary or even important for the mentor to have done the GCHE. It is clear that the mentor needs to be interested and experienced in the teaching of their discipline.

Another way to focus on the discipline of the academic is to focus activities and assessment on the teaching that the academic already does. This has the added benefit of providing opportunities for the academic to apply and make sense of the work done in the GCHE to their own disciplinary teaching. This approach requires the academic to be teaching. Examples of ways in which to focus activities and assessments on current teaching include: analysis of (and improvement of) assessment strategies and instruments; observation (peer/tutor/mentor) of already scheduled classes and the reciprocal observation of the mentor or peer; interviews with current students; lesson development for upcoming classes; discussion of specific disciplinary issues; and the flexibility of projects to encourage academics to work in an area that they want to explore or design a curriculum they want to design.

Links with institutional structures

While recruitment, promotion, pay increases and career advancement are linked exclusively and demonstrably with the research component of the academic role, many, if not most, academics will be strategic enough to put their limited time into their research. Institutional structures such as promotion need to be demonstrably linked to education development. Different universities achieve this in different ways. Scheurs *et al.* (1999), reported that in Maastricht University in the Netherlands '… only staff members who have passed the workshops of the faculty development project can perform senior educational roles'. Since the late 1990s, at Monash University in Australia, academics can use the completion of the university's GCHE to demonstrate engagement with teaching for promotion purposes. In Chapter 4 Chalmers and O'Brien describe how at the University of Queensland, a large, research-intensive Australian university, academic portfolios are used for 'annual performance review, mid-term and final review for confirmation of continuing appointment, and applications for promotion, study leave and teaching awards. Academic portfolios are made up of evidence and reflection on teaching, research and service' (Chapter 4: 61).

Clearly, given the current government funding arrangements for universities in many countries (for example, the Research Assessment Exercise in the UK), there is little incentive for individual universities to encourage academics to devote valuable time to education development when it could be used to improve funding through further research. This issue is discussed further in Chapter 11.

CONCLUSION

GCHEs developed for today's academics need to be significantly different from those developed in the 1980s and 1990s. A great deal more is known about the discipline of teaching in higher education and that research base needs to underpin programmes. They also need to acknowledge and reflect the disciplinary teaching contexts in which academics teach.

In many universities, in particular research-intensive universities, the commitment to link recruitment, pay and promotion to different components of the academic role, including teaching, depends very much on the formulas used for government funding. Only when those funding approaches change will many universities significantly restructure their recruitment and promotion structures to value and reward teaching effort and excellence. Until that time, regardless of the rhetoric of governments and central university administrations, the professionalisation of university teaching (as discussed by Ryan *et al.* in Chapter 11), is unlikely to proceed and the percentage of academics enrolling in GCHEs that introduce them to the discipline of higher education will remain insignificant (Dearn *et al.*, 2002).

NOTES

1   A broad range of university staff directly support student learning including librarians, IT specialists, graduate teaching assistants, studies skills tutors, to name only a few. Increasingly GCHEs are being adapted to be relevant to a broader range of participants, i.e. not only academics. I will use the term 'academic' throughout the chapter to refer to GCHE participants. In most but not all cases the concepts being discussed are equally applicable to the broad range of GCHE participants.
2   In Australia, Monash University established the Higher Education Advisory Research Unit (HEARU) in 1972 and Queensland University established the Teaching Education Development Institute in 1973. Both universities are research-intensive universities.
3   I use the term 'mode' to refer to types of teaching such as distance education, online teaching, tele-teaching, computer classes, small class teaching, large class teaching, etc.

10

Education development through funded projects

Bob Matthew and Ray Land

Over the last two decades considerable sums of public money have been invested, in different countries, in a wide range of education development projects in higher education. The effectiveness of these projects, in terms of their adoption, impact and penetration has been perceived, where they have been evaluated, as variable. It is timely to consider both what might be the source of this variation and what may be learned from it. This chapter arises from our personal experiences of working as education developers in the contexts of Scottish-, English- and European-funded higher education projects. We are clear that this chapter is not a comprehensive review of education development projects; that has already been carried out by Murphy (2003). Instead our intention is to discuss, on the basis of our own experience, how education development might be more successfully facilitated through funded projects. Of course the world of education developers comprises a number of overlapping 'tribes' or communities of practice (Wenger, 1998), and these communities operate through a variety of different approaches and conceptual frameworks (Land, 2001). Hence the reader must take what we, as developers with our own tribal affiliations, say and contextualise it into their own organisation and their own way of working. Our own reflections on how we work as developers alongside academic colleagues lead us to conclude that our practice needs both to include, and to be informed by research, with clear awareness of the theoretical perspectives and conceptual frameworks on which we draw (Fry *et al.*, 2004). This has implications for how we see education development, particularly through funded projects, and the following discussion will reflect such perspectives.

In this chapter we will first discuss the problem of engagement with academic colleagues, and then go on to review our own experience of engaging with academics through various funded projects. This then leads us to reflect on a variety of more theoretical perspectives on the tactics and process of engagement. In the final section of the chapter we highlight some of our experiences of working with staff who are employed on funded education development projects and this raises, particularly, the issue of the gender of such staff.

THE PROBLEM OF ENGAGEMENT

The use of development projects is of course just one operational approach from a broad repertoire available to, and employed by, education developers. However, it is an approach which in our experience is well suited to the often tricky process of engaging research-minded academic colleagues. Frielick (2002) has pointed out how difficult it is 'to advance the cause of teaching and learning – particularly in a traditional research university'. The reasons for this difficulty in engaging colleagues are complex, and would seem to emanate from a number of factors including contested notions of the concept of 'development' and the need for it, the purposes of university education, mechanisms of reward and recognition within the academic labour process, the organisational and disciplinary cultures, contexts and communities within which academics find themselves operating, and the ways in which competing conceptual frameworks and discourses differently frame the practice of academics within the university (Elvidge, 2004). A particularly significant issue of engagement is that of academic identity, in regard to the ways in which both academics and education developers construct identities for themselves and for each other.

> The identities *attributed* to academic developers by others are equally varied. Positively, they may be seen as genuine facilitators and valued allies in the development of learning and teaching. Negatively, they may be seen as enforcers of edicts from on high – or even as a kind of quack, a wastrel with no respectable knowledge base and no under-standable epistemological justification for their claims about teaching and learning.
>
> (Ashworth *et al.*, 2004, in press)

The politics of identity would seem to be a more than occasional source of mistrust and misrecognition that can lead to an unwillingness to become involved in collaborative endeavours. The following is a salutary, and probably not uncommon, insight into the view that is held by academics of education developers seemingly bearing gifts.

We've given up three precious days of research for this. There is frustra-
tion and resistance among us, and most certainly considerable levels
of suspicion. We've already heard that this is a waste of time, from
those who have passed through this phase of development before us
and returned with this as settled news. Most of us haven't had a chance
to do any research at all during the course of this term. It's been just
too overwhelming. We are anxious about this. We have book proposals
to write, articles to finish, and untold piles of marking to get through
before the end of the week. Our discussions are not on the subject of
teaching and learning, … 'What are you working on?' is the question
between us. The question is never 'What courses do you teach?' …
And who are you anyway? You have an academic title. You tell me
something of your background. You say that you are, or were, an …
ologist, of sorts. But in telling us who you were you tell us nothing of
who you are now. You have moved into this area because it is important.
You are here because most of the time we academics do this important
work badly. We bristle …

(from Ashworth *et al.*, 2004, in press)

In a recent developmental project on making the curriculum 'accessible',
Stefani and Matthew (2002) report that agreement on a common educational goal is the first pre-requisite for a successful project. Now that may
seem to many to be a self-evident truth and yet how often do education
developers explain to academic colleagues what they are trying to do and
why they are trying to do it? It seems to us that in our work, just like
academics and research, we need to make explicit to all concerned the
nature and the purpose of our engagement.

As a result of these difficulties of engagement and rapprochement, our
view is that much of what we do is carried out obliquely, often by stealth,
and in a sense is akin to a 'Trojan horse' approach for getting our colleagues
to discuss teaching and learning issues. This is particularly the case in research-
intensive universities where teaching and learning matters, whilst not discussed
clandestinely, are certainly not often to the fore in common room discussions.
Our experience, however, has been that education development projects can
offer useful and important conceptual and developmental spaces in which
we, as developers, are able to engage with colleagues to explore and discuss
learning and teaching issues so that the process we go through together can
be seen as developing us, as a community.

ENGAGING COLLEAGUES THROUGH PROJECTS

Many developers would attest to the view that academics are more easily engaged in education developmental activity when involvement is likely to arouse their intellectual curiosity and permit the sense of professional autonomy that many academics jealously defend and preserve. Collaborative work through funded projects often provides the interpretive space in which a 'hermeneutic' form of engagement might be established. Projects can enable a 'Dialectic approach of "intelligent conversation" with colleagues in which balancing of different views, relation of local to wider perspectives, part to whole, etc., leads to critical synthesis and production of new shared insights and practice' (Land, 2001). What would seem to be a strong advantage of projects as a useful element of kit in the development toolbag is the way in which project work of this kind goes very much with the grain of academics' preferred *modus operandi* and, for many academics, though certainly not all, project work has much in common with the culture and activities of the research practices they are familiar with. Developers also recognise the strength of the disciplinary communities of practice from which academic colleagues derive their own professional identities and how they are often driven by their subject-specific 'guild' culture. Hence development is sometimes considered only to be effective when going with the grain of disciplinary needs. Where projects can be located within disciplinary settings, development can be seen as 'situated learning' within the disciplinary community of practice.

So the project approach allows colleagues to retain their academic identity and also allows developers to position themselves in academic and research roles as well as in more conventional facilitative or 'service' roles. 'Enhancing Teaching–Learning Environments in Undergraduate Courses' (ETL), a four-year project funded by the ESRC as part of its Teaching and Learning Research Programme, provides an interesting case in point. The project has been designed to support departments involved in undergraduate teaching in 'thinking about new ways of encouraging high-quality learning'. This project adopts an explicitly collaborative approach, 'underpinned by research into the quality of student learning and how it is influenced, not just by teaching and assessment, but by the whole teaching–learning environment.' Engagement of fellow academics within the disciplines is crucial to the achievement of the project aims, and the disciplinary dimension is to the fore.

> The project seeks to develop subject-specific conceptual frameworks to guide institutional and faculty or departmental development of teaching–learning environments. The frameworks are being deployed to integrate findings from research both with the professional knowledge

of academic staff and with national and institutional criteria describing high quality teaching and learning. By working collaboratively with departmental partners, ways of enhancing the system-wide capacity for research-based practice are being explored and disseminated.

(ETL, 2003)

PROJECTS, OUTCOMES AND CONTINGENCY

Sometimes a landscape seems to be less a setting for the life of its inhabitants than a curtain behind which their struggles, achievements and accidents take place. For those who, with the inhabitants, are behind the curtains, landmarks are no longer geographic but also biographical and personal (Berger and Mohr, 1967).

Rudduck (1991: 19) wrote that 'All of us who were actively involved then in research and development have looked out on the landscape of change, but we will have experienced it and responded to it differently'. This is a sentiment which we as education developers who have been in higher education (HE) over the past couple of decades recognise immediately.

In recent years in HE the words 'innovation' and 'change' have often been used interchangeably (Hannan and Silver, 2000). The words have entered the language of both academics and institutions, though the responsibilities have often been confused. For us it is individuals who innovate (or change). Institutions also innovate but more importantly *manage* innovation, whilst funding agencies *sponsor* innovation in fields of activity where they fund education development projects. Hannan and Silver (2000: 11) also note that whilst 'innovation may aim to bring about improvement, it does not necessarily produce it'.

For us innovation and change are facets of development. Innovation in a higher education context is about a deliberate planned process whereby change is introduced. This change is intended to improve some aspect of student learning (or in some cases solve a problem relating to education development), though the improvement does not always ensue. The innovation or change can be new, can be adapted from practice elsewhere, but what is important is that the changes are new to the individual, course, department or institution as a whole. Given that there is no certainty of success then management of the risk involved is a key factor for education developers. Implicit in our argument is that for innovation or change to take place people must change and develop as a result. This means that education developers need to understand something of how development actually takes place if we are to manage the risks involved.

Our view is that development needs to be looked at in a system-wide way, i.e. as developers we need to have some understanding of system dynamics. In particular we need to understand how our own institutions function, where the power lies and who influences the way things are done. Much has been written recently about learning/teaching systems and in particular the Biggs (1999) presage-process-product (3P) model. However, for us the Biggs 3P model is premised on a 1940s understanding of system dynamics which does not include more recent thinking particularly on non-linear dynamics, e.g.

> a change to any one component will, depending on the state of equilibrium already achieved, either effect change throughout and thereby create a new equilibrium and hence a new system, or the changed component will be absorbed, the system reverting to the status quo.
>
> (Biggs, 1993: 76)

Recent thinking on system theory has led to an understanding that living systems, including organisations, are self-organising dissipative structures, which can be self-maintained in a stable state, which are on the edge of chaos, and spontaneously re-order themselves at levels of complexity (Waldrop, 1994). Looked at in this way education developers can create all kinds of favourable environments for learning, but there is no guarantee that any of these will result in learning in our colleagues. Our best 'development' intentions may be complicated not only by the complexity of the organisations within which we work but also by our colleagues' prior experience, habituated practices and assumptions (Bourdieu, 1977). Equally, as Tutt's (1985) theory of unintended consequences would attest, our interventions can lead to unexpected developments. Cryer and Elton (1990) have used the thinking behind catastrophe theory to try and explain this phenomenon. Berg and Östergren (1979) suggest that there is a lack of conformity in any system, giving rise to 'cracks' in the system, where change can start, particularly in organisations facing strong external pressures. It is these 'cracks' that education developers look for as the starting point. However, on many occasions the 'cracks' though present are not 'visible' to the developer and so the outcome is unexpected. Thus as education developers we have to be prepared to 'go with' the unexpected and learn to live with such unpredictability.

Of course unpredictability can in many instances lead to positive outcomes. A concrete example of this type of outcome can be obtained from the setting up of Learning and Teaching Development Funds in our institutions. These are schemes that offer small sums of money to academic colleagues to support small-scale development projects. What constitutes innovation is locally determined in these projects, but the way in which other colleagues elsewhere in the institution have picked up and used the ideas has been surprising and unpredicted. For example in one of our institutions development work on using handsets to obtain feedback during lectures in computing science has spread to veterinary medicine and social anthropology (Draper *et al.*, 2002). A project funded to introduce reflective practice in civil engineering has spread to social and economic history, archaeology and restorative dentistry – hardly areas we could have predicted.

ACTION POETRY, COUNTDOWN FACTORS AND BLOW-UP FACTORS

Though much modern management theory acknowledges the possible effects of complexity theory and non-linear change (Fullan, 1993), senior managers and funders revert, understandably, to a noticeably linear concept when they come to estimate the achievement and outcomes value of projects. It behoves us as developers to consider ways in which projects we deem to be serving useful goals might be made less susceptible to the contingency factors we have mentioned. In the light of the vulnerability of projects to such environmental instability Perkins (2000: 17) has identified a series of 'countdown factors' which would appear to provide helpful conditions for the success of education development projects.

One of the factors Perkins identifies is to create *an expectation for action*, and hence avoid 'the problem of talking forever' (p. 17). The latter is resolved by the setting up of smaller 'lens groups' to tackle and address specific issues (action projects) within the wider project. These smaller groupings are provided with coaching but also have a 'gentle public accountability' (p. 17) brought to bear upon them – not too strong to be threatening but enough to motivate them to produce what is asked of them. The action projects should be chosen to be 'safe enough', with a sense of 'low-risk realism' and the opportunity to explore new practices or approaches in 'practice fields' without the anxiety of usual 'on-site high-stakes' (p. 19) pressure. Linked to this is the important need to avoid 'complex unmemorable language and strategies' in favour of identifying an appropriate *action poetry* (p. 18). The latter is a form of shared and accessible language and terminology to which all parties feel they can sign up without discomfort to their existing academic or professional identities and without a sense of entering an alien discourse. In this way action poetry both motivates and empowers and time should be allocated within the project to ensuring that such a language of participation has been agreed. The ASSHE project (Assessment Strategies in Scottish Higher Education project) (Hounsell *et al.*, 1996) and the PROMOTE project (Professional Recognition of Methods of Promoting Teaching and Learning Enhancement) in

Scotland (Land and McArthur, 2003) were interesting examples of how developers and academics across all Scottish higher education institutions were able to collaborate and contribute successfully when the 'lens' was on specific examples of interesting local practice and a simple common conceptual framework was employed. On the other hand our experience of involvement in large-scale European and UK collaborative projects where diverse conceptual frameworks and competing discourses have remained contested for much of the project has shown how the inability to establish 'action poetry' has protracted the discussions on goals and slowed progress.

Even when action poetry is generated, however, there remains the danger of 'getting the idea but missing the moment' (Perkins, 2000: 20). Developers need to build into their projects specific occasions when the emphasis will be on scanning for potential problems and opportunities before planning the next stage. At a pragmatic level this involves defining the '*whens* and *hows*' (p. 20) of development project activity, or particularising the completion of tasks beyond mere broad intentions. Similarly, at the personal level, developers may need, Perkins argues, to 'introduce *active inhibition* as a deliberate practice' (p. 21). Given the powerful disciplinary identities of academics discussed earlier there is often a tendency, Perkins found, for well-established existing habits to override new practices, even when the aim to change is quite genuine. For example, recent work at one of our universities was aimed at introducing teaching 'ethics' to undergraduate biological scientists and a model for doing this was developed, piloted and tested (Clarkeburn *et al.*, 2002). The final strand of the project was one of training academic staff in the departments to facilitate this learning of 'ethics'. However, some three years later this introduction has stalled as staff have found a variety of reasons for not getting involved in teaching ethics to the students.

Moreover the satisfactory accommodation of countdown factors is no guarantee of successful project outcomes. They would appear to be necessary but not sufficient conditions. What Perkins (2000: 23) identifies as 'blow-up factors' are usually unpredictable and intractable occurrences which can prove fatal to the success and even continuation of projects. In these instances all that can be advocated is vigilance and preparedness, to 'look to the skies' (p. 32). Blow-up factors would include *problem blindness* (p. 23) when project members cannot or will not see the problems that begin with them. Our experience, confirmed by Perkins' findings, is that this tends to be lessened in smaller-scale action projects, where project members work on problems closer to home and feedback processes are simpler and more effective. Related to this, Perkins advocates also that developers should be vigilant for signs of a *polarisation of allegiance* (p. 25) within project teams. There will inevitably be a degree of backsliding and variable performance in project teams. 'A bell-shaped curve of involvement' he points out, 'is good news. The bad news is a U-shaped curve – polarization' (p. 25). This indeed has been our experience on one large funded national project where two distinct ideological camps emerged and found it difficult to reconcile conceptual differences and hence find practical ways forward or an action poetry. Perkins' advice in these circumstances is to provide *participation ramps* (p. 25) – ways in which 'many degrees of participation' can be tolerated and encouraged. Our experience is that these ramps need to be built particularly across project divides where gender, age or conceptual frameworks lead to salient differences in perspective. The situation is often exacerbated by *negative symbolic conduct* (p. 26) which 'sends divisive or discouraging side-messages' to other members of the project team. An over-concentration on 'getting things done' may lead to neglect of seemingly 'trivial things' which are in fact symbolically important, such as showing up for certain events. Again in line with Perkins' findings, our experience has been that awareness of symbolic conduct is a particular consideration for project leaders. Neglect of these deceptively minor issues can lead in projects to *stirring the swamp*, in which 'rivalries, resentments, issues that have only been "corridor talk" are brought onto the public stage' (p. 27) and the development project is already on its way downhill.

FUNDING AND CONSENSUS

Our experience leads us to believe that what is important in a funded project, be it a national funded project or a locally (i.e. institutional level) funded project is that it is key to have consensus at the start about the purpose and direction. For us, obligations can be negotiated and/or imposed later. This consensus is best obtained in a practitioners' community forum, so that it has the endorsement of all at the start. This minimises both the 'not invented here syndrome' and the pulling-in-different-directions issues. One of us has written about the experience of being involved in a nationally funded project which has had minimum impact in their own and others' institutions. This was as a direct result of the two main parties involved having very different ideas about both the goals of the project and the ways in which they would work towards them (Stefani and Matthew, 2002). A clear case again of polarised allegiance. Equally one of us was involved in another nationally funded project where the goals were discussed by all, agreed upon through good action poetry and delivered, resulting in an education development package which has been widely used by the partner universities and others outside the project (Bolander *et al.*, 2001).

In an ideal world the 'project' would be enquiry-based (as stated earlier that is what we are and what we do) and open-ended so that it would grow organically. In a sense the project would be an exploratory journey not a blueprint (Fullan, 1993). As a journey it would not be a complete mystery tour, but would be flexible enough to allow us to visit interesting 'sites' along the way. In others words it's a research project – we have a good idea but don't know if it will work or exactly where it will take us. However, in the present climate we are realistic enough to acknowledge that in order to get funded projects we need to honour certain parameters or 'deliverables'. This means the 'project' needs to be defined within certain bounds.

Let us for a moment consider the real underlying issues between the funders of development projects and those doing the work. The issues for us are risk, trust and tolerance. Recently, in Scotland a new system of Institutional Audit has been announced, namely 'Enhancement-Led Institutional Review'. In the *Handbook for Reviewers* (QAAHE, 2003), it is explicitly acknowledged that innovation (which is usually the desired outcome of a development project) involves risk, and what is of interest to the reviewers is how that risk is managed. As the funding council, in this case SHEFC (Scottish Higher Education Funding Council), has been one of the major supporters of development projects this is a major step forward.

It needs to be acknowledged at this point that one of the problems of development projects has been an expectation of the 'successful' dissemination of the outcomes. As Murphy (2003: 61) states

> distinctions need to be made between publicising, disseminating and making an impact on practice on the basis of research findings of research and development projects.

Like all research projects the outcomes of development projects are not always successful nor do they lead to the identification of 'best', 'good' or 'excellent' practice. This leads us to a view that it is *management of the risk* behind conducting a development project that is important, not the dissemination. That is not to say that dissemination is not important, but like all research outcomes the dissemination and application to the practice of others is not in the hands of those doing the work in the first instance. We do not normally expect those who conduct research in the disciplines to be responsible for the dissemination of their work other than through publications so why should we expect differently of those doing research and development in the field of education development?

It must be acknowledged by all concerned – sponsors, funders, education developers and academics – that education development projects can and do falter (they really wouldn't be research if they all succeeded) and even when successful they come with a limited shelf-life. In our work we firmly believe that there is no such thing as complete 'failure', just more interesting feedback. In other words we learn from our mistakes.

PROJECTS AND PEOPLE

One aspect of education development projects that is often ignored is the people involved and the knowledge and skill they both produce and acquire. Reflecting on our experience of involvement with such projects leads us to two tentative observations. The first is that projects which are concerned primarily with the development of new materials, conceptual tools or innovative practices (what we might term 'stuff' development) tend to be more successful than those from the outset designed to develop individuals ('staff' development), though, interestingly, the development of individuals often seems likely to follow from materials development. If you aim for people development up-front you are possibly more likely to be disappointed. The second observation is that the participants in education development projects are increasingly women, and it is interesting to speculate why that might be.

So where do these conclusions come from? In a recent SHEFC funded series of projects – Scottish Communication and Information Technology (SCROLLA, 2003) – designed to support the use of communications and information technology in learning and teaching (C&IT), a project entitled 'NetCulture' was funded. This project was designed to develop and enhance the network of all those involved in staff development-related C&IT initiatives in Scotland – education developers, C&IT specialists, librarians, technical support people, software developers, etc. At the outset a number of those involved argued for a 'stuff' development theme to the project but this was not agreed on. All the Scottish HEIs were involved in the project and the project was funded and ran for two years. In the external evaluation report of the ScotCIT initiative, the Scottish Centre for Research in On-Line Learning and Assessment, stated that

> There is a general understanding that NetCulture provided an opportunity to achieve what was considered to be the valuable function of regional efforts to broker good practice across all Scottish HEIs. However, an underlying sense remains that what was certainly a good idea in theory did not genuinely provide value for money in practice.
> (SCROLLA, 2003: 14)

However the report also stated that 'some respondents attributed subsequent career progression directly to their involvement with ScotCIT' and that some of the 'expertise gained was subsequently lost to Scotland specifically through the departure of key individuals for organisations in England and overseas' (p. 14). Equally, discussion with colleagues in other institutions leads us to believe that particularly in the C&IT field there are now numbers of well-qualified and experienced people in the system as a result of the short contract work that they carried out on many project initiatives. What is important to us is that of those employed to be part of the project, all except one had track records in 'stuff' development, not people development. However, people development was perceived through the external evaluation to be an important, if unplanned, outcome of the funded programme. It is worth speculating also that the large investments in the differing phases of the Teaching and Learning Technology Programme (TLTP), though primarily about stuff development, probably have as their legacy a large and talented cohort of information technology specialists who are still in the HE system and have gone on to be involved in a wide range of subsequent projects and activities.

As regards the second issue our own (male!) experience and that of (female!) others (Wiles, 2003) leads us to believe that a significant number of those who work in education development and in learning technology are female. We think that it is worthwhile pausing for a moment to reflect on why that might be. We asked a number of those who had been involved in education development projects in Scotland how they saw the education development field, the extent to which they considered it to be a male normative, or 'macho', environment in comparison with other academic working environments, an area that people enter because money isn't everything, or an area where (younger) female staff are more vulnerable to being exploited through short-term contracts.

The responses on the whole in this very small-scale survey suggest that education developers need skills like multi-tasking, networking and communication which are often stereotypically represented as being 'feminine' skills. One respondent stated

> I think that the women working in this field do it because they want a lot, a lot of change, be part of seeing people change – they have a vision, and it is perhaps difficult to say 'no' – but I suppose this is the same everywhere in academia. For some reason men are better at saying 'no' to things that are fun, and say 'yes' to things that get them somewhere in their career.

Another respondent stated

> I'm not denying some gender thing going on, but I think it's complex. I would say that education developers I respect and have enjoyed working with have a strong sense of nurturing and co-operating with colleagues in all spheres, though this may not be explicitly stated. But I don't want to be the one to label that as feminine.

This same group were also asked about why they were attracted to work on a funded project in the first instance. Again the responses yield an insight into how people end up in education development with a desire to change things for the better.

> I had developed an interest in teacher training in higher education because of my experience as a student of 'not-so-good' teaching; and my interest in developing quality in higher education. I think in a way it was some kind of 'mission' feeling; I wanted to change the world, and this is an opportunity for me to get involved and also to learn more about the educational area.

Another replied

> I felt driven to the post by the shaping of my career in my institution. I was being driven more towards the commercial side whereas my interest lay in learning and teaching. This may say something about my own values and attitudes – giving something back.

A third respondent wrote that

> I believe there is a real strength to funded projects that bring people from different institutions and that this can bring great spin-off benefits to both the institutions and the individuals involved.

Finally we asked this group of people how they would describe their own development. Was it planned, unplanned, serendipitous? The replies received suggest that initially people enter the field somewhat accidentally.

> I initially 'fell in' to education development and didn't have a clue what it was!

> I feel as if all of this was unplanned, but I can see that I have always been drawn to the role of development of others – I get a lot of personal satisfaction from that.

What became apparent once this group of people had entered the field was that they themselves were developed in a planned way.

> My development remained largely unplanned until I began the project. Then it became more planned largely due to the influence of two members of the group. They made it explicit to me that this funded

project was an opportunity for me to develop and to begin to establish myself in this professional area.

> I think it all started for real then, when I started working in the department. And yes, I did have a plan, I wanted to work with this, I wanted to learn how to do it (be an education developer), and I wanted to teach.

It is clear from our small survey that whilst none of the projects that these people worked on had an explicit remit to develop them as an individual, that is exactly what happened. All of them are now in full-time permanent posts in European universities as education developers.

FINAL THOUGHTS

Schumacher's famous advocacy of the small as beautiful (Schumacher, 1973) has, in our view, considerable relevance to education development. Our experience of large multi-institution projects is not, on the whole, a happy one, whereas small projects involving three or four institutions with a clearly stated common purpose have been the ones that have been both most successful and enjoyable to work on. Large-scale projects can tend to siphon off considerable allocations of the project funding to the administrative maintenance of the project itself rather than its research and development activity. On the other hand a positive benefit resulting from all the projects in which we have been engaged is that all of those involved, but particularly the contract staff, have been developed themselves as a result of involvement with the project team and home institution(s).

To those who fund education development projects we would offer two recommendations. First, trust the project team. Whilst the work may not deliver exactly what was promised the results are likely to be just as useful to the community. Second, don't get hooked on dissemination. A number of commentators have analysed the relationship between new policies and implementation. Reynolds and Saunders (1985: 200) talk of the 'implementation staircase' at the various levels of which the original policy purposes get re-conceptualised and re-interpreted. Trowler (1998) also illustrates the way in which policy necessarily changes during implementation. Taylor (1999:75) points out that implementation is 'a mutually adaptive process' in which both intentions and practices change. 'Thus, cultures and traditions are also changed, and always at the local level' (p. 75). There has been so much dissemination of education development projects (particularly in the UK) in recent years that most of us are saturated with dissemination. It is often said that dissemination saves reinventing the wheel, but there is benefit to reinventing wheels. Without reinvention, or perhaps more correctly development, then the use and forms of wheels might have stagnated a long time ago. The world of education is no different.

ACKNOWLEDGEMENT

The authors would like to thank Klara Bolander, Jan McArthur, Heather McKiggan-Fee and Kathy Wiles for both the work they did on various funded projects and for taking the time to respond so thoroughly to all our questions. We would also like to thank Colin Mason of St Andrews University for his suggestions and advice in the early planning of this chapter.

11

Towards a profession of tertiary teaching: academic attitudes in Australia

Yoni Ryan, Kym Fraser and John Dearn

From an historical perspective, interest in the quality of university teaching by government, university management and the public, as evidenced, for example, in the West Report in Australia (1998), and the Dearing Report in the UK (1997), is not surprising.

Until the late nineteenth century, teaching was conceived of as the major function of the university, but the export of 'the German model' of research and teaching (Coaldrake and Stedman 1999) to the UK and the USA led to research being seen as the *sine qua non* of a university. From the twentieth century a university's reputation was determined largely by its research profile in 'traditional' disciplinary areas, resulting in the emergence of a university 'elite': in Australia, 'the Group of Eight' (Go8), in the UK, the 'Russell Group'.

By the latter half of the twentieth century, research success as measured by publications and grants had become the primary determinant of promotion and success for academic staff, at least from the perspective of staff themselves. Almost every analysis of staff perceptions towards research and teaching duties in universities attests to this perception (Ramsden *et al.* 1995; McInnes 1999). The research dimension of the academic role has become dominant over the teaching dimension, entry to the profession being determined by a specialised and high-level entry qualification (the masters, and preferably the PhD) in a disciplinary area, ongoing professional development in the discipline (conference attendance), and scrutiny by one's peers (through the process of peer review of publications).

However, the advent of mass participation in higher education in the developed world in the 1960s and more dramatically again in the 1980s and 1990s, shifted the actual activities of academics towards teaching in all but a small number of these elite institutions. Large numbers[1] of students not only put immense pressure on a system (the lecture/ laboratory/tutorial model) designed for a smaller student population, but also opened the university to greater scrutiny from government funding bodies, and more recently, to the new 'funding bodies', students and their parents.

During the 1990s, further expansion of the higher education system, along with the advent of technological innovations such as learning management systems which require academics to enter grades and unit[2] information, along with cuts in public funding, broadened the academic role to include administrative tasks previously undertaken by 'general' staff, leading to the 'blurring of borders' between academic and administrative staff noted by Coaldrake and Stedman (1999).

In an era of quality assurance, public scrutiny has put pressure on higher education systems to focus more on assuring the quality of teaching, and to question whether the indicators of research professionalism such as a PhD are relevant to teaching professionalism. Can the possession of a PhD be taken as a proxy for teaching competence? Can all academics combine the originality of high-quality research with the time, effort, skill and flair required of the good teacher? Should all academic staff be actively engaged in research as well as teaching? And should teaching, as Boyer (1990) argued in his landmark study, be accorded a higher status than it had been in the late twentieth-century university, and assume a specialised role, as one of four types of scholarship engaged in by the modern academic?

Clearly, academic roles today are multi-faceted, incorporating more management tasks (coordinating sessional[3] staff, reporting on quality assurance processes, etc.). It is also clear that a minority of staff (certainly if sessional staff are included) are research-active. Ramsden (1998a) reports that in Australia, 80 per cent of publications are produced by 40 per cent of academic staff; and 50 per cent of publications are produced by only 14 per cent of staff. There are moves in both the UK and Australia which will further reduce the requirements on universities to contribute to research. Indeed, worldwide, the uncoupling of the dual teaching and research functions of the academic role is gathering pace, as university managers seek efficiencies in a massified higher education sector: see for example, proposals for the French system (Belloc 2003). 'Teaching-only' institutions are likely to become common, as there is little evidence to support the importance of the 'teaching–research nexus' at the level of the individual academic (Hattie and Marsh 1996; Smeby 1998). Given the figures above, and the casualisation of the academic workforce (estimated at 25 per cent of equivalent full-time staff by the National Tertiary Education Union in 2003 in Australia), government, university management and academics themselves have a compelling interest in raising the profile and status of teaching. This would suggest that professionalisation of the teaching role is urgently needed.

PROFESSIONALISATION

Two commonly accepted characteristics of a profession are a degree of autonomy in professional practice (within the broader ethical framework of acting in the public interest), and self-regulation by a professional body (Boreham *et al.* 1976). Autonomy in pursuing personal research interests, and in determining curricula within one's disciplinary specialism, has long been a characteristic of the academic role, although Altbach (1995) is one of many noting a tendency towards dilution of that autonomy through commercialisation of research, reduced funding for research, and increasing regulatory control of university governance processes. The Gillespie and Walsh (2000) study of stress levels in Australian universities also reflects a loss of autonomy as one of the factors leading to increased stress levels amongst academics; see also the Winefield Report (2001).

However, unlike most professions, a professional body spanning universities and dedicated to self-regulation has not emerged in respect of university teaching in any western country. The largest university-oriented professional bodies tend to be industrial bodies working for the benefit of members' pay rates and conditions, such as the US American Association of University Teachers (AAUT), or the UK's National Association of Teachers in Further and Higher Education (NATFHE) and the Association of University Teachers (AUT) or the National Tertiary Education Union (NTEU) in Australia.

In Australia, the peak body dedicated to improving teaching and learning in universities, the Higher Education Research Society for Australasia (HERDSA), had a small membership of 872 in 2003 from a total population of university academics of over 82,000 full-time equivalent staff. HERDSA consistently attracts more education developers than faculty-based staff. It has made a number of attempts to initiate debate on the professionalisation of university teaching through accreditation, but has not pursued the matter with its membership or through taking a position in various government inquiries into university teaching. In 2003, the society introduced a HERDSA Fellowship Professional Recognition and Development Scheme based on teaching portfolios to recognise staff who demonstrate good teaching against a set of standards-based criteria. It is noteworthy that of the ten inaugural fellows awarded in 2003, five were faculty academics, four were education developers and one a manager (*Herdsa News*, 25(2) 2003: 1–2).

In the UK, as early as the 1960s the Robbins' review of higher education reported that '… the emphasis on research in the universities is excessive, and that university teachers devote too much time and energy to their personal research to the detriment of their teaching' (Robbins Committee on Higher Education 1963: 181). Bamber (2002) discusses the reasons that the recommendations of the Robbins review did not lead to significant change in the UK. It was not until the 1990s that the professionalisation of university of teaching has progressed in the UK. This has been as a result of the work of the long-established Staff and Education Development Association (SEDA) and more recently through the establishment of the Institute for Learning and Teaching (ILT) and the Learning and Teaching Support Network (LTSN), following the Dearing recommendations of 1997. ILT (now ILTHE) claims 14,000 individual members (HEFCE Press Release, 2003) or 14 per cent of eligible UK academics (DES 2003: 15), and has accredited 133 staff development programs at 107 UK universities (of a possible 116 UK universities, Universities UK 'Higher education in facts and figures'). In early 2003, the British government proposed the amalgamation of ILTHE, the LTSN, and the management-focused Higher Education Staff Development Agency (HESDA) to form a single teaching and learning body, the Academy for the Advancement of Learning and Teaching in Higher Education, which would take responsibility for accrediting staff development programs, and would also accredit all new university staff, from 2004 (HEFCE 2003). Responses from university staff have not been uniformly enthusiastic, the most common objection being that such moves will exacerbate the growing trend to further differentiate researchers from teachers.

Why has there been so little support for professionalisation of the teaching role in Australia? And why is there such limited success in attracting staff to gaining accreditation as teaching professionals via the ILTHE and SEDA programs in the UK?

Any debate over professionalising higher education teaching would appear to have a compelling logic and inevitability. As primary and then secondary education became compulsory in the west, regulatory requirements were introduced to validate the ability of teachers in discipline knowledge and pedagogical knowledge and skills. School teachers themselves supported specialised training as a pre-entry marker to the profession, and in some jurisdictions, such as Queensland in Australia, a registration process which required regular renewal of registration through evidence of in-service training. Victoria introduced compulsory registration via its Institute of Teaching in 2003. Such in-service training is tied into industrial agreements. (It is only in the last decade in the US and the UK that teacher shortages induced by the perceived unattractiveness of the profession in government schools have led to relaxation of regulatory entry requirements and 'fast-track' teacher training.)

As we have seen, there has been no equivalent move to professionalise university teaching, even as teaching has assumed a greater proportion of the time of most academics (Altbach 1995; McInnes 1999; Coaldrake and Stedman 1999), and affects a far greater proportion of the population than ever before, with university attendance now at all-time highs in the west, and with even higher participation projected by the UK government and, in Australia, by the Australian Vice-Chancellors' Committee (AVCC). As Coaldrake and Stedman (1999: 10) note, the common understanding of a profession as involving 'specialised initial and ongoing training and external quality assurance of output (usually through peer review)', does not apply to teaching within a university. In the next section of this chapter we report on the views of Australian academics towards the professionalisation of university teaching.

ACADEMIC ATTITUDES IN AUSTRALIA

As part of a 2002 Department of Education, Science and Training (DEST) sponsored research study (Dearn *et al.* 2002), we collected data on how Australian universities prepared and developed staff for teaching and learning. We also sought to discover the attitudes of academics and university peak bodies to accreditation of teaching. Diffidence towards professionalisation of the tertiary teaching role and particularly towards a mandated teaching qualification were the most interesting results of the research.

This section of the chapter refers to focus group data gathered in that project. Focus groups were held with experienced, inexperienced and sessional teachers in a broadly representative sample of the Australian higher education sector. The sample included universities from the Australian Technology Network (ATN) and the Group of 8 as well as a regional university and a new university. There was no attempt to mirror the proportions of staff in particular categories (i.e. sessional staff), or different levels of staff, nor were focus group staff controlled for gender representation (coincidentally, the majority of staff interviewed were female). Staff came from a wide variety of disciplines.

The 13 focus groups consisted of six groups of experienced academics, four groups of inexperienced academics (conceived as having taught in universities for less than three years), two groups of inexperienced and part-time academics, and one group of sessional academics. Group sizes ranged from 2 to 15 with a total of 59 academics involved in the focus groups. All of the interviews and focus groups were audio recorded and the tapes transcribed. All transcripts were analysed for themes and patterns of responses between the transcripts. Quotes were extracted to support and contradict themes. The focus groups were asked seven questions. This section draws on responses to five of those questions and these are included at the end of the chapter. Quotes used to illustrate the themes are representative of the comments made by the focus groups. At the end of each quote, the type of focus group the quote is drawn from is indicated, e.g. 'experienced'.

Responses to the questions were often mixed within groups as individuals brought to the discussions different opinions, beliefs and perspectives. A range of issues and concerns were raised both in support of 'teacher education' and in the rejection of 'teacher education'. An analysis of the data identified five themes. These themes were reiterated across groups and are:

1   university teaching as a profession;

2   standards of and support for university teaching;

3   current reward structures, workload and resources;

4   the multifaceted nature of the academic role; and

5   models of teaching development.

Each of these themes will be explored in the rest of this chapter.

University teaching as a profession

Both experienced and inexperienced academics in the main expressed the belief that university teaching is indeed a profession. They perceived that there exists an inherent contradiction when universities provide an education and a qualification for other professions, including primary and secondary teachers, but not for university teachers.

> You can't be a lawyer, you can't be an accountant, you can't be really any other profession without actually saying 'I've gone along to uni, I've done all those things, I've passed, now I want a job in your area' …
>
> (Experienced teacher)

Some academics expressed the view that as with any profession, university teachers need to stay up to date by engaging in continuing professional development related to their teaching. Two sessional groups believed that while these opportunities needed to be available, they needed to be optional, with sessional staff paid for their time.

> Anyone in any job in forty years … can't possibly stay fresh [for] forty years and believe in themselves 100 per cent.
>
> (Experienced teacher)

> I think it [regular revalidation of teaching] is essential. The profession is open for criticism … because of its inability to define its own sense of excellence.
>
> (Inexperienced teacher)

> For instance, university lecturers do two basic things. They teach and they research. Research is peer reviewed, teaching is not.
>
> (Inexperienced teacher)

Other focus group members did not perceive that a qualification was of interest to academic staff and some believed that not all academics wanted to teach.

> The idea of formal teacher training, i.e.: people going and getting Masters of Education or Grad. Certs. in higher education or tertiary teaching is not an issue that I think higher ed staff are so interested in.
>
> (Experienced teacher)

> I mean it is possible to get the qualification and say 'yes I've got my piece of paper that says I have done a graduate diploma in higher education or whatever' but that is not going to take away from the fact that there are academics that would rather be doing research than teaching and put more effort into that area than another.
>
> (Inexperienced teacher)

Not all focus group members saw themselves as 'university teachers' and some questioned whether academia is a profession.

> When you say we spend most of our time teaching, it's true we do, but I am not a teacher. I'm a historian who teaches because I am thinking and analysing as a historian and imparting that to others .... If you just talk about it as a teacher it is as if somehow we spend a lot of our time doing something for which a lot of people seem to think we ought to have specific skills or specific training but there is something that seems to me dangerously content void in that approach, in that way of representing what it is that I do as an academic teacher.
>
> (Experienced teacher)

> I think it revolves around 'are we a profession anyway?' and I think there's a whole issue about 'who are we?' ... I think that there is a real issue around what is an academic's job.
>
> (Experienced teacher)

Standards of and support for university teaching

The reasons focus group members gave for making teaching development compulsory included the need for clear standards, staff support (especially for inexperienced teaching staff), improving staff confidence and morale, and that doing so would demonstrate that institutions truly valued teaching.

Support

I have been at [...] for 22 years and in that time I don't think anyone has offered any help or advice to me individually.... In my experience the attitude of the university in developing teaching skills is simply like head in the sand and hope that nothing goes wrong.

(Experienced teacher)

In my case I was thrown into it here. I had an enormous class, no one told me what to do. I practised on students for three years, nobody told me about content, nobody told me what second years knew and what second years didn't know ... I would have saved at least one year's worth of students a lot of trauma if somebody had just told me all of those basic things.

(Experienced teacher)

It is fine for governments and Deputy Vice-Chancellors to make these glowing statements about the importance of teaching but it doesn't filter down to the departmental level where a significant amount of your own personal time [is invested in] improving teaching materials and things like this. You do not get a positive response.

(Experienced teacher)

There's no preparation for part-timers. There needs to be a course before university starts, and people should be paid to come. It's not content we want; it's skills and processes.

(Inexperienced and part-time teacher)

Standards/quality

In terms of quality, yes absolutely. They should [provide compulsory teacher education]. There is a responsibility toward the students to be providing people who know what they are doing. One of the things that shocked me as a student coming into the university was how hit and miss it all is. You would expect tertiary education to be presenting you with people who are at least as well trained as in secondary education and perhaps even more so. And it doesn't! You know, you are taught by third year students.

(Sessional teacher)

I have had some pretty awful teachers at university level.

(Inexperienced teacher)

I went into the person that I was tutoring for and said 'look, what do I do?' And their response was 'it's your tute, do whatever you like'. That was my absolute total training for tutorials and for my first lecture I ever gave.

(Experienced teacher)

I mean for us it boiled down to two quite simple questions, the answers aren't easy but the questions are. One is 'how do you know when these people [sessional staff] that we're employing have the skills that are required to [teach]?' And the second one is, 'if they don't, … what do you do about them?' And rather than simply say 'both of those are too hard' it seems to me we should be making some kind of effort to addressing them.

(Experienced teacher)

Valuing teaching

Making it mandatory may be the only way to increase the profile of teaching. Sometimes legislation does change culture over a period of time. If your legislators say that from now on university teachers must be able to demonstrate competency, eventually the value of teaching will improve.

(Experienced teacher)

But we give people six months for sabbatical leave to help them with their research and everybody considers that quite legitimate and the thing one should do. The idea we're talking about now, we shouldn't go much more than two or three weeks [per year] if we're going to talk about teaching, it comes back to continuing to devalue the teaching side. Universities devalue teaching and unless something is done, unless there's some policy brought in that actually starts to change that perception, we're going to be sitting around having the same conversation in ten years' time…

(Experienced teacher)

If I was doing research, my top priority was research, I could let my teaching slip right down, take all the time I want for research and just kick in the minimal amount of teaching which is what some academic staff do and I could be a really bad teacher …

(Experienced teacher)

Rewards, workload, staffing and resources

Workloads and a lack of resources were seen as key impediments to academics devoting time to the development of their teaching. In an already stretched sector where academics average over 49-hour working weeks (McInnes 1999), academics did not support adding teaching development on top of their already heavy workload. Many focus group members expressed the belief that the development of sessional staff was particularly problematic. There is a perception (supported by the Australian University Teaching Committee, Sessional Teaching Project), that part-timers' involvement in teaching development would need paid attendance and that there was not the capacity within the sector to resource that. One sessional staff member raised the question 'If a sessional staff member teaches three hours a week, how much investment in their teaching should [the university] put into them?'

> I would be interested [in teaching development] but given the savage staff cuts in the humanities I am grossly overworked ...
>
> (Experienced teacher)

> I work with a number of casual tutors and they are extraordinarily committed people but the level of work they are required to do and the complete vacuum in which they are expected to do it [makes it hard]. I think the fact that they don't get paid for any sort of supervision or support is really significant. I meet regularly with my tutors but they don't get paid for that. They are doing it in their own time, they often have other jobs, other commitments, and yet they will meet with me for a couple of hours because they desperately want support and supervision in the system, but there is no capacity to pay them apparently, absolutely no induction program.
>
> (Inexperienced teacher)

> ... good teaching like any other activity ... requires time, all of this requires time and the time is just not there.
>
> (Experienced teacher)

> In terms of how effective the current form [of teaching development] is I don't think it's very effective at all. One of the reasons is ... there is no recognition in workloads ... and the assumption that one does this in the evenings or in the weekends, I don't think applies to academics because quite frankly that's when we do our research.
>
> (Experienced teacher)

University systems were perceived by the vast majority of the focus group members to reward research, and therefore time devoted to improving teaching was seen to be both unrewarded and unsupported.

> When I look at the criteria for example if I go for a promotion, one of the things to be counted is the number of papers I have published ... If you want to get good teachers then I suggest you have got to lower research as an entry bar into lecturing at university and that is exactly the opposite of the recent output I have heard from the people here. I don't mind. I actually came here to do research. I did not come here to do teaching.
>
> (Inexperienced teacher)

Some focus group members concluded that teaching development needed to be optional because of recruiting and staffing difficulties in their disciplines. In some disciplines, finding sessional staff was particularly difficult. A requirement for teaching development, it was argued, would further exacerbate the situation. Often sessional staff were employed 'at the last moment', making it difficult to provide prior teaching development.

Other interviewees observed that some staff have been employed primarily to do research (e.g. 70 per cent research). Teaching development was seen as a low priority and time devoted to it took them away from the main reason for their employment. As Ryan *et al.* (2004) note 'In the UK, the Research Assessment Exercise (RAE) is clearly driving employment directions in many universities. Full page advertisements in the *Times Higher Education Supplement* for significant numbers of new chairs and professorships have become a common feature in late 2003 and early 2004, presumably to put in place research active staff in time for the next RAE.' It is difficult to argue that teaching development should take priority when departmental funding is determined primarily by research output and quality.

> We are scraping the bottom of the barrel to get enough warm bodies as it is ... requiring all our staff to be trained reduces the potential pool again.
>
> (Sessional teacher)

> We've got people [prospective staff] who will say to us 'what about this graduate certificate? I haven't got time to do that if I'm here to do research'. And we've lost very good applicants because of that. I think these people need to learn to teach. That needs to be put in perspective to what their overall role is going to be so if it's a research role ... and as a head of department that's what I would direct for them to do, develop their research, get that underway but too, at the same time

begin something in terms of learning about teaching and develop their skills there, but that's a lower priority. Three or four years time it might change.

(Experienced teacher)

I can only speak for computer science. Our poor kids are just dropped in it. It really is sink or swim … But we are so desperate for staff, and we're recruiting more and more third years, … most of our first year classes are now run by third years.

(Sessional teacher)

Multi-faceted nature of the academic role

The academic role is a multi-faceted one. At any one time research, teaching and administration are elements of the vast majority of academic roles. Community service, management and leadership are also elements of the roles of many. Some focus group members stressed the need for development in the various aspects of the academic role.

… I am quite concerned about the totality of the job, whatever the job is and it is very complex and you know it is multi-skilled and it is kind of growing and I just wondered how we are picking up the other component, and I know we are talking about teaching here but I actually think it will be better for us if we talk about an academic profession which does a whole lot of things and perhaps puts different emphasis on some of those different points in the career as part of a team and a program …

(Experienced teacher)

… we've got two professions running side by side if we are teaching, I think and we've got to give attention to that.

(Inexperienced teacher)

Our professional qualification is the higher degree and so forth. In a way what you are talking about is a kind of double profession that we have the profession of scholar but because we are teaching other scholars, or helping people to become scholars then we have to have some kind of teaching qualification established too …There used to be a quite substantial apprenticeship in the disciplines that I am familiar with because people would be a part-time tutor then a full-time tutor, Level A[4] as it is now called, though more is expected of Level A these days …

(Experienced teacher)

Models of teaching development

Many questions and possibilities were raised as to the models that might be used and the practicalities of administering a system.

> I would prefer a system [in] which the teachers themselves, as professionals, had control over the conditions of entry and the maintenance of standards in the profession.
>
> (Experienced teacher)

> The point is valid; the practicalities are pretty difficult. The Australian Psychological Society has come up with this continuous training development and it is a monster to police. You are supposed to have 20 hours of professional development each two years, of which 10 years will be acknowledged, and somebody has got to keep a register of it. You have got to go to certain things that are authorised or accredited by the APS to be acceptable and you have got to get a certificate and you have got to send this in. I haven't bothered, it is only college members at the moment but I can't imagine the difficulty of doing it, the cost of administering it.
>
> (Inexperienced teacher)

> I think it will be actually much better for us to be thinking about professional development for academics, which could be in leadership or it could be IT, it could be all of those things. Around the key tasks the key functions that academics perform – of which teaching and learning, let's face it, is a huge one. So, I don't think we would lose the emphasis, but I think it would actually make it more realistic … so I think it would be better maybe if we moved perhaps towards a professional portfolio or some system that incorporated the range of activities.
>
> (Experienced teacher)

> I do think if we were to say we are a profession and part of our professional responsibility is continuing professional development as many other professions have, there's probably some kind of a point system or something where you have many different ways of accruing the points. It could be attending workshops, it could be undertaking an action learning project, it could be many different possibilities.
>
> (Experienced teacher)

SUMMARY OF FINDINGS

Both within and across focus groups, individuals expressed contradictory beliefs. Some clearly saw university teaching as a profession and consequently acknowledged the need for both introductory and continuing professional development. Some individuals did not see themselves as 'teachers' and others questioned the notion of university teaching as a profession.

Most of the academics who took part in the study expressed concerns about the lack of support that they received when first starting to teach, and many expressed continuing concerns about the quality of university teaching generally. Some expressed concerns about the ability to attract and retain staff if teaching development became a legislated requirement.

All focus groups agreed that the sector was not resourced to support systematic institution-wide teaching development and that current workloads mitigated against undertaking professional development in this area. They also agreed that current reward structures and the primacy of research in both recruitment and promotion did not encourage academics to devote time to the development of their teaching.

The changing and multi-faceted nature of academic work was perceived as distinctly different from that of many other professions and as a consequence presented particular challenges for development of that role.

CONCLUSIONS

It would appear then, that the factors that militate against professionalisation of university teaching are strong. The implications of this for government policy in the UK and Australia are considerable, and will be discussed further below.

There is a reluctance to support a further differentiation of function between research and teaching among academic staff, notwithstanding the reality that a high proportion of academic staff in universities effectively only engage in teaching. Indeed, Australian attitudes regarding academic identity as researcher-teacher are strongly replicated in the UK (*THES* 2003a). Second, while the Australian study showed some support for the notion that new staff should participate in teaching development, there was great reluctance amongst current staff to engage in teaching development because of workload and time pressures, with many staff arguing that they had little time to even keep up with scholarship in their discipline areas. Third, there was a strong belief amongst the Australian academics that requiring sessional and part-time staff to undertake teacher training was unrealistic and could not be justified in a tight funding environment, notwithstanding a clear recognition that the proportion of sessional staff is increasing, and that they are ill-trained for their teaching role.

It is indeed difficult to professionalise a part-time workforce, unless some form of registration is required by a regulatory body as in nursing or medicine. World-wide, the numbers of part-time academics continue to increase as a proportion of all academic staff, and they are increasingly employed to teach large first- and second-year classes. In the US, it is estimated that they constitute 40 per cent of all academics (National Center for Postsecondary Improvement, 2002). Their skills in teaching are therefore critical to learning in the early years of university study.

However laudable the intentions of Australian and UK government agencies to encourage and reward good teaching through teaching awards, and through the work of the Higher Education Academy and National Institute for Learning and Teaching in Higher Education (NILTHE) in Australia, if this Australian study is any guide, only mandated and funded teaching development will alter the current situation. The British move to accredit university academics in teaching is commendable, and perhaps vital to the future credibility of academia as a profession. Yet mandating subscription to the Academy, the remit of which is to 'establish and police recognised professional standards for teachers in higher education' has raised strong opposition in UK universities, as HEFCE has found (*THES* 2003b).

Much of the recent literature on academic life and governance within universities bemoans the decline in academic autonomy and a parallel diminution of the status of 'the profession'. Ramsden (1998a: 351) for example, speaks of a shift from 'academics as professionals to academics as proletarians'; Becher and Trowler (2001: 13) note that 'the deprofessionalisation of academic work is clearly occurring' because of increased regulatory control. (It should be noted, however, that regulatory control has entered every profession, from accountancy to medicine.)

Yet in a globalised education sector, any move by one or two countries alone to professionalise university teaching through qualifications and accreditation not widely recognised outside that country would appear to be doomed. University academics have historically been globally mobile, and current pressures to 'export' education from home institutions to overseas campuses have made them more so. Just as the European Commission is encouraging the 'harmonisation' of the degree structure throughout Europe, it may prove necessary to initiate discussions on accreditation outside national boundaries, perhaps through UNESCO, which could act as a super-accreditation body for national schemes such as the UK Higher Education Academy. In any event, it is clear that individual institutions, and relevant bodies such as the Academy in the UK and the National Institute of Learning and Teaching in Australia, must address the changing reality of the academic role, and de-emphasise research activity as the hallmark of recruitment, promotion and university funding, while rigorously pursuing development needs in teaching. Our students should expect no less in the way of accreditation from their university teachers than they do from their school teachers.

APPENDIX 1

Interview questions

Focus groups were asked the following questions:

1   How effective do you think current forms of teacher education are?

2   Should universities be required to provide some form of teacher education for their teaching staff?

3   Do you think that teacher education should be compulsory for all teaching staff in universities?

4   Should some form of nationally recognised validation be required for teaching staff?

5   If so, do you think some form of formal regular revalidation should take place as is found in other professions?

NOTES

1   Between 1963 and 1997 in the UK, the number of higher education institutions 'grew from 25 universities … with 180,600 full-time students to over 170 HEIs … with more than 1.6 million students' (Bamber 2002: 435).

2   A unit refers to a unit of study and may be called a 'subject', a 'module', a 'course', etc.

3   Sessional teachers are defined as any university instructors not in tenured or permanent positions. This may include part-time tutors or demonstrators, postgraduate students or research fellows involved in part-time teaching, external people from industry or professions, clinical tutors, casually employed lecturers or any other teachers regularly employed on a course-by-course basis (Chalmers *et al.* 2002a: 1).

4   Level A refers to associate lecturers, the lowest level on the lecturer scale and traditionally this is an 'apprenticeship' for academia.

References

Akerlind, G., Newell, B., Pearson, M., and Pettigrove, M. (1993) *Responding to Changing Needs: Enhancing Teaching Practice*, Report to the Department of Employment, Education and Training, Canberra: Centre for Educational Development and Academic Methods, Australian National University.

Alexander, S., McKenzie, J. and Giessinger, H. (1998) *An Evaluation of Information Technology Projects for University Learning*, Committee for University Teaching and Staff Development Report to the Department of Employment, Education and Training. Canberra: Australian Government Publishing Service. Executive summary available online: http://www.autc.gov.au/in/in_pu_cu_ex.htm (accessed 28 January 2004).

Altbach, P. (1995) 'Problems and possibilities: the US academic profession', *Studies in Higher Education*, 20, 1: 27–44.

Andresen L. (1995) 'Accredited courses in teaching and learning', in A. Brew (ed.) *Directions in Staff Development*, Buckingham: The Society for Research into Higher Education and Open University Press.

Argyris, C. and Schön, D.A. (1978) *Organisational Learning: A Theory of Action Perspective*, Wokingham: Addison-Wesley.

Ashworth, P., Handl, G., Hole, C., Land, R., Orr, M. and Phipps, A. (2004) 'Who are "we", who are "you", who are "they"? Issues of role and identity in academic development', in Elvidge, L. (ed.) *Exploring Academic Development in Higher Education – Issues of Engagement*, Cambridge: Jill Rogers Associates.

Austin, A. (1998) 'Collegial conversation as metaphor and strategy for academic staff development', paper presented at the Links/SAAAD/SARDHE Conference, Capacity-building for quality teaching and learning in further and higher education, September, Bloemfontein, South Africa.

Australian Human Rights and Equal Opportunity Commission. Available online: http://www.hreoc.gov.au (accessed 11 February 2004).

Australian University Teaching Committee. Sessional Teaching Project (undated) 'Sessional Teaching Survey Results'. Available online: http://www.tedi.uq. edu.au/SessionalTeaching/pdfs/Lit_review/Survey_results.pdf (accessed 28 February 2004).

AVCC (Australian Vice-Chancellors' Committee) (1996) 'Exploiting information technology in higher education: an issues paper', Sydney: Australian Vice-Chancellors' Committee. Available online: http://www.avcc.edu.au/policies_ activities/information_tech_copyright/standing_committee_ information/ terms_reference/eithe.htm (accessed 5 March, 2004).

AVCC (Australian Vice-Chancellors' Committee) (1999) 'Promoting education as a major export industry', Sydney: Australian Vice-Chancellors' Committee media release. Available online: http://www.avcc.edu.au/news/public_ statements/media_releases/1999/99mr19.htm (accessed 22 February, 2004).

Badhni, S. and Aungles, P. (2002) 'The role of the Course Experience Questionnaire in quality assurance for the higher education sector', paper presented to the 'Seventh Quality in Higher Education International Seminar: Transforming Quality', October, Melbourne, Australia.

Bamber, V. (2002) 'To what extent has the Dearing policy recommendations on training new lecturers met acceptance? Where Dearing went that Robbins didn't dare', *Teaching Development*, 6, 3: 433–57.

Barnacle, R. (2002) 'Investigating part-time research students in professional work: a pilot study', report for the Research and Development Section in conjunction with the Faculty of the Constructed Environment, Melbourne: RMIT University. Available online: http://mams.rmit.edu.au/47quxo5ca2mp.pdf (last accessed 29 June 2004).

Barnett, R. (1997) *Higher Education: A Critical Business*, Buckingham: The Society for Research into Higher Education and the Open University Press.

Barnett, R., Parry, G. and Coate, K. (2001) 'Conceptualising curriculum change', *Teaching in Higher Education*, 6, 4: 435–49.

Bass, R. (1999) 'The scholarship of teaching: what's the problem?', *Inventio*, 1, 1: 1–8.

Becher, T. (1989) *Academic Tribes and Territories: Intellectual enquiry and the cultures of disciplines*, Buckingham: Society for Research into Higher Education and Open University Press.

Becher, T. and Trowler, P. (2001) *Academic Tribes and Territories: Intellectual Enquiry and the Culture of Discipline*, 2nd edn, Buckingham: Society for Research into Higher Education and Open University Press.

Bell, M., Bush, D., Nicholson, P., O'Brien, D. and Tran, T. (2002) 'Universities online: a survey of online education and services in Australia', Occasional Paper Series 02–A, Canberra: Department of Education, Science and Training. Available online: http://www.dest.gov.au/highered/occpaper/02a/02_a.pdf (accessed 26 February 2004).

Belloc, B. (2003) 'Propositions pour une modification du decret 84-431 portant des enseignants chercheurs'. Available online: http://www.education.gouv.fr/ rapport/proposition_belloc.pdf (accessed 28 February 2004).

Bender, E. and Gray, D. (1999) 'The scholarship of teaching', *Research & Creative Activity*, 22, 1. Available online: http://www.indiana.edu/%7Ercapub/v22n1/ p03.html (accessed 28 January 2004).

Benjamin, J. (1997) 'Academic staff's conceptions of and approaches to collaboration in the teaching of large first-year university courses', paper presented at the Higher Education Research and Development Society of Australasia conference, July, Adelaide, Australia.

Bennett, N. (1984) *The Quality of Pupil Learning Experiences*, London: Lawrence Erlbaum.

Bereiter, C. and Scardamalia, M. (1993) *Surpassing Ourselves*, La Salle, IL: Open Court.

Berg, B. and Östergren, B. (1979) 'Innovation processes in higher education', *Studies in Higher Education*, 4, 4: 261–8.

Berger, J. and Mohr, J. (1967) *A Fortunate Man*, London: Writers' and Readers' Co-operative.

Bergquist, W. (1992) *The Four Cultures of the Academy*, San Francisco: Jossey-Bass.

Biggs, J. (1993) 'From theory to practice: a cognitive systems approach', *Higher Education Research and Development*, 12, 1: 73–85.

Biggs, J. (1999) *Teaching for Quality Learning at University: What the Student Does*, Buckingham: Society for Research into Higher Education and Open University Press.

Birnbaum, R. (1992) *How Academic Leadership Work*, San Franciso: Jossey-Bass.

Blackmore, P., Gibbs, G. and Shrives, L. (1999) *Supporting Staff Development within Departments*, Oxford: Oxford Centre for Learning Development, Oxford Brookes University.

Bolander, K., Mason, C.,Matthew, B. and Morss, K.(2001) *Effective Lecturing: A Resource for Staff Developers*, Edinburgh: Scottish Higher Education Funding Council. Available online: http://www.gla.ac.uk/services/tls/STAFF/ras/ELPwebpage/project/index.htm.

Boreham, P., Pemberton, A. and Wilson, P. (1976) *The Professions in Australia*, Brisbane: University of Queensland Press.

Boud, D. (1995) 'Meeting the challenges', in Brew, A. (ed.) *Directions in Staff Development*, Buckingham: Society for Research in Higher Education and Open University Press.

Boud, D. (1999) 'Situating academic development in professional work: using peer learning', *International Journal for Academic Development*, 4, 1: 3–10.

Bourdieu, P. (1977) *Outline of a Theory of Practice* (trans. R. Nice), Cambridge: Cambridge University Press.

Bowden, J. and Marton, F. (1998) *The University of Learning*, London: Kogan Page.

Boyer Commission on Educating Undergraduates in the Research University (1998) *Reinventing Undergraduate Education: A Blueprint for America's Research Universities*, New York: SUNY. Available online: http://naples.cc.sunysb.edu/Pres/boyer.nsf/ (accessed 4 February 2004).

Boyer, E. (1990) *Scholarship Reconsidered, Priorities of the Professoriate*, Princeton, NJ: Carnegie Foundation for the Advancement of Teaching.

Brennan, J. and Shah, T. (2000) *Managing Quality in Higher Education: an International Perspective on Institutional Assessment and Change*, Buckingham: Open University Press.

Brew, A. (ed.) (1995) *Directions in Staff Development*, Buckingham: Society for Research in Higher Education and Open University Press.

Brew, A. (2003a) 'Teaching and research: new relationships and their implications for inquiry-based teaching and learning in higher education', *Higher Education Research and Development*, 22, 1: 3–18.

Brew, A (2003b) 'The future of research and scholarship in academic development', in H. Eggins and R. Macdonald (eds) *The Scholarship of Academic Development*, Buckingham and London: SRHE and Open University Press.

Brookfield, S. (1995) *Becoming a Critically Reflective Teacher*, San Francisco: Jossey-Bass.

Bryant, C. and Jary, D. (2001) *The Contemporary Giddens: Social Theory in a Globalizing Age*, London: Palgrave Macmillan.

Candy, P. (1994) *Developing Lifelong Learners through Undergraduate Education*, Commissioned Report No. 28 for the National Board of Employment, Education and Training, Canberra: NBEET.

Centre for Learning Enhancement and Research, The Chinese University of Hong Kong (undated). Available online: http://www.cuhk.edu.hk/clear/ (accessed 26 February 2004).

Chalmers, D., Bath, D., Hannam, R., Whelan, K., and Smeal, G. (2002a) *Training, Managing and Supporting Sessional Teachers*, Australian University Teaching Committee project. Available online: http://www.tedi.uq.edu.au/sessional teaching (accessed 14 January 2004).

Chalmers, D., Bath, D., Hannam, R., Weber, R., Macdonald, D., Bahr, N., Terry., D. and Lipp, O. (2002b) 'Teaching large classes', Australian University Teaching Committee project. Available online: http://www.tedi.uq.edu.au/largeclasses (accessed 14 January 2004).

Clark, B.R. (1996a) 'Substantive growth and innovative organisation: new categories in higher education research', *Higher Education*, 32, 4: 417–30.

Clark, B.R. (1996b) 'Diversification of higher education: viability and change', in V.L. Meek, V. Goedegebuure, O. Kivinen and R. Rinne (eds) *The Mockers and Mocked: Comparative Perspectives on Differentiation, Convergence and Diversity in Higher Education*, Oxford: Pergamon.

Clarkeburn, H., Downie, J.R. and Matthew, B. (2002) 'Impact of an ethics programme in a life sciences curriculum', *Teaching in Higher Education*, 7, 1: 65–79.

Coaldrake, P. and Stedman, L. (1999) 'Academic work in the twenty-first century: changing roles and policies', Occasional Paper Series 99H, Canberra: Australia Higher Education Division, Department of Education, Training and Youth Affairs.

Commonwealth Disability Strategy (Australia) (undated) 'Fact Sheet 2: Some facts and figures about people with disabilities in Australia'. Available online: http://www.facs.gov.au/disability/cds/fs/fs_02.htm (accessed 11 February 2004).

Connolly, W.E. (1974) *The Terms of Political Discourse*, Lexington, MA: D.C. Heath.

Cross, K. P. and Steadman, M. H. (1996) *Classroom research: Implementing the scholarship of teaching*, San Francisco: Jossey-Bass.

Cryer, P. and Elton, L. (1990) 'Catastrophe theory: a unified model for educational change', *Studies in Higher Education*, 15, 1: 75–86.

Cuban, L. (1984) *How Teachers Taught: Constancy and Change in American Classrooms 1890–1980*, New York: Longman.

Cunningham, S., Tapsall, S., Ryan, Y., Stedman, L., Flew, T. and Bagdon, K. (1998) *New Media and Borderless Education*, Report 97/22 to the Evaluations and Investigations Programme, Canberra: Department of Education, Training and Youth Affairs. Available online: http://www.dest.gov.au/archive/highered/eippubs/eip97-22/eip9722.pdf (accessed 26 February 2004).

Cunningham, S., Ryan, Y., Stedman, L., Tapsall, S., Bagdon, K., Flew, T. and Coaldrake, P. (2000) *The Business of Borderless Education*, Report 00/3 to the Evaluations and Investigations Programme, Canberra: Department of Education, Training and Youth Affairs. Available online: http://www.dest.gov.au/archive/highered/eippubs/eip00_3/bbe.pdf (accessed 26 February 2004).

Daniels, C. (1998) 'Quality assessment: Cardiff University of Wales, United Kingdom', case study conducted for the OECD (in Brennan and Shah, *Managing Quality in Higher Education: an International Perspective on Institutional Assessment and Change*, Buckingham: Open University Press.). Available online: http://www.oecd.org/dataoecd/49/22/1871497.pdf (accessed 19 October 2003).

Data Protection Act 1998 (UK). Available online: http://www.legislation.hmso.gov.uk/acts/acts1998/19980029.htm (accessed 11 February 2004).

Dearing, R. (1997) *The National Committee of the Inquiry in Higher Education Report*, to Secretaries of State for Education and Employment, Wales, Scotland and Northern Ireland. Available online: http://www.leeds.ac.uk/educol/ncihe/sumrep.htm (accessed 11 February 2004).

Dearn, J., Fraser, K. and Ryan, Y. (2002) *Investigation into the Provision of Professional Development for University Teaching in Australia: A Discussion Paper*, a report to the Higher Education Innovations Programme, Department of Education, Science and Training, Canberra: Department of Education, Science and Training.

de la Harpe, B. and Radloff, A. (2000) 'Supporting generic skill development: reflections on providing professional development for academic staff', in *Refereed Proceedings of the Lifelong Learning Conference*, Yeppoon, Queensland: Central Queensland University.

de la Harpe, B. and Radloff, A. (2001) 'Learning to be strategic about helping staff to increase graduate employability', in C. Rust (ed.) *Improving Student Learning: Improving Student Learning Strategically*, Oxford: The Oxford Centre for Staff Development, Oxford Brookes University.

de la Harpe, B. and Radloff, A. (2002) 'From practice to theory in developing generic skills', paper presented at the 10th Improving Student Learning International Symposium, September, Brussels, Belgium.

de la Mare, W. (1913) *Peacock Pie*, London: Constable.

Delanty, G. (2001) *Challenging Knowledge: The University in the Knowledge Society*, Buckingham: The Society for Research into Higher Education and the Open University Press.

Department of Education, Science and Training (undated) 'Equity Groups as a share of non-overseas students 1992–2000'. Available online: http://www.dest.gov.au/archive/highered/statistics/characteristics/tables/9.xls (accessed 11 February 2004).

Department of Education, Science and Training (2003) *Higher Education Statistics on Student*. Available online: http://www.dest.gov.au/highered/statpubs.htm#studpubs (accessed 20 May 2003).

Department of Health and Social Security, National Statistics (undated) 'Survey of adults with a disability in the UK population'. Available online: http://www.statistics.gov.uk/STATBASE/Product.asp?vlnk=8008 (accessed 11 February 2004).

DfES (Department for Education and Skills) (2003) *The Future of Higher Education*, (referred to as 'the White Paper'), London: DfES. Available online: http://www.dfes.gov.uk/highereducation/hestrategy/foreword.shtml (accessed 11 February 2004).

Dill, D.D. (1993) 'Quality by design: toward a framework for academic quality management', *Higher Education: A Handbook of Theory and Research Vol VIII*, New York: Agathon Press.

Dill, D.D. (1999) 'Academic accountability and university adaptation: The architecture of an academic learning organisation', *Higher Education*, 38, 2: 127–54.

Disability Discrimination Act 1992. Available online: http://scaleplus.law.gov.au/html/pasteact/0/311/top.htm (accessed 28 July 2004).

Disability Discrimination Act – UK: 'Special Educational Needs and Disability Act'. Available online: http://www.natdisteam.ac.uk/resources_knowledge_SEN.html (accessed 11 February 2004).

Disability Rights Commission (undated a) 'Codes of practice'. Available online: http://www.drc.org.uk/thelaw/practice.asp (accessed 22 July 2004).

Disability Rights Commission (undated b) 'A range of good practice guides'. Available online: http://www.skill.org.uk/info/drc-guides/index.asp (accessed 22 July 2004).

Downey, J. (1995) 'The university as trinity: balancing corporation, collegium and community'. Louise McBee Lecture, The University of Georgia , Institute of Higher Education. Available online: http://www.uga.edu/ihe/lectures/Downey.pdf (accessed 26 February 2004).

Draper, S., Cargill, J. and Cutts, Q. (2002) 'Electronically enhanced classroom interaction', *Australian Journal of Educational Technology*, 18, 1: 13–23.

Dunkerley, D. and Wong, W. (2001) *Global Perspectives on Quality in Higher Education*, Aldershot: Ashgate.

Ecclestone, K. (1996) 'The reflective practitioner: mantra or model for emancipation?', *Studies in the Education of Adults*, 28, 2: 146–61.

Elton, L. (1987) *Teaching in Higher Education: Appraisal and Training*, London: Kogan Page.

Elvidge, L. (ed.) (2004) *Exploring Academic Development in Higher Education: Issues of Engagement*, Cambridge: Jill Rogers Associates.

Emery, M. and Purser, R.E. (1996) *The Search Conference: A Powerful Method for Planning Organizational Change and Community Action*, San Francisco: Jossey-Bass.

ETL (Enhancing Teaching–Learning) (2003) Economics and Social Research Council project, 'Enhancing teaching–learning environments in undergraduate courses'. Available online: http://www.ed.ac.uk/etl/project.html#overall purpose (accessed 29 February, 2004).

Flexner, A. (1930 [1968]) *Universities: American, English, German*, London: Oxford University Press.

Fraser, K. (2001) 'Australasian academic developers' conceptions of the profession', *The International Journal for Academic Development*, 6, 1: 54–64.

Frielick, S. (2002) 'Adventures in the zone of educational development', paper presented at International Consortium for Educational Development (ICED) Conference, July, Perth.

Fry, H., Hewes, I., Kiley, M., Marincovich, M., Meyer, J.H.F., Pearson, M., Way, D. (2004) 'Conceptual frameworks in action', in L. Elvidge (ed.) (2004) *Exploring Academic Development in Higher Education – Issues of Engagement*, Cambridge: Jill Rogers Associates.

Fullan, M. (1993) *Change Forces: Probing the Depths of Educational Reform*, London: The Falmer Press.

Gibbs, G. (1995) 'Changing lecturers' conceptions of teaching and learning through action research', in A. Brew (ed.) *Directions in Staff Development*, Buckingham: Society for Research in Higher Education and Open University Press.

Gibbs, G. (2001) *Analysis of Strategies for Learning and Teaching*, Research Report 01/37a to the Higher Education Funding Council for England, Bristol: HEFCE.

Gibbs, G. and Coffey, M. (2000) 'What is training of university teachers attempting to achieve, and how could we tell if it makes any difference?', paper presented at the International Consortium for Educational Development Conference, July, University of Bielefeld.

Gibbs, G. and Coffey, M. (2001) 'The impact of training on university teachers' approaches to teaching and on the way their students learn', paper presented at the European Association for Research on Learning and Instruction Conference, August, Freibourg, Switzerland.

Giddens, A. (1984) *The Constitution of Society: Outline of the Theory of Structuration*, Cambridge: Polity Press.

Giddens, A. (1999) *Runaway World: How Globalisation is Reshaping our Lives*, London: Routledge.

Giddens, A. (2000) *The Third Way and its Critics*, Cambridge: Polity Press.

Gillespie, N. and Walsh, M. (2000) *Occupational Stress within Australian Universities: Staff Perceptions of the Determinants, Consequences and Moderators of Stress*, Melbourne: National Tertiary Education Union.

Gosling, D. (2003) 'Philosophical approaches to academic development', in H. Eggins and R. Macdonald (eds) *The Scholarship of Academic Development*, Buckingham: Society for Research in Higher Education and Open University Press.

Gow, L. and Kember, D. (1993) 'Conceptions of teaching and their relationship to the student learning', *British Journal of Educational Psychology*, 63, 1: 20–33.

Graduate Careers Council of Australia (1994) *The Course Experience Questionnaire*, Parkville: Graduate Careers Council of Australia.

Gray, K. and McNaught, C. (2001) 'Evaluation of achievements from collaboration in a learning technology mentoring program', in G. Kennedy, M. Keppell, C. McNaught and T. Petrovic (eds) *Meeting at the Crossroads*, proceedings of the 18th annual Australian Society for Computers in Learning in Tertiary Education 2001 Conference, 9–12 December, University of Melbourne. Available online: http://www.ascilite.org.au/conferences/melbourne01/pdf/papers/grayk.pdf (accessed 26 February 2004).

Gumport, P.J. and Puser, B. (1999) 'University restructuring: the role of economic and political contexts', in J. Smart (ed.) *Higher Education: Handbook of Theory and Research*, Vol. XIV, New York: Agathon Press.

Gumport, P.J. and Sporn, B. (1999) 'Institutional adaptation: demands for management reform and university administration', in J. Smart (ed.) *Higher Education: Handbook of Theory and Research*, Vol. XIV, New York: Agathon Press.

Habermas, J. (1991) *The Theory of Communicative Action*, Cambridge: Polity press.

Habermas, J. (2001) *The Postnational Constellation*, Cambridge, MA: MIT Press.

Hacking, I. (1999) *The Social Construction of What?*, Cambridge, MA: Harvard University Press.

Hancock, P. and Tyler, M. (2001) *Work, Postmodernism and Organization: A Critical Introduction*, Thousands Oaks, CA: Sage.

Hannan, A. and Silver, H. (2000) *Innovating in Higher Education – Teaching, Learning and Institutional Cultures*, Buckingham: Society for Research in Higher Education and Open University Press.

Hattie, J. and Marsh, H. (1996) 'The relationship between teaching and learning: a meta-analysis', *Review of Educational Research*, 66, 4: 507–42.

Hayden, M. and Speedy, G. (1995) *Evaluation of the 1993 National Teaching Development Grants*, NSW, Australia: Southern Cross University.

HEFCE (Higher Education Funding Council for England) (1995) HEFCE Circular 29/95, 'Fund for the Development of Teaching and Learning', Bristol: HEFCE.

HEFCE (Higher Education Funding Council for England) (1998a) Report 98/68, 'Evaluation of the Fund for Teaching and Learning', Bristol: HEFCE.

HEFCE (Higher Education Funding Council for England) (1998b) Report 98/47, 'An evaluation of the computers in teaching initiative and teaching and learning technology support network', Bristol: HEFCE. Available online: http://www.hefce.ac.uk/Pubs/hefce/1998/98_47.htm (accessed 8 March 2004).

HEFCE (Higher Education Funding Council for England) (1998c) Report 98/40 'Learning and teaching: strategy and funding proposals', Bristol: HEFCE.

HEFCE (Higher Education Funding Council for England) (2001) Report 01/37, 'Strategies for Learning and Teaching in Higher Education: a guide to good practice', Bristol: HEFCE.

HEFCE (Higher Education Funding Council for England) (2003) Press Release. 27 January.

HEFCE (Higher Education Funding Council for England) (undated a) 'Review of the Computers in Teaching Initiative (CTI) and the Teaching and Learning Technology Support Network (TLTSN)'. Available online: http://www.hefce.ac.uk/learning/tinits/cti/reviewof.htm (accessed 5 March 2004).

HEFCE (Higher Education Funding Council for England) (undated b) 'Widening Participation at HEFCE'. Available online: http://www.hefce.ac.uk/Widen/ (accessed 11 February 2004).

HEFCE (Higher Education Funding Council for England), Universities UK (UUK) and the Standing Conference of Principals (SCOP) (2003) *Final Report of the TQEC on the Future Needs and Support for Quality Enhancement of Learning and Teaching in Higher Education*, Bristol: HEFCE.

Heifetz, R.A. and Laurie, D.L. (1997) 'The work of leadership', *Harvard Business Review*, January–February: 124–33.

HERDSA News (Higher Education Research and Development Society of Australasia) Sydney: HERDSA. Available online: http://www.herdsa.org.au/newsletter.php (accessed 7 March 2004).

HERDSA News, 'First HERDSA Fellowships awarded', 25, 2: 1–2.

HESA (Higher Education Statistics Agency (UK)) (undated) 'Statistics on the number of students who have a disability in UK higher education institutions for 1994–2001'. Available online: http://jarmin.com/demos/course/awareness/hesa.html (accessed 11 February 2004).

Ho, A., Watkins, D. and Kelly, M. (2001) 'The conceptual change approach to improving teaching and learning: an evaluation of a Hong Kong staff development programme', *Higher Education*, 42, 2: 143–69.

Hounsell, D. (1994) 'Educational development', in J. Bocock and D. Watson (eds) *Managing the University Curriculum: Making Common Cause*, Buckingham: The Society for Research into Higher Education and Open University Press.

Hounsell, D., McCulloch, M., Scott, M., Burley, E., Day, K., Falchikov, N., Haywood, J. and Land, R. (1996) *The ASSHE Inventory: Changing Assessment Practices in Scottish Higher Education*, Sheffield: Universities' and Colleges' Staff Development Agency.

Huber, M.T. and Morreale, S.P. (eds) (2002) *Disciplinary Styles in the Scholarship of Teaching and Learning: Exploring Common Ground*, Washington, DC: American Association for Higher Education and The Carnegie Foundation for the Advancement of Teaching.

Hughes, C., Hewson, L. and Nightingale, P. (1997) 'Developing new roles and skills', in Yetton, P. and associates (eds) *Managing the Introduction of Technology in the Delivery and Administration of Higher Education*, Report 97/3 to the Evaluations and Investigations Programme, Canberra: Australian Government Publishing Service. Aavailable online: http://www.detya.gov.au/archive/highered/eippubs/eip9703/front.htm (accessed 26 February 2004 using Inspiration software, available online: http://www.inspiration.com.

Hutchings, P. and Shulman, L.S. (1999) 'The scholarship of teaching: new elaborations, new developments', *Change*, 31, 5: 10–15.

Jackson, B. and Phillips, J. (2002) *A Review of the Evaluation Reports of Recent Major Funded Initiatives Aimed at Enhancing the Quality of Learning and Teaching: The Implications of Educational Development*, LTSN Generic Centre. Available online: http://www.ltsn.ac.uk/application.asp?app=resources.asp&process=full_record&section=generic&id=34 (accessed 15 February 04).

Jenkins, A. (1996) 'Discipline-based educational development', *International Journal for Higher Education*, 1, 1: 50–62.

Johnston, S. (1996) 'What can we learn about teaching from our best university teachers?', *Teaching in Higher Education*, 1, 2: 213–25.

Johnston, S. (1997) 'Educational development units: aiming for a balanced approach to supporting teaching', *Higher Education Research and Development*, 16, 3: 331–42.

Katz, L.F. (1999) 'Technological change, computerization, and the wage structure', paper presented at the 'Understanding the Digital Economy: Data, Tools and Research' Conference, May, Washington, DC. Available online: http://post.economics.harvard.edu/faculty/katz/papers/lkdig2.pdf (accessed 5 March 2004).

Kayrooz, C., Pearson, M. and Quinlan, K. (1997) 'Development from within academe: eschewing imperialism, managerialism and missionary zeal', *International Journal for Academic Development*, 2, 2: 64–71.

Kember, D. (1997) 'A reconceptualisation of the research into university academics' conceptions of teaching', *Learning and Instruction*, 7, 3: 255–75.

Kember, D. (1998) 'Teaching beliefs and their impact on students' approach to learning', in B. Dart and G. Boulton-Lewis (eds), *Teaching and Learning in Higher Education*, Camberwell, Victoria: Australian Council for Education Research Press.

Kember, D. (2000) *Action Learning and Action Research: Improving the Quality of Teaching and Learning*, London: Kogan Page.

Kember, D. and McKay, J. (1996) 'Action research into the quality of student learning: a paradigm for faculty development', *Journal of Higher Education*, 67, 5: 528–54.

Kerr, C. (1991) *The Great Transformation in Higher Education 1960–1980*, Albany, NY: State University of New York Press.

Kerr, C. (2001) *The Uses of the University* (5th edn), Cambridge, MA: Harvard University Press.

Kirkpatrick, D. (1998) *Evaluating Training Programs*, New York: Berrett-Koehler.

Knight, P.T. (2002) *Being a Teacher in Higher Education*, Buckingham: The Society for Research into Higher Education and the Open University Press.

Knight, P.T. and Trowler, P.R. (2001) *Departmental Leadership in Higher Education*, Buckingham: The Society for Research into Higher Education and Open University Press.

Kotter, J.P. (1990) 'What leaders really do', *Harvard Business Review*, May–June: 103–11.

Kotter, J.P. (1996). *Leading Change*, Boston, MA: Harvard Business School Press.

Land, R. (2001) 'Agency, context and change in academic development', *The International Journey for Academic Development*, 6, 1: 4–20.

Land, R. and McArthur, J. (2003) 'PROMOTE – issues of reward and recognition in educational development', *Educational Developments*, 4, 2: 1–4.

Lash, S. and Urry, J. (1994) *Economies of Signs and Space*, Thousands Oaks, CA: Sage.

Light, G. and Cox, R. (2001) *Learning and Teaching in Higher Education: The Reflective Professional*, London: Paul Chapman Publishing.

Lines, R. (2002) 'Capabilities as a framework for program design: reflections on the design of a Bachelor of Commerce', in M. Kalantzis, G. Varnava-Skoura and B. Cope (eds) *Learning for the Future*. Common Ground Publishing. Available online: http://learningconference.Publisher-Site.com/ProductShop (accessed 5 June 2003).

LSTN (Learning and Teaching Support Network) (2002) 'Evaluating the Learning and Teaching Support Network: from awareness to adaptation', Deliverable D10. Second Annual Report to the LTSN Executive (2002).

Macdonald, R. (2003) 'Developing a scholarship of academic development: setting the context', in H. Eggins and R. Macdonald (eds) *The Scholarship of Academic Development*, Buckingham: Society for Research in Higher Education and Open University Press.

Macdonald, R. and Wisdom, J. (2002) *Academic and Educational Development: Research, Evaluation and Changing Practice in Higher Education*, London: Kogan Page.

McGill, I. and Beaty, L. (1995) *Action Learning: A Guide for Professional, Management and Educational Development*, London: Kogan Page.

McInnes, C. (1999) 'The work roles of academics in Australian universities', Evaluations and Investigations Programme, Canberra: Higher Education Division: Department of Education, Training and Youth Affairs. Available online: http://www.dest.gov.au/archive/highered/eippubs/eip00_5/fullcopy.pdf (accessed 27 January, 2004).

McKeachie, W. (1997) 'Critical elements in training university teachers', *International Journal of Academic Development*, 2, 1: 67–74.

McNaught, C. (2001a) 'Views on staff development about flexible learning', in C. Steeples and C. Jones (eds) *Networked Learning: Perspectives and Issues*, London: Springer.

McNaught, C. (2001b) 'Quality assurance for online courses: from policy to process to improvement?', in G. Kennedy, M. Keppell, C. McNaught and T. Petrovic (eds) *Meeting at the Crossroads*, Proceedings of the 18th annual Australian Society for Computers in Learning in Tertiary Education 2001 conference, December, Melbourne. Available online: http://www.ascilite.org.au/conferences/melbourne01/pdf/papers/mcnaughtc.pdf (accessed 26 February 2004).

McNaught, C. (2003) 'The effectiveness of an institution-wide mentoring program for improving online teaching and learning', *Journal of Computing in Higher Education*, 15, 1: 27–45.

McNaught, C., Phillips, P., Rossiter, D. and Winn, J. (2000) 'Developing a framework for a usable and useful inventory of computer-facilitated learning and support materials in Australian universities', Report 99/11 to the Evaluations and Investigations Programme, Canberra: Higher Education Division, Department of Employment, Education, Training and Youth Affairs. Available online: http://www.detya.gov.au/highered/eippubs.htm#99_11 (accessed 26 February 2004).

McNay, I. (1995) 'From the collegial academy to corporate enterprise: The changing cultures of universities', in T. Schuller (ed.) *The Changing University*, Buckingham: Society for Research into Higher Education and Open University Press.

Marginson, S. and Considine, M. (2000) *The Enterprise University: Power, Governance and Reinvention in Australia*, Cambridge: Cambridge University Press.

Marshall, S.J., Adams, M.J., Cameron, A. and Sullivan, G. (2000) ' "Academics" perceptions of their professional development needs related to leadership and management: What can we learn?', *International Journal for Academic Development*, 5: 42–53.

Martin, E. (1999) *Changing Academic Work: Developing the Learning University*, Buckingham: Open University Press.

Marton, F. and Booth, S. (1997) *Learning and Awareness*, Mahwah, NJ: Lawrence Erlbaum and Associates.

Marton, F. and Saljo, R. (1976) 'On qualitative differences in learning 1: outcome and process', *British Journal of Educational Psychology*, 46: 4–11.

Massy, W.F. and Zemsky, R. (1995) *Using Information Technology to Enhance Academic Productivity*, Occasional Paper, Washington, DC: Educom.

Middlehurst, R. (1993) *Leading Academics*, Buckingham: Society for Research into Higher Education and Open University Press.

Millar, C. (1991) 'Critical reflection for educators of adults: getting a grip on the scripts for professional action', *Studies in Continuing Education*, 13, 1: 15–23.

Mintzberg, H. (1980) *The Nature of Managerial Work*, Englewood Cliffs, NJ: Prentice-Hall.

Mintzberg, H. (1994) *The Rise and Fall of Strategic Planning*, New York: Prentice-Hall.

Monash University Disability Liaison Unit. website (undated). Available online: http://www.adm.monash.edu.au/sss/pc/equity/dlu/ (accessed 11 February 2004).

Moodie, G. (2002) 'Fish or fowl? Collegial processes in managerialist institutions', *Australian Universities Review*, 45, 2: 18–22.

Moses, I. and Roe, E. (1990) *Heads and Chairs*, Brisbane: Queensland University Press.

Murphy, D. Edwards, H., Jamieson, P. and Webb, G.(2000) 'Becoming flexible: changing academic staff development', paper presented at the Australian Society for Educational Technology/Higher Education Research and Development Society of Australasia conference, July, Toowoomba, Australia.

Murphy, J. (1994) ' Improving the effectiveness of educational development: concerns, constraints and recommendations', *Higher Education Research and Development*, 13, 2: 213–30.

Murphy, R. (2003) 'The use of research and development projects in higher education', in H. Eggins and R. Macdonald (eds) *The Scholarship of Academic Development*, Buckingham: Society for Research into Higher Education and Open University Press.

National Center for Postsecondary Improvement (2002) *Beyond Dead Reckoning: Research Priorities for Redirecting American Higher Education*, Stanford, CA: Stanford University. Available online:: http://siher.stanford.edu (accessed 19 December 2002).

National Committee of Inquiry into Higher Education (1997) *National Committee of Inquiry into Higher Education and the Learning Society*, London: NCIHE.

National Foundation for Educational Research (1991) *Second Year National Evaluation of EHEI (Enterprise in Higher Education Initiative)*, Slough: NFER.

Nelson, B. (2003) *Our Universities: Backing Australia's Future*, Canberra: Commonwealth of Australia.

Nicholls, G. (2001*) Professional Development in Higher Education: New Dimensions and Directions*, London: Kogan Page.

Nicolettou, A. and Wright, S. (2002) 'Project intrepid – a learner-centred approach to professional development', paper presented at the Higher Education Research and Development Society of Australasia conference, July, Perth, Australia.

Nightingale, P. (1987) 'Multiple and conflicting expectations of "units" of higher education', *Programmed Learning and Educational Technology*, 24, 1: 55–61.

O'Brien, M. (2004) 'Understanding knowledge for the development of curriculum', unpublished PhD thesis, Griffth University.

Palmer, J. (2001) *Fifty Modern Thinkers on Education*, London: Routledge.

Parker, S. (1997) *Reflective Teaching in the Postmodern World*, Buckingham: Open University Press.

Parker, L., Goodell, J., Radloff, A., Kulski, T. and Butorac, A. (1998) 'Devolved academic staff development: successful initiatives at Curtin University', symposium presented at the International Consortium for Educational Developers (ICED) Conference, April, Austin, TX.

Partington, P. and Stainton, C. (2003) *Managing Staff Development*, Buckingham: Open University Press.

Patrick, K. (2003) 'The CEQ in practice: using the CEQ for improvement', paper presented at the Graduate Careers Council of Australia symposium: 'Graduates, Outcomes, Quality and the Future', March, Canberra, Australia.

Patrick, K., Lines, R., Joosten, V., Watts, R. and Weisz, M. (2002) 'Quality and innovation in university education: synergy or contradiction?', paper presented to the Seventh Quality in Higher Education International Seminar, Transforming Quality, Melbourne, Australia, October 2002.

Pearson, M. (1983) 'Approaches to individualising instruction: a review', *Higher Education Research and Development*, 2, 2: 155–81.

Pearson, M. (1996) 'Strategic and systematic university leadership and management development – what are the issues?', in S. Leong and D. Kirkpatrick (eds) *Different Approaches: Theory and Practice in Higher Education*, Proceedings of Higher Education Research and Development Society of Australasia Annual Conference, Perth: HERDSA.

Pearson, M. (1998) 'Issues in funding and supporting projects to improve quality and encourage innovation in teaching in departments', paper presented at the International Conference on Educational Development, April, Austin, TX.

Pearson, M., Roberts, P., O'Shea, C. and Lupton, M. (2002) 'An inclusive approach to transition in a research-led university', paper presented at the 6th Pacific Rim First Year in Higher Education Conference: 'Changing Agendas', July, Christchurch, New Zealand.

Perkins, D. (2000) 'Building organisational intelligence', unpublished seminar given at Edinburgh University as adviser to the Economic and Social Research Council funded project *Enhancing Teaching-Learning Environments in Undergraduate Courses*. Available online: http://www.ed.ac.uk/etl/publications.html (accessed 5 March 2004).

Pirsig, R. (1974) *Zen and the Art of Motorcycle Maintenance: An Inquiry into Values*, London: Bodley Head.

Pitkethley, A. and Prosser, M. (2001) 'The first year experience project: a model for university-wide change', *Higher Education Research Development*, 20, 2: 185–98.

Power, M. (1997) *The Audit Society*, Oxford: Oxford University Press.

Prosser, M. and Trigwell, K. (1999) *Understanding Learning and Teaching: The Experience in Higher Education*, Buckingham: Open University Press.

QAAHE (Quality Assurance Agency for Higher Education) (1999) 'Code of Practice: Section 3 Students with disabilities' (UK). Available online: http://www.qaa.ac.uk/public/cop/copswd/contents.htm (accessed 11 February 2004).

QAAHE (Quality Assurance Agency for Higher Education) (2003) *Handbook for Enhancement-led Institutional Review: Scotland*, Gloucester: Quality Assurance Agency for Higher Education.

Quinn, L. (2003) 'Reflections on a theoretical framework for a professional development course for lecturers at a South African university', a paper given at the SEDA/SRHE Conference, April, Bristol.

Race, P. (1999) *2000 Tips for Lecturers*, London: Kogan Page.

Radloff, A., de la Harpe, B. and Wright, L. (2001) 'A strategic approach to helping university teachers foster student self-directed learning', in C. Rust (ed.) *Improving Student Learning: Improving Student Learning Strategically*, Oxford: The Oxford Centre for Staff Development, Oxford Brookes University.

Ramsden, P. (1992) *Learning to Teach in Higher Education*, London: Routledge.

Ramsden, P. (1998a) 'Managing the effective university', *Higher Education Research Development*, 17, 3: 347–70.

Ramsden, P. (1998b) *Learning to Lead in Higher Education*, London: RoutledgeFalmer.

Ramsden, P., Margetson, D., Martin, E. and Clarke, S. (1995) *Recognising and Rewarding Good Teaching in Australian Higher Education*, Canberra: Committee for the Advancement of University Teaching.

Readings, B. (1996) *The University in Ruins*, Boston, MA: Harvard University Press.

Reid, A. (1999) 'The national educational agenda and its curriculum effects' in Reid, A. and Johnson, B. (eds) *Contesting the Curriculum*, Sydney: Social Science Press.

Reynolds, J. and Saunders, M. (1985) 'Teacher responses to curriculum policy: beyond the "delivery" metaphor', in J. Calderhead (ed.) *Exploring Teachers' Thinking*, London: Cassell.

RMIT University (undated) 'Teaching and Learning at RMIT'. Available online: http://www.rmit.edu.au/teachingandlearning (accessed 26 February 2004).

Robbins Committee on Higher Education (1963) *Higher Education: A Report of the Committee Appointed by the Prime Minister under the Chairmanship of Lord Robbins* ('The Robbins Report'), London: HMSO.

Rowland, S. (2001) 'Surface learning about teaching in higher education: the need for more critical conversations', *International Journal for Academic Development*, 6, 2, 162–7.

Rowland, S. (2003) 'Academic development: a practical or theoretical business?', in H. Eggins and R. Macdonald (eds) *The Scholarship of Academic Development*, Buckingham: Society for Research in Higher Education and Open University Press.

Rowley, D., Lujan, H. and Dolence, M. (1998) *Strategic Choices for the Academy: How Demand for Lifelong Learning will Re-create Higher Education*, San Franciso, CA: Jossey-Bass.

Rudduck, J. (1991) *Innovation and Change: Developing Involvement and Understanding*, Buckingham: Open University Press.

Rust, C. (1998) 'The impact of education development workshops on teachers' practice', *The International Journal of Academic Development*, 3, 1: 72–80.

Ryan, Y. and Stedman, L. (2002) *The Business of Borderless Education 2001 Update*, Report 02/1 to the Evaluations and Investigations Programme, Canberra: Higher Education Group. Available online: http://www.dest.gov.au/highered/eippubs/eip02_1/eip02_1.pdf (accessed 26 February 2004).

Ryan, Y., Fraser, K., Bryant, L. and Radloff, A. (2004) 'The multiple contexts of higher education staff and academic development', in L. Elvidge (ed.) *Exploring Academic Development in Higher Education: Issues of Engagement*, Cambridge: Jill Rogers Associates.

Sallis, E. (2002) *Total Quality Management in Education*, 3rd edn, London: Kogan Page.

Sarros, J.C., Gmelch, W.H. and Tanewski, G.A. (1997) 'The role of department head in Australian universities: tasks and stresses', *Higher Education Research and Development*, 16, 3: 283– 92.

Schon, D.A. (1987) *Educating the Reflective Practitioner*, San Francisco, CA: Jossey-Bass.

Schreurs, M., Roebertsen, H and Bouhuijs, P. (1999) 'Leading the horse to water: teacher training for all teachers in a faculty of health sciences', *International Journal for Academic Development*, 4, 2: 115–23.

Schumacher, E.F. (1973) *Small is Beautiful: A Study of Economics as if People Mattered*, London: Blond and Briggs.

Scott, G. (2002) 'Faculty of Life Sciences: Review of the Faculty's implementation of the Program Quality Assurance system', commissioned report, Melbourne: RMIT University.

Scott, P. (1995) *The Meanings of Higher Education*, Buckingham: Society for Research in Higher Education and Open University.

SCROLLA (Scottish Centre for Research on On-Line Learning and Assessment) (2003) *ScotCIT Communications and Information Technology Programme, External Evaluation*, Final Report to Scottish Higher Education Funding Council. Edinburgh: SHEFC.

Senge, P.M. (1990) *The Fifth Discipline*, New York: Doubleday.

Sinclair, A. (1992) 'The tyranny of a team ideology', *Organisational Studies*, 13, 4: 611–26.

Slowey, M. (ed.) (1995) *Implementing Change from Within Universities and Colleges*, London: Kogan Page.

Smeby, J. (1998) 'Knowledge production and knowledge transmission: the interaction between teaching and research at universities', *Teaching in Higher Education*, 3, 1: 5–20.

Somekh, B. (1998) 'Supporting information and communication technology innovations in higher education', *Journal of Information Technology for Teacher Education*, 7, 1: 11–32.

Somekh, B. and Thaler, M. (1997) 'Contradictions of management theory, organisational cultures and the self', *Educational Action Research*, 5, 1: 141–60.

Staff and Educational Development Association (undated). Available online: http//www.seda.ac.uk/ (accessed 23 February 2004).

Standing Conference on Academic Practice (2002) Overview of Teaching/Academic Practice Provision 2002, Coventry: University of Warwick, SCAP.

Stefani, L. and Matthew, B. (2002) 'The difficulties of defining development: a case study', *International Journal for Academic Development*, 7, 1: 41–50.

Tan, J. (1995) 'Managing transformations in university departments', in M. Slowey (ed.) *Implementing Change from Within Universities and Colleges*, London: Kogan Page.

Taylor, M. (2003) 'Teaching capabilities and professional development and qualifications framework project: stage one', unpublished report, Melbourne: RMIT University.

Taylor, P.G. (1999) *Making Sense of Academic Life: Academics, Universities and Change*, Buckingham: Society for Research in Higher Education and Open University Press.

THES (*Times Higher Educational Supplement*) (2003a) 'Academics wish to keep dual role', 12 September: 64.

THES (*Times Higher Educational Supplement*) (2003b) 'Hefce "farce" makes sign-up to teaching academy compulsory', 10 October: 8.

Tierney, W. (1997) 'Organizational socialization in higher education', *Journal of Higher Education*, 68, 1: 1–16.

Tierney, W. (1999) *Building the Responsive Campus*, Thousands Oaks, CA: Sage.

Times Higher Education Supplement Online. Available online: http://www.thes.co.uk/ (accessed 7 March 2004).

Trevitt, A.C.F. (2003) 'Coaching the transition to flexible learning: re-thinking instructional design', paper presented at the Higher Education Research and Development Society of Australasia conference, July, Christchurch, NZ.

Trigwell, K., Prosser, M. and Waterhouse, F. (1999) 'Relations between teachers' approaches to teaching and students' approaches to learning', *Higher Education*, 37, 1: 57–70.

Trowler, P.R. (1998) *Academics Responding to Change: New Higher Education Frameworks and Academic Cultures*, Buckingham: Society for Research in Higher Education and Open University Press.

Trowler, P. and Knight, P. (1999) 'Organizational socialization and induction in universities: reconceptualizing theory and practice', *Higher Education*, 37, 2: 177–95.

Tucker, A. (1984) *Chairing the Academic Department*, New York: American Council on Education/Macmillan.

Tutt, N. (1985) 'The unintended consequences of integration', *Educational and Child Psychology*, 2: 30–8.

University Grants Committee (undated a) 'UGC-funded institutions'. Available online: http://www.ugc.edu.hk/english/fund_inst.html (accessed 26 February 2004).

University Grants Committee (undated b). Available online: http://www.ugc.edu.hk/ (accessed 26 February 2004).

University of Nottingham (undated a) 'Inclusive teaching strategies'. Available online: http://www.nottingham.ac.uk/disability/ITS%20leaflets.htm (accessed 20 July 2004).

University of Nottingham (undated b) 'Staff and educational development short courses'. Available online: http://www.nottingham.ac.uk/sedu/courses/EO_courses.php (accessed 20 July 2004).

University of Queensland (1999) 'University of Queensland staff development policy'. Available online: http://www.uq.edu.au/hupp/contents/view.asp?s1=5&s2=80&s3=1 (accessed 14 January 2004).

Universities UK (undated) 'Higher education in facts and figures'. Available online: http://www.universitiesuk.ac.uk/bookshop/downloads/factssummer03.pdf (accessed 28 February 2004).

Välimaa, J. (1998) 'Culture and identity in higher education research', *Higher Education*, 36, 2: 119–38.

Victorian Auditor-General's Office (Australia) (2003) 'Report on public sector agencies: results of special reviews and financial statement audits as at 30 June

2002'. Available online: http://www.audit.vic.gov.au/reports_mp_psa/psa03–101.html (accessed 26 February 2004).

Wahr, F., Radloff, A. and Gray, K. (2002) 'Reflections on a developing quality management system: another management fad or a sustainable approach to enduring, outcomes focussed enhancement of educational programs?', paper presented at the 7th Quality in Higher Education International Seminar, October, Melbourne.

Waldrop, M.M. (1994) *Complexity: The Emerging Science at the Edge of Order and Chaos*, Harmondsworth: Penguin Books.

Walker, M. (1993) 'Developing the theory and practice of action research: a South African case', *Educational Action Research*, 1, 1: 95–109.

Walker, M. (2001) *Reconstructing Professionalism in University Teaching*, Buckingham: Society for Research in Higher Education and Open University Press.

Warren-Piper, D. (1994) 'The role of educational development units in universities', *Tertiary Education News*, 4, 1: 1–2.

Watson, D. and Taylor, R. (1998) *Lifelong Learning and the University: A Post-Dearing Agenda*, London: RoutledgeFalmer.

Watts R. (2002) 'Down and out in the modern university: the discourse of quality assurance and the fate of language and truth', discussion paper, available from the author, RMIT University (rob.watts@rmit.edu.au).

Webb, G. (1996 *Understanding Staff Development*, Buckingham: Society for Research in Higher Education and Open University Press.

Weimer, M. and Lenze, L.F. (1991) 'Instructional interventions: a review of the literature on efforts to improve instruction', in J.C. Smart (ed.) *Higher Education: A Handbook of Theory and Research* Vol VII, New York: Agathon Press.

Wenger, E. (1998) *Communities of Practice: Learning, Meaning and Identity*, Cambridge: Cambridge University Press.

Wergin, J.F. (1994) *The Collaborative Department: How Five Campuses Are Inching Toward Cultures of Collective Responsibility*, Washington, D.C.: American Association for Higher Education.

Wergin, J.F. (2003) *Departments That Work: Building and Sustaining Cultures of Excellence in Academic Programs*, Bolton, MA: Anker Publishing.

West Report (1998) *Learning for Life: Review of Higher Education Financing and Policy*, Canberra: Department for Education, Training and Youth Affairs. Available online: http://www.dest.gov.au/archive/highered/hereview/default/htm (accessed 5 March 2004).

Wiles, K. (2003) personal communication.

Winefield Report (2001) Available online: http://www.unisanet.unisa.edu.au/nuss/NationalUniversityStressStudy.htm (accessed 16 October 2003).

Winter, R. and Sarros, J. (2002) 'The academic work environment in Australian Universities: a motivating place to work?', *Higher Education Research and Development*, 21, 3: 241–58.

www.crikey.com.au (undated) (accessed 26 February 2004).

Yetton, P. (1997) *Managing the Introduction of Technology in the Delivery and Administration of Higher Education*, Canberra: Australian Government Printing Services. Available online: http://www.deetya.gov.au/divisions/hed/highered/eippubs.htm (accessed 4 February, 2004).

Zuber-Skerritt, O. (1992) *Professional Development in Higher Education: A Theoretical Framework for Action Research*, London: Kogan Page.

Zuber-Skerritt, O. (1994) 'Academic staff development in Australia in the 1990s: a government driven agenda', Occasional Paper No. 3, Brisbane: Griffith Institute for Higher Education.

Index